THE SCIENTIFIC WAY OF WARFARE

CRITICAL WAR STUDIES

Series editors

TARAK BARKAWI
Centre of International Studies, Cambridge University

SHANE BRIGHTON
Birkbeck College, University of London

War transforms the social and political orders in which we live, just as it obliterates our precious certainties. Nowhere is this more obvious than in the fate of truths offered about war itself. War regularly undermines expectations, strategies and theories, and along with them the credibility of those in public life and the academy presumed to speak with authority about it. A fundamental reason for this is the frequently narrow and impoverished intellectual resources that dominate the study of war. Critical War Studies begins with the recognition that the unsettling character of war is a profound opportunity for scholarship. Accordingly, the series welcomes submissions from across the academy as well as from reflective practitioners. It provides an open forum for critical scholarship concerned with war and armed forces and seeks to foster and develop the nascent encounter between war and contemporary approaches to society, history, politics and philosophy. It is a vehicle to reconceive the field of war studies, expand the sites where war is studied, and open the field to new voices.

ANTOINE BOUSQUET

The Scientific Way
of Warfare
Order and Chaos on the
Battlefields of Modernity

Columbia University Press
New York

Columbia University Press
Publishers Since 1893
New York Chichester, West Susses

Copyright © 2009 Antoine Bousquet

Library of Congress Cataloging-in-Publication Data

Bousquet, Antoine.
 The scientific way of warfare : order and chaos on the battlefields of modernity / Antoine
Bousquet.
    p. cm. — (Critical war studies)
 First published in the United Kingdom by Hurst Publishers, London, c2009.
 Includes bibliographical references and index.
 ISBN 978-0-231-70078-8 (cloth : alk. paper)
        978-0-231-70079-5 (pbk: alk. paper)
 1. Military art and science—Technological innovations—History. 2. Military art and
science—Methodology—History. 3. Science—Military aspects—History. 4. Technology—
Military aspects—History. 5. Military art and science—Philosophy. 6. Military history,
Modern. 7. Military policy—History. 8. Military research—History. I. Title. II. Series.

 U39.B68 2009
 355.02.01'1—dc22

                                       2008048758

Columbia University Press books are printed on permanent and durable acid-free paper.
This book is printed on paper with recycled content.
Printed in India

c 10 9 8 7 6 5 4 3 2 1

References to Internet Web sites (URLs) were accurate at the time of writing. Neither
the author nor Columbia University Press is responsible for URLs that may have expired
or changed since the manuscript was prepared.

Contents

Figures

Acknowledgments

Begun over five years ago, the writing of this book has been an intellectual journey which has taken me in directions and places I had never envisaged, but whose guiding compass has been an enduring fascination for the subject matter, some of which I hope will be conveyed to the reader.

Obviously, no undertaking of this sort, however solitary it is in the main, can ever be brought to fruition without the help and support of many others. I owe special gratitude to Christopher Coker for his encouragement and diligent supervision of this work in its earlier incarnation as a doctoral thesis. Thanks are also due to my examiners Colin Gray and Theo Farrell for their thorough probing and questioning of my argument as well as the constructive comments and advice they have offered. Neither can I overstate the importance of the friendship and intellectual companionship provided by my fellow doctoral candidates at the London School of Economics and Political Science during those crucial years.

I am thankful to Michael Dwyer and all at Hurst Publishers for their professionalism and backing, as I am to Tarak Barkawi and Shane Brighton for having selected this book for their new Critical War Studies series that I have no doubt will spearhead a renewed productive engagement on questions of war and society. I also owe thanks to Michael Innes for his comments and unprompted enthusiasm for the book.

I am grateful to Neil Wells for having read through an early draft of the book for any glaring inaccuracies or misinterpretations in my presentation and use of scientific theories. In this respect as in all others, any flaws with the present text naturally remain entirely my own.

Ultimately nothing would have been possible without the enduring support and belief of my family over the years and to whom I am forever indebted. Last but not least is the gratitude I owe Naoko for her love and patience.

To my parents, Alison and Michel

Every age had its own kind of war, its own limiting conditions, and its own peculiar preconceptions. Each period, therefore, would have held to its own theory of war, even if the urge had always and universally existed to work things out on scientific principles.

Carl von Clausewitz

Introduction

When Baghdad fell to the American army on April 9, 2003 after a lightening war of barely three weeks, military officials were prompt to pronounce it a spectacular early demonstration of the Pentagon's new doctrine of network-centric warfare. For the commander of Coalition forces General Tommy Franks, the experience was nothing short of religious: "I've died and gone to heaven and seen the first bit of net-centric warfare at work!"[1] Although the reality of operations was still a far cry from the vision of swarming self-synchronised warfighting units expounded by the theorists of network-centric warfare, its advocates were keen to claim that the deployment of a vast network of surveillance and communication technologies had granted the Coalition forces unparalleled awareness of the battlefield and unprecedented military effectiveness. Following on soon after the similarly swift toppling of the Taliban in Afghanistan, the network-empowered American Leviathan seemed briefly unstoppable.

Four years later, with the Coalition mired in a guerrilla war against the insurgency that soon erupted in the aftermath of the invasion of Iraq, a very different assessment can be heard from the freshly retired successor to Franks at the head of US Central Command. "The enemy is in fact more networked, more decentralised, and operates within a broader commander's intent than any twentieth-century foe we've ever met," General John Abizaid tells his audience at a convention on military transformation. "In fact, this enemy is better networked than we

---

1   Office of Force Transformation, *The Implementation of Network-Centric Warfare* (2005), p. 18.

are." Using mobile phones and the Internet for communications and operating within loose and diffuse organisational structures, it is indeed the insurgents that have appeared more adept at embracing the network form than their adversaries. For Abizaid only one thing can still turn the tide: more of the same. Networking and tactical decision-making capabilities must be made fully accessible to lowest levels of the battlefield, that of the individual soldier. After all, "it takes a network to beat a network, and our network must be better." [2]

How has war, an activity traditionally dominated by institutions extolling the virtues of hierarchical command and submission to orders, come to be understood essentially in terms of decentralised networks of combatants connected together by horizontal information links?

The most popular account of this momentous transformation usually centres on the availability of a new cornucopia of information and communication technologies that has radically altered the possibilities of human interaction and social organisation. It is a seductive tale combining both simplicity and apparent explanatory power, and indeed widespread applications of such technology can be readily identified. Yet technology is first and foremost a tool and one that only takes on meaning and purpose within the specific social and cultural formations in which it is deployed. Nor does it appear *ex nihilo* but as the product of a particular human engagement with the world. As Martin van Creveld has observed, "behind military hardware there is hardware in general, and behind that there is technology as a certain kind of know-how, as a way of looking at the world and coping with its problems." [3]

In the present age, it is science that provides the dominant way of looking at the world whether as a methodological disposition to problem-solving or in informing our conceptions of how the world works. Our present understanding of the social world in terms of information and networks is directly reflected in the central preoccupations of contemporary science. Indeed the genealogy of the concepts of swarming and self-synchronisation dear to network-centric warfare can be traced back to the scientific theories of chaos and complexity which

2   *Transformation Warfare '07*, Virginia Beach, VA Convention Center, June 2007.

3   Martin van Creveld, *Technology and War: From 2000 B.C. to the Present* (New York: Free Press, 1989), p. 1.

have emerged over the past few decades. Where technology has played a role, it is in conjunction with the scientific conceptual frameworks that have accompanied its development and diffusion. From the very introduction of the term of network-centric warfare in 1998, military doctrine and scientific theory were being explicitly linked: "military operations are enormously complex, and complexity theory tells us that such enterprises organise best from the bottom-up."[4]

Nor is this a novel phenomenon. Scientific concepts and theoretical frameworks have been influencing military thought and practice since the inception of the Scientific Revolution in the late sixteenth century. Moreover the interface between science and warfare has been far from restricted to one-way traffic, with military imperatives stimulating both technological and scientific discoveries. From the earliest synergies between the study of the motion of bodies and military ballistics, science and the military arts have been inextricably bound, long before the scientific breakthrough of the Manhattan project yielded the atomic weapon.

This book forms an enquiry into this profound interrelationship of science and warfare. Its central claim is that throughout the modern era the dominant corpus of scientific ideas has been reflected in the contemporary theories and practices of warfare in the Western world. From the ascendancy of the scientific worldview in the seventeenth and eighteenth centuries to the present day, an ever more intimate symbiosis between science and warfare has established itself, with the increasing reliance on the development and integration of technology within complex social assemblages of war. This extensive deployment of scientific ideas and methodologies in the military realm allows us to speak of the constitution and perpetuation of a *scientific way of warfare*.

The notion of a scientific way of warfare seeks not merely to capture the growing role played by science in developing and perfecting military technologies, important as it has been. Rather the primary concern here is with the manner in which scientific ideas have been systematically recruited to inform thinking about the very nature of combat and the forms of military organisation best suited to prevail in it. The success of modern science and technology in providing reliable predictions about

---

4   Arthur K. Cebrowski and John J. Garstka, "Network-Centric Warfare: Its Origin and Future", *Proceedings*, US Naval Institute, Jan. 1998.

the world and increasing human control over it through the discovery of fundamental laws and the construction of apparatus capable of taking advantage of them has naturally proven highly attractive to military thinkers and practitioners in search of decisiveness on the battlefield. From the eighteenth century onwards, attempts have been made to apply scientific method and insights to warfare in its totality, and many have believed, like the Baron de Jomini, that "all strategy is controlled by invariable scientific principles" only awaiting discovery by the rational mind.[5] The scientific way of warfare therefore refers to an array of scientific rationalities, techniques, frameworks of interpretation, and intellectual dispositions which have characterised the approach to the application of socially organised violence in the modern era.

If a scientific approach has remained a consistent feature of warfare, there are however significant variations in the theories and practices espoused within the scientific way of warfare according to the prevalence of certain scientific ideas and technological apparatuses in given periods of the modern era. The following text will be structured according to four distinct regimes of the scientific way of warfare, each of which is characterised by a specific theoretical and methodological constellation: mechanistic, thermodynamic, cybernetic, and chaoplexic warfare. At the core of every scientific regime we find an associated paradigmatic technology, respectively the clock, the engine, the computer and the network. Technologies are here considered not simply in terms of the material changes they have wrought but also as central conceptual and metaphorical figures around which particular scientific frameworks are organised.

With each regime a different dimension of warfare comes to the fore and dominates its exercise, whether it is the ordering and disciplining of motion on the battlefield, the channelling and projection of energy, or the flow and distribution of information. Every one of these regimes is furthermore marked by a differing approach to the central question of order and chaos in war, on which hinge the related issues of centralisation and decentralisation, predictability and control. The book will analyse in turn each scientific regime, charting its emergence and drawing

---

5   Philip K. Lawrence, *Modernity and War: The Creed of Absolute Violence* (Basingstoke: Macmillan, 1997), p. 22.

out its fundamental principles and assumptions before investigating its impact on military organisation and war.

Chapter 1 sets out the broad conceptual framework underpinning the study, along with the theoretical and methodological foundations it rests upon. The ideas of order and chaos are introduced and related to the theories and practices of both warfare and science. The intimate relationship of technology and science is elaborated, notably through the idea of a unitary phenomenon of technoscience. The notions of discursive formations and abstract mechanisms of operation are called upon for the task of the combined treatment of both the material and ideational dimensions of sociocultural change undertaken in the rest of the book. The figure of the metaphor is developed as a useful conceptual lens to analyse the movement of ideas and practices from one domain to another, particularly in the context of the machinic metaphors at play in different scientific eras. The chapter concludes with a summary outline of the proposed periodisation of the scientific way of warfare.

The historical study proper starts with Chapter 2 and the first regime of the scientific way of warfare: *mechanistic warfare*. The invention and dissemination of the clock and clockwork mechanism is related to the emergence of the first major scientific body of ideas constituted by the principles of mechanism and Newtonian physics. Its ontological and epistemological implications, along with the mathematical and geometrical methodology that supports it, are discussed. The manifestation of these ideas and particularly that of the clockwork metaphor in fields as diverse as cosmology, anatomy, and political theory are all charted before turning to their instantiation in the military sphere. The role of geometry and physics in the development of fortifications and ballistics is analysed here but attention is especially focused on the army of Prussia's Frederick the Great as the epitome of mechanistic warfare in which soldiers are heavily drilled and disciplined to execute pre-ordained manoeuvres on the battlefield.

Chapter 3 turns to the next period in the development of the scientific way of warfare, that of *thermodynamic warfare*. The appearance of the engine, first driven by steam and later by internal combustion and electricity, is placed in the context of the industrialisation and motorisation of Western societies. Within the new science of energy that is thermodynamics, the engine as a physical contraption and conceptual device occupies a central place. Theories of energy proliferate in the physical and biological sciences, as well as in other fields of social and cultural life. Warfare becomes thermodynamic in both the motorisation of its forces that extends their reach across space and time as never before and in its quest for ever-more powerful energy weapons, culminating in the atom bomb. The chapter concludes with a reading of Clausewitz's writings through the lens of thermodynamics.

Chapter 4 covers the genesis of the computer within the lineage of electromagnetic communication technologies and their applications in the military context. The emergence of the computer itself is tied to the Second World War and the momentous technological and scientific innovations which it stimulated. The sciences of information and cybernetics are presented here with particular attention paid to the conceptual apparatus which lays down the foundations of a new informational paradigm in the natural and social sciences. This chapter's purpose is to establish the key ideas and principles which inform the accompanying regime of the scientific way of warfare discussed in the following chapter.

Accordingly, Chapter 5 charts the ascendancy, dominance, and subsequent failure of *cybernetic warfare* in Cold War America. Closely bound to the process of computerisation of the military in the wake of the Second World War, a conception of warfare resting on the notion that information is the paramount factor determining success emerges in this period, along with a belief that war can be fully managed and controlled scientifically. Its various manifestations are analysed here, from the development of "command and control" as both operational principle and socio-technical system to the meteoric rise to power of operations researchers and system analysts. The chapter concludes with an analysis of the spectacular debacle of cybernetic warfare in Vietnam.

The next phase in the development of the informational paradigm is the subject of Chapter 6. Chaos theory and complexity science are presented here, with particular attention to the manner in which they grow out of cybernetic ideas yet also significantly break with some of their key assumptions, thereby forging a new body of ideas with a wide-ranging effect on both the natural and social sciences. Of particular importance are the concepts of non-linearity and self-organisation, imposing both limitations on the predictability of systems and restoring the potential for creative transformation of those same systems. The dominant metaphor which surfaces here is that of the distributed network which eclipses the computer as a centralising information-processing unit.

Chapter 7 analyses the implication of these new scientific ideas on military theories and practices and postulates the emergence of the latest regime of the scientific way of warfare: *chaoplexic warfare*. We first turn to the ideas of the fighter pilot and strategist John Boyd, connecting his key insights to those of chaos theory and complexity science. A return to Clausewitz and the non-linear aspects of his thoughts, particularly those pertaining to the question of uncertainty, allows a further appraisal of the potential applications of the new sciences to warfare. The role of networks in contemporary warfare is then considered, first through a discussion of the operational methods of terrorist networks and guerrilla groups, and then through an in-depth analysis of the Pentagon doctrine of network-centric warfare which, despite nods to chaos theory and complexity science, is found to be still largely in thrall to the principles of cybernetic warfare.

1

Technoscientific Regimes of Order in Warfare

Scientific theory is a contrived foothold in the chaos of living phenomena.

Wilhelm Reich

The army general, the scientific inventor or the military theorist is caught up in an interminable quest to hold the internal and external forces of disruption in check.

Daniel Pick[1]

Throughout the ages, military leaders have sought to organise and direct their armies so that they can best preserve their order and coherence when faced with the centrifugal forces of chaos unleashed on the battlefield. Thus they have tried to avert for as long as possible the state of disorganised free-for-all that threatens all armies under the stress of battle. The forces that have succeeded in remaining organised while precipitating their adversaries into disarray have almost invariably prevailed.

Hence for van Creveld "the history of command in war consists essentially of an endless quest for certainty – certainty about the state and intentions of the enemy's forces; certainty about the manifold factors that together constitute the environment in which the war is fought, from the weather and the terrain to radioactivity and the presence of

---

1   Daniel Pick, *War Machine: The Rationalisation of Slaughter in the Modern Age* (New Haven, CT: Yale University Press, 1993), p. 34.

chemical warfare agents; and last, but definitely not least, certainty about the state, intentions, and activities of one's own forces."[2] Likewise, John Keegan notes that the fundamental purpose of training "is to reduce the conduct of war to a set of rules and a system of procedures – and therefore to make orderly and rational what is essentially chaotic and instinctive."[3] The practice of warfare can thus be understood as the attempt to impose order over chaos, to exert control where it most threatens to elude, and to find predictability in the midst of uncertainty.

States, along with other political entities, seek to employ organised violence in a manner such as to attain certain political objectives. Military force is only one of the instruments of statecraft and its rational and measured employment demands that its use be commensurate with the overall objective to which it is intended to contribute. Indeed the pursuit of war solely for its own sake or as part of a warrior lifestyle that seeks merely the perpetuation of its own existence is antithetical to any *raison d'état*. This is the meaning of Clausewitz's oft-repeated dictum that war is the continuation of policy by other means, formulated as the modern state and its particularly instrumental understanding of the use of force were ascendant. The exercise of judgement over the appropriate means to be deployed in the pursuit of a given political end belongs to the domain commonly known as strategy. However the formulation of strategy and an assessment of the role of military force within it requires an understanding of the likely effects any course of action is likely to result in – "if the essence of strategy is instrumentality, the essence of instrumentality is predictability."[4] Strategic thought and behaviour are thus necessarily accompanied by a rationalisation of military force as an instrument of broader political objectives and a theorisation of the potential and limits of the use of organised violence, all in an effort to bring order and predictability to activities which would otherwise be left entirely to chance and contingency.

A clear parallel can be drawn between the ordering of military organisation and instrumental application of armed force on one hand and

---

2   Martin van Creveld, *Command in War* (Cambridge, MA: Harvard University Press, 2003), p. 264

3   John Keegan, *The Face of Battle* (London: Cape, 1976), pp. 18-19.

4   Colin S. Gray, *Strategy for Chaos: Revolutions in Military Affairs and the Evidence of History* (London: Frank Cass, 2002), p. 98.

scientific endeavour on the other. Indeed scientists continuously strive to extract "patterns" from "noise", to identify regularities in the fog of randomness, to uncover the "laws" governing the behaviour of nature and reveal the hidden order behind its apparent chaos. For the scientist Norbert Wiener, one of the pivotal characters in this study, the "highest destiny" of mathematics, the universal "language" of science, was "the discovery of order among disorder".[5] Alfred North Whitehead expressed the same idea, albeit in a more poetic fashion, when he proposed that the pursuit of mathematics was "a divine madness of the human spirit, a refuge from the goading urgency of contingent happenings."[6] With the discovery and formulation of regularities comes greater predictability of phenomena and an enhanced control over the natural world. Auguste Comte, the founder of positivism, explicitly made this link: "from science comes prevision; from prevision comes control."[7] The scientific project is thus inextricably connected to the drive for greater control and power over the world, as originally formulated by one of its earliest expositors, Francis Bacon: *scientia potentia est.*

Engineering is here again analogous since it seeks to constitute technological artefacts designed to be ordered and predictable through the utilisation of natural laws and resist those other physical forces which would undo them. For van Creveld, it is the repetitive and predictable character of physical nature which first made technology possible in primitive societies. Technological progress from then on depended increasingly on the specialisation and integration of different tasks and tools. The coordination necessary to constitute such systems "hinges on the ability of management to predict the behaviour of each and every part of the system. Ultimately, what is involved is nothing less than an attempt to insulate the system from uncertainty by creating a perfectly controlled and perfectly stable – since change means disruption – artificial world."[8] Thus the quest for order and predictability necessary for

---

5   Steve J. Heims, *John Von Neumann and Norbert Wiener: From Mathematics to the Technologies of Life and Death* (Cambridge, MA and London: MIT Press, 1980), p. 68.

6   Heims, *John Von Neumann and Norbert Wiener*, p. 116.

7   Ian T. King, *Social Science and Complexity: The Scientific Foundations* (Huntington, NY: Nova Science Publishers, 2000), p. 20.

8   Van Creveld, *Technology and War*, p. 315.

the operation of any tool soon extends to the larger systems, including social, of which they are only a part.

In his piece entitled *The Question Concerning Technology*, Martin Heidegger claims that "the essence of technology is nothing technological" but rather that, along with science, it is an expression of *enframing* (*Ge-Stell*) that is "ordering as the supposed single way of revealing."[9] The philosopher sees in enframing a will to dominate nature, to convert the whole universe into an undifferentiated "standing reserve" (*Bestand*) available to be put to work when needed. Heidegger seems to suggest this attitude to the world is implicit in the scientific project:

Man's ordering attitude and behaviour display themselves first in the rise of modern physics as an exact science. Modern science's way of representing pursues and entraps nature as a calculable coherence of forces. Modern physics is not experimental physics because it applies apparatus to the questioning of nature. Rather the reverse is true. Because physics, indeed already as pure theory, sets nature up to exhibit itself as a coherence of forces calculable in advance, it therefore orders its experiments precisely for the purpose of asking whether and how nature reports itself when set up in this way.[10]

Science and technology are therefore the means by which the world is made to "reveal" itself in a certain way so as to order it. If Heidegger accepts that the instrumental understanding of modern technology is correct in viewing it as a means to an end, he goes further by seeming to suggest that instrumentality itself flows from the way in which technology "brings forth" or reveals the world through enframing, that is in our way of "knowing" it.

If the ordering Heidegger is speaking of is one that corresponds to a specific technoscientific rationality, ordering as a codification of the world which seeks to abstract regularities and correlations from it and dictate ways of being within it appears to be central to all human societies, whether manifested in the form of law, religion, tradition, or morality.[11] For Freud, it can be traced to a fundamental psychological impulse:

---

9   Martin Heidegger, *The Question Concerning Technology and Other Essays* (New York: Harper Torchbooks, 1977), p. 32.

10   Heidegger, *The Question Concerning Technology and Other Essays*, p. 21.

11   For Hedley Bull, "to say of a number of things that together they display order is, in the simplest and most general sense of the term to say that they are related

Order is a kind of compulsion to repeat which, when a regulation has been laid down once and for all, decides when, where and how a thing shall be done, so that in every similar circumstance one is spared hesitation and indecision. The benefits of order are incontestable. It enables men to use space and time to the best advantage, while conserving their psychical forces.[12]

If the process of ordering appears to be a defining characteristic of civilisation and social life, the specific forms it takes are not inconsequential, particularly with regards to the manner in which they mediate between order and chaos. What follows is an account of the specific technoscientific regime of order that emerged in the modern era, its relationship to the theories and practices of warfare, and the various ways in which the tensions between order and chaos are played out.

The Technoscientific Regime of Order

In the Western world, a particular regime of order emerged with modernity, displacing previously established mechanisms for the production of order.[13] Order came to be increasingly justified and organised on the basis of a scientific and technical rationality. Knowledge produced through the inductive methods of scientific enquiry gained ascendancy over deductive theological and scholastic claims about the world. Both the state entities and capitalistic forms of economic organisation which emerged in this era relied on the rationalisation and systematisation of processes and social interactions to manage enlarged bureaucracies and sites of production. Efficiency considerations and cost-benefit or profit calculations increasingly supplanted tradition, custom or other

---

to one another according to some pattern" and social order is "an arrangement of social life such that it promotes certain goals and values." Hedley Bull, *The Anarchical Society: A Study of Order in World Politics* (London: Macmillan, 1977), pp. 4-5.

12   Sigmund Freud, *Civilisation and its Discontents* (London: Penguin, 2004), p. 40.

13   The term regime is endowed here with a meaning analogous to what Fritjof Capra calls a "social paradigm": "a constellation of concepts, values, perceptions, and practices shared by a community, which forms a particular vision of reality that is the basis of the way the community organises itself." Fritjof Capra, *The Web of Life: A New Synthesis of Mind and Matter* (London: Flamingo, 1997), pp. 5-6.

grounds as the ordering principle of social organisation, thereby fuelling a systematic and continually complexifying division of labour alongside accelerating technological development. A new regime of order meant that a new way of speaking about the world and dictating social arrangements within it had acquired predominant legitimacy.

Michel Foucault would here speak of a "regime of truth" produced by discourse and through which relations of power are established and perpetuated:

> In a society such as ours, but basically in any society, there are manifold relations of power which permeate, characterise and constitute the social body, and these relations of power cannot themselves be established, consolidated nor implemented without the production, accumulation, circulation and functioning of a discourse. There can be no possible exercise of power without a certain economy of discourse of truth which operates through and on the basis of this association. We are subjected to the production of truth through power and we cannot exercise power except through the production of truth.[14]

It is crucial in this context that discourse should not be reduced to the semantical field of spoken interaction and written text. Paul Edwards makes clear that "discourse goes beyond speech acts to refer to the entire field of *signifying* or *meaningful practices*: these social interactions – material, institutional, and linguistic – through which human knowledge is produced and reproduced. A discourse, then, is a way of knowledge, a background of assumptions and agreements about how reality is to be interpreted and expressed, supported by paradigmatic metaphors, techniques, and technologies and potentially embodied in social institutions."[15] In accordance with this broad understanding of discourse as a nexus of ideas and practices which (re)produce social reality and a certain set of power relations with it, modernity is to be viewed in Philip Lawrence's terms as "a structural organisation of state, economy, society and culture; a power complex and a mode of consciousness."[16]

---

14   Michel Foucault, *Power/Knowledge* (Hemel Hampstead: Harvester Press, 1980), p. 93.

15   Paul Edwards, *The Closed World: Computers and the Politics of Discourse in Cold War America* (Cambridge, MA: MIT Press, 1996), p. 34.

16   Lawrence, *Modernity and War*, p. 6.

With the advent of the Scientific Revolution at the dawn of the seventeenth century, a new set of beliefs, tools and practices was established and according to which nature could be interrogated and its fundamental laws revealed. The agenda of its initiators was explicitly one of extending control over the physical world, as evidenced by both Descartes's invitation to seek a "practical philosophy" through which to "render ourselves the masters and possessors of nature" and Bacon's injunction to "extend the power and dominion of the human race itself over the universe."[17] Scientific discourse rapidly grew in influence as it accumulated successes, soon acquiring a pre-eminent role in the ordering of social life within Western civilisation.[18] Some of this authority derived from its ability to predict natural phenomena but an even greater prestige was derived from its close association with technology. The synthesis that would emerge remains one of the defining characteristics of modernity. [19]

---

17   Langdon Winner, *The Whale and the Reactor: A Search for Limits in an Age of High Technology* (Chicago, IL: University of Chicago Press, 1986), p. 123.

18   This is not to say that science is the only ordering discourse of modernity or that it has not been contested since its very inception. Nor could it have achieved pre-eminence without chiming with other contemporary discourses. Mathematics and various modes of scientific endeavour also played major roles in Western and non-Western societies previous to the modern era. However the present work is concerned with the particular forms of scientific knowledge and method that emerged with the "Scientific Revolution".

19   The debates over the postulated historical transition to a new post-modern era will not be directly addressed in this book. Much ink has been spilt over this question with authors seeking to capture a number of social, economic, and cultural changes with a plethora of different terms such as post-modernity (Harvey, Jameson), "late" or "high" modernity (Giddens), "second" or reflexive modernity (Beck), and liquid modernity (Bauman). While this debate has yielded valuable insights into recent and on-going processes of societal transformation, this literature will not be directly engaged here nor will any of the above terminology be adopted. Instead, this study will rely on an understanding of modernity as a historical era characterised by the widespread application of technoscientific rationality to the organisation of society, and which in this sense has not been in any way overcome or superseded. The periodisation that will be established within modernity is therefore primarily based on evolutions in scientific theory and practice and the development of related technologies, rather than on other social, political, or cultural changes. No pretence is made here that this definition of modernity is any sense more proper or correct than many of the other alternatives that have been formulated, simply than it is most

Tools and technical artifacts had always existed as necessary requisites of human civilisation but they had previously remained distinct from the theoretical contemplation of nature's laws. Indeed Prigogine and Stengers claim that it is with Plato and Aristotle and their development of natural philosophy that:

the distinction between *theoretical thinking* and *technological activity* was established. The words we still use today – machine, mechanical, engineer – have a similar meaning. They do not refer to rational knowledge but to cunning and expediency. The idea was not to learn about natural processes in order to utilise them more effectively, but to deceive nature, to "machinate" against it – that is, to work wonders and create effects extraneous to the "natural order" of things. The field of practical manipulation and that of rational understanding of nature were thus rigidly separated. Archimedes' status is merely that of an engineer; his mathematical analysis of the equilibrium of machines is not considered to be applicable to the world of nature, at least within the framework of traditional physics. In contrast, the Newtonian synthesis expresses a systematic alliance between manipulation and theoretical understanding.[20]

Within this systematic alliance between science and technology, artefacts such as the clock, engine and computer were to play a key role. They allowed for the isolation and study of physical forces, the resulting new theoretical understandings of which would then feed back into the design of these and other devices. For this reason, it is more apropos to speak of the emergence of *technoscience* in the modern era, an ever tighter symbiotic bond between these two fields to the extent than any distinction is largely nominal and of limited conceptual value. Although this convergence is present at the very foundation of modern science, the proximity between science and technology from the Second World War onwards is such that any major technological advance has been inextricably linked to scientific knowledge. Derrida correctly signalled that "one can no longer distinguish between technology on the one

---

appropriate to the thesis being advocated in this book. David Harvey, *The Condition of Postmodernity: An Enquiry into the Origins of Cultural Change* (Oxford: Basil Blackwell, 1990); Frederic Jameson, *Postmodernism or The Cultural Logic of Late Capitalism* (London: Verso, 1991); Anthony Giddens, *The Consequences of Modernity* (Cambridge: Polity, 1990); Ulrich Beck, *Risk Society: Towards a New Modernity* (London: Sage Publications, 1992); Zygmunt Bauman, *Liquid Modernity* (Cambridge: Polity, 2000).

20   Ilya Prigogine and Isabelle Stengers, *Order out of Chaos: Man's New Dialogue with Nature* (Fontana: London, 1985), p. 39.

hand and theory, science and rationality on the other. The term techno-science has to be accepted."[21]

We must therefore also dispense with the now widely discredited view of technology as merely applied science. Heidegger had already observed in 1954 that:

It is said that modern technology is something incomparably different from all earlier technologies because it is based on modern physics as an exact science. Meanwhile we have come to understand more clearly that the reverse holds true as well: modern physics, as experimental, is dependent upon technical apparatus and upon progress in the building of apparatus.[22]

Technological artefacts have therefore been crucial in serving as instrumental apparatus and isolating physical phenomena for scientific study. There is much historical evidence for this, substantiating such claims as that "thermodynamics owed much more to the steam engine than the steam engine ever owed to thermodynamics."[23] Several other examples of this process will be discussed throughout this study, illuminating the co-constitutive interrelationship of science and technology. While the constraints of exposition in the following chapters may occasionally entail placing greater emphasis on the effect one of these domains had on the other, we are in fact always dealing with a unitary phenomenon of technoscience as a way of knowing and being in the world.

Similarly the technological and industrial development of Western societies in the modern era cannot be merely understood as the introduction and application of successive forms of machinery. Equally important are the forms of social organisation that allow for the implementation of specific technologies, enforcing new arrangements and combinations of individuals and machinery. Fay states:

the obvious but important truth that the exploitation of nature for the production of goods and services can only occur through the cooperative effort of men who undertake to do the work involved. This truth becomes a pre-eminent fact

21   Chris Hables Gray, *Postmodern War: The New Politics of Conflict* (New York: The Guilford Press, 1997), p. 262.

22   Heidegger, *The Question Concerning Technology and Other Essays*, p. 14.

23   Derek J. De Solla Price, "Notes Towards a Philosophy of the Science/Technology Interaction" in Rachel Laudan (ed.), *The Nature of Technological Knowledge: Are Models of Scientific Change Relevant?* (Dordrecht,: D. Reidiel Publishing, 1984), p. 106.

in a society which is devoted to a constant increase in production through the self-conscious organisation of social labour; for in these societies rational administration directed towards ensuring continuity of operation, speed, precision, and an efficient employment of men and machines leads to an increasing division-of-labour in which men come to perform quite specialised functions, and in such a complex economy productive activity can go forward only when this activity is performed according to some highly abstract and general plan.[24]

What Fay says of social organisation for the production of goods and services is no less true for the social organisations seeking to "produce" destructive force. Kranzberg is eager to underline that "the introduction of new analytical techniques in management forms the part of technological history just as much as it does of economic history and, now, of military history."[25] If a "highly abstract and general plan" is thus crucial to the organisation of modern modes of both production and destruction, we should not assume that such a plan is exogenous or secondary to the process of technological development. In Pacey's words, "technology can never be adequately understood in terms of machines and techniques alone. Machines are always used within a framework of organisation and management, and often there are organisational changes at the heart of important technological developments."[26]

One could go even further in viewing those abstract organisational schemes as constitutive of broader social machines or assemblages in which specific technical apparatuses are given function and meaning. Deleuze and Guattari's analysis of technology is here particularly relevant:

The principle behind all technology is to demonstrate that a technical element remains abstract, entirely undetermined, as long as one does not relate it to an assemblage it presupposes. It is the machine that is primary in relation to the technical element: not the technical machine, itself a collection of elements, but the social or collective machine, the machinic assemblage that determines

---

24   King, *Social Science and Complexity*, p. 29.

25   Melvin Kranzberg, "Science-Technology and Warfare: Action, Reaction, and Interaction in the Post-World War II Era" in Monte D. Wright and Lawrence J. Paszek (eds), *Science, Technology and Warfare: The Proceedings of the Third Military History Symposium* – United States Air Force Academy 8-9 May 1969, p. 133.

26   Arnold Pacey, *Technology in World Civilization* (Oxford: Basil Blackwell, 1990), p. 157.

what is a technical assemblage at a given moment, what is its usage, extension, comprehension, etc.[27]

Deleuze and Guattari develop in their work a "machinic" conception of society in which the machine is not first and foremost technical but rather describes any assemblage of parts which combine to work together. This allows for an understanding of social developments in which technologies, organisational arrangements, and ideational arrays all combine to constitute mixed assemblages that allow certain actions, or "ways of being", and forbid others. Analysis does not therefore focus primarily on determining a pre-eminent causal flow between either the ideational and material realms or the technological and social domains. Instead it seeks to uncover the modes of assembly and operation of the "machinic" entities which are composed of elements from all these fields.

Throughout each of the different regimes of the scientific way of warfare that will be distinguished below, those abstract and general plans, according to which armies have been assembled and that manifest themselves simultaneously in technical apparatuses, social organisations and military thinking, will be foregrounded. While embodied in all these respective forms, such plans and diagrams can also be viewed as independent from any specific stratum of reality. In his discussion of the Panopticon, Jeremy Bentham's plans for a model prison in which all inmates could be simultaneously supervised from a single omniscient position, Foucault considered the architectural disposition from the perspective of "a generalisable model of functioning, [...] the diagram of a mechanism of power reduced to its ideal form [...] it is in fact a figure of political technology that may and must be detached from any specific use."[28] As a diagrammatic condensation of the disciplinary principles that were forming in the modern era, the Panopticon was destined to spread across the social field, governing the operation of a wide range of institutions and social organisations. DeLanda speaks of the formation

---

27   Gilles Deleuze and Felix Guattari, *A Thousand Plateaus* (London and New York: Continuum, 2003), pp. 397-8. Also in Deleuze's book on Foucault: "Machines are social before being technical. Or rather there is a human technology before there is a material technology. No doubt the latter develops its effects throughout the entire social field; but, for it to be possible, the tools, the material machines, must have first been selected by a diagram, taken on by an assemblage." Gilles Deleuze, *Foucault* (Paris: Les Editions de Minuit, 1986), p. 47.

28   Michel Foucault, *Surveiller et Punir* (Paris: Editions Gallimard, 1975), p. 239.

of "abstract machines" as the point at which mechanical contraptions become "mechanism independent, that is as soon as they can be thought of independently of their physical embodiments."[29] Another way of thinking about such diagrams and models would be in terms of metaphors, more on which will be said below. First we must consider further the relationship and discursive mediation between scientific activity and the broader cultural formations it is contemporary to.

Science, Culture, and Discursive Resonance

Having established the importance of abstract machines and diagrams of power to this book's field of inquiry, it is crucial to note the role of discourse in establishing and perpetuating them. Once again, following Foucault, the use of discourse as an analytical tool implies much more than speech acts or written enunciation:

Discursive practices are not purely and simply ways of producing discourse. They are embodied in technical processes, in institutions, in patterns for general behaviour, in forms for transmission and diffusion, and in pedagogical forms which, at once, impose and maintain them.[30]

In this sense, the power of discourse is in permitting the arrangement of bodies, machines and *matériel* according to abstract organisational diagrams through the production and circulation of the conceptualisations, theorisations, representations and practices that support such dia-

---

29   Manuel DeLanda, *War in the Age of Intelligent Machines* (New York: Swerve Editions, 1991), p. 142. DeLanda borrows the term "abstract machine" from Deleuze and Guattari but uses the concept in a narrower sense than its originators, in accordance with the above definition. This study will mainly follow DeLanda's understanding but it is useful to refer to the original formulation as it makes clear that abstract machines are to be understood as diagrams which cut across the physical and ideational realms but are not to be elevated as a first cause since they are socially and historically produced: "an abstract machine in itself is not physical or corporeal, any more than it is semiotic; it is diagrammatic [...] [it] is neither an infrastructure that is determining in the last instance nor a transcendental idea that is determining in the supreme instance." Deleuze and Guattari, *A Thousand Plateaus*, pp. 141-142.

30   Michel Foucault (ed. Donald Bouchard), *Language, Counter-memory, Practice: Selected Essays and Interviews* (Ithaca, NY: Cornell University Press, 1977), p. 200.

grams. Science and the worldview it promotes are particularly pervasive instances of such power, and are all the more enduring due to science's ability to overhaul regularly some of its most fundamental theories while still claiming a single cohesive body of knowledge superior to "non-scientific" enquiry.

Thomas Kuhn's seminal work on paradigms and scientific revolutions did much to challenge the established view of a linear progression in the acquisition of scientific knowledge.[31] Kuhn argued that most scientific endeavour ("normal science") occurs within well-established paradigms, defined as a set of ideas and practices which determine what phenomena are to be observed and scrutinised, which kind of questions are to be asked, what constitutes a valid means of interrogation and how results are to be presented and interpreted. Periods of stability are punctuated by violent intellectual revolutions and episodes of intense controversy in which an existing paradigm is found to be no longer adequate and is replaced by a new one. While Kuhn's work has been often, legitimately or not, called upon to undermine science's claims to truth and cumulative knowledge, it also serves to make evident one of the fundamental strengths of scientific discourse, that is its ability to transform radically its constitutive theories and frameworks while still claiming a single corpus and methodology. It is this ability to remould itself that has secured science's lasting legitimacy as the central authoritative discourse in the Western world.

If the accounts of the development of scientific theories presented here examine the historical role of specific scientists, their purpose is to outline the context and chronology of these theories *per se* rather than to present them as a series of individual accomplishments. The romantic image of the lone and misunderstood scientist or technologist toiling in his laboratory before being struck by a sudden "Eureka" moment may be narratively satisfying but is a far cry from the reality of scientific endeavour. Science is always a collective enterprise conducted within a scientific community which shares and (re)produces the ideas, norms, and practices that constitute science. Theories and concepts are not produced in a vacuum but are the result of an accumulation of experiments, publications, and debates and only gain broad currency

31   Thomas S. Kuhn, *The Structure of Scientific Revolutions* - 3rd edn (Chicago, IL: University of Chicago Press, 1996).

through their review by the scientific community. This explains the oft-observed phenomenon of multiple independent discoveries whereby similar breakthroughs are made by scientists working independently of each other.[32] This suggests that certain ideas or theories are ripe for formulation and diffusion at a given moment in history, as the result of both the accumulated work of previous scientists and the aptness of the cultural climate. Katherine Hayles argues in this way that the scientists behind the development of chaos theory did not act in isolation; "they rather acted like lightening rods in a thunderstorm or seed crystals in a supersaturated solution. They gave a local habitation and a name to what was in the air. It was because the cultural atmosphere surrounding them was supercharged that these ideas seemed so pressing and important."[33]

Science is not an activity separate from other contemporary social developments and intellectual trends, much as some scientists may insist that the theories produced by the scientific method are formulated free from any of ideological constraints or subjective judgments prevalent in other forms of enquiry into the world. For Margaret Wertheim, science is always a "cultural project", in the sense that the widespread acceptance of any understanding of reality is necessarily the product of the social and linguistic negotiation of its epoch.[34] Wertheim has charted the rise of the purely physicalist notion of space in the modern age to the detriment of the dualistic conception of body space and soul space prevalent in the Middle Ages. Medieval metaphysical dualism posited that reality was composed of both a finite earthly realm and a spiritual dimension which contemporary art made no attempt to represent in a naturalistic manner. This worldview was increasingly challenged in the late Middle Ages and Renaissance and eventually gave way to the desanctified vision of a single unified physical reality that now dominates Western consciousness. While the scientific theories of Kepler, Newton and Einstein

---

32   Famous examples of multiple independent discoveries include the discovery of calculus by Newton and Leibnitz, oxygen by Lavoisier and Priestley, evolution by Darwin and Wallace, and the first law of thermodynamics by Joule, Mayer and Helmholtz.

33   N. Katherine Hayles, *Chaos Bound: Orderly Disorder in Contemporary Literature and Science* (Ithaca and London: Cornell University Press, 1990), p. 174.

34   Margaret Wertheim, *The Pearly Gates of Cyberspace: A History of Space from Dante to the Internet* (New York: W.W. Norton, 1999), p. 133.

underpin the elevation of a homogenised space in which the totality of reality is located, Wertheim argues that cultural developments such as the introduction of perspective and spatial integrity in painting played a key role in allowing for the psychological shift that enabled minds to accept this radically new conception of space.[35]

Along similar lines, the Nobel Prize physicist Erwin Schrödinger has claimed that:

All science is bound up with human culture in general, and [...] scientific findings, even those that which at the moment appear the most advanced and esoteric and difficult to grasp, are meaningless outside their cultural context. A theoretical science unaware that those of its constructs considered relevant and momentous are destined eventually to be framed in concepts and words that have a grip on the educated community and become part and parcel of the general world picture – a theoretical science, I say, where this is forgotten, and where the initiated continue musing to each other in terms that are, at best, understood by a small group of close fellow travellers will necessarily be cut off from the rest of the cultural mankind; in the long run it is bound to atrophy and ossify however virulently esoteric chat may continue within its joyfully isolated groups of experts.[36]

In order for any scientific truth to gain universal or even widespread acceptance beyond its tiny communities of expertise, it must therefore necessarily be socially and culturally reproduced and validated. This entails presenting its core ideas and notions in terms that are coherent and comprehensible to the non-initiated, generally expressed through the medium of language but also possibly in a visual or experiential fashion.

One crucial means by which the new can be apprehended in terms of the familiar is through metaphor. Prigogine and Stengers attribute the ascendance of the clock as a symbol of world order to its metaphorical resonance with broader discursive formations:

A watch is a *contrivance* governed by a rationality that lies outside itself, by a plan that is blindly executed by its inner workings. The clock world is a metaphor suggestive of God the Watchmaker, the rational master of a robotlike nature. At the origin of modern science, a "resonance" appears to have been set up between theological discourse and theoretical and experimental activity – a resonance that was no doubt likely to amplify and consolidate the claim that scientists were in the process of discovering the secret of the "great machine of

---

35   Wertheim, *The Pearly Gates of Cyberspace*, p. 115.

36   Prigogine and Stengers, *Order out of Chaos*, p. 18.

the universe." [...] It is not our intention to state, nor are we in any position to affirm, that religious discourse in any way determined the birth of theoretical science, or of the "world view" that happened to develop in conjunction with experimental activity. By using the term *resonance* – that is, mutual amplification of two discourses – we have deliberately chosen an expression that does not assume whether it was theological discourse or the "scientific myth" that came first and triggered the other."[37]

The authors later note that the manner in which irreversible time is introduced into physics in the nineteenth century with the development of thermodynamics, namely the claim to a universal "tendency towards homogeneity and death", is reminiscent of "ancient mythological and religious archetypes" which they relate to a deep contemporary anxiety caused by "the rapid transformation of the technological mode of interaction with nature [and] the constantly accelerating pace of change."[38] Certainly Crosbie Smith's masterful history of the development of the science of energy in Victorian Britain persuasively argues for the influence of the specific Protestant environment in which its formulators were immersed.[39]

Of particular methodological note is Prigogine and Stenger's notion of "resonance" between discourses and their refusal to commit to postulating the primacy of any particular discourse, preferring to opt for a more flexible contextual history. Smith shares this disposition, seeking to present "scientific work not as the product of isolated individuals but as crucially contingent upon the cultural resources of the age in which it was produced" and which include "such seemingly diverse ingredients as industrial machines, social and institutional networks, and religious and political ideologies."[40] The uses of contingency and resonance here echo Foucault's ambition to replace the "uniform, simple notion of assigning causality" with a "whole play of dependencies" and by "by eliminating the prerogative of the endlessly accompanying cause, bring out the bundle of polymorphous correlations."[41] Adopting a similar methodological and

---

37   Ibid., p. 46.

38   Prigogine and Stengers, *Order out of Chaos*, p. 116.

39   Crosbie Smith, *The Science of Energy: A Cultural History of Energy Physics in Victorian Britain* (London: Athlone, 1998).

40   Smith, *The Science of Energy*, p. ix.

41   Michel Foucault (edited by Sylvère Lotringer), *Foucault Live – Interviews 1961-1984* (New York, NY: Semiotext(e), 1996), p. 38.

epistemological outlook, the analysis contained herein will not be seeking to assign primary or exclusive causality to any particular substrate or domain of reality for the developments in technoscience and warfare that will be charted. Rather it will privilege an account which brings forth the resonances, dependencies, tensions, and breaks of competing and complementary discourses across the sociocultural spectrum.

The Power of Metaphors

The main conceptual tool that will be employed to understand how different discourses can interact with one another and even co-constitute one another is the metaphor, which has already been touched upon above. Traditionally viewed as a mere rhetorical flourish reserved to poetry and literature and viewed as the sign of muddled thinking in philosophy, the role of the metaphor in language and human cognition has benefited from a major re-evaluation in recent times. In opposition to the notion of the metaphor as a mere statement of similarity, paraphrase, or ornamental figure of prose ("saying one thing and meaning another"), Max Black has argued that the metaphor consists in viewing a principal conceptual domain – that is any coherent organisation of experience – through the lens of another subsidiary conceptual domain. The word "metaphor" itself is from the Greek for "transfer" with metaphors effectively transfering meaning from one domain to another. But as two different domains cannot by definition be the same, metaphor necessarily involves an arbitrary simplification of both domains since it must rely on illuminating certain features while obscuring others in order for the metaphor to work. Hence "the metaphor selects, emphasises, suppresses, and organises features of the principal subject by implying statements about it that normally apply to the subsidiary subject."[42] The reverse is also true in that metaphors work both ways; the subsidiary subject comes to be seen to be more like the principal subject.

It has furthermore been argued that many "literal" expressions are in fact simply "dead" or "frozen" metaphors that we no longer recognise as such. Obvious examples would include such expressions as the

---

42   Max Black, *Models and Metaphors: Studies in Language and Philosophy* (Ithaca, NY: Cornell University Press, 1962), pp. 44-45.

wings of a building, the branches of science, or the foot of a mountain.[43] Thus according to Schon all language is metaphorical and the creation of metaphors is the process through which concepts are formed and displaced from old to new domains. "The metaphorical character of language [...] is due to the fact that our language, at any given time, gives us a cross-section of our processes of concept formation or discovery. The metaphors in language are to be explained as signs of concepts at various stages of displacement, just as fossils are to be explained as signs of living things in various stages of evolution."[44]

If conceptual thought is therefore largely structured according to specific metaphors, it follows that many (if not all) social activities and human representations of the world around us are organised by metaphorical understandings. For Lakoff and Johnson, this implies that:

new metaphors have the power to create a new reality. This can begin to happen when we start to comprehend our experience in terms of a metaphor, and it becomes a deeper reality when we begin to act in terms of it. If a new metaphor enters the conceptual system that we base our actions on, it will alter that conceptual system and the perceptions and actions that the system gives rise to.[45]

While new metaphors can modify our conceptual system, they also help us apprehend novelty. Indeed, through them we can understand the new and unfamiliar in the terms of images, objects or conceptual frameworks we are already comfortable with (we should not necessarily limit the concept of "metaphor" to language – "metaphors can be not merely linguistic but experiential and material as well"[46]). As Richard Robbins observes:

Metaphors give a feeling of power and control. If we have a thorough understanding of one system of relations [...] we can use it to comprehend a system of relations we only begin to grasp, and, as a result, we get a feeling of security,

---

43   Alan D. Beyerchen, "Clausewitz, Nonlinearity, and the Importance of Imagery" in David S. Alberts and Thomas J. Czerwinski (eds), *Complexity, Global Politics, and National Security* (Washington, D.C.: National Defense University, 1997), p. 74.

44   Donald A. Schon, *Displacement of Concepts* (London: Tavistock Publications, 1963), p. 51.

45   George Lakoff and Mark Johnson, *Metaphors We Live By* (Chicago, IL: University of Chicago Press, 1990), pp. 145-146.

46   Edwards, *The Closed World*, p. 30.

well-being and power. Simply by naming features of a new experience, we fix and control that experience. In every instance of the use of a known metaphor to interpret a new experience there is a transition from helplessness to power. Where something was puzzling, it suddenly becomes clear.[47]

Metaphors can therefore constitute a means of ordering experience by imposing existing structures of meaning over the chaos and confusion produced by the eruption of novelty. It is on the basis of the new understanding afforded by metaphor that future actions can be justified and control exerted. The parallels with the ordering processes in science, technology in warfare previously discussed are clear, indicating perhaps that we have with the metaphor one of the basic mechanisms through which human consciousness imposes order on experience. Certainly for Nietzsche "the drive toward the formation of metaphors is the fundamental human drive, which one cannot for a single instant dispense with in thought, for one would thereby dispense with man himself." [48]

Black argues that the theoretical model in science does function very much like the metaphor as a "distinctive mode of achieving insight" which brings disparate domains into cognitive relation and constitutes new relationships that cannot be antecedently predicted:

Much the same can be said about the role of models in scientific research. If the model were invoked *after* the work of abstract formulation had already been accomplished, it would be at best a convenience of exposition. But the memorable models of science are "speculative instruments" [...] They, too, bring about a wedding of disparate subjects, by a distinctive operation of transfer of the *implications* of relatively well-organised cognitive fields. And as with other weddings, their outcomes are unpredictable. Use of a particular model may amount to nothing more than a strained and artificial description of a domain sufficiently known otherwise. But it may also help us to notice what otherwise would be overlooked, to shift the relative emphasis attached to details – in short, to *see new connections*.[49]

Black proposes a much more general understanding of metaphor than that allowed by its traditional literary definition since it applies to

---

47   Richard H. Robbins, *The Belief Machine* (1985).

48   Friedrich Nietzsche, 'On Truth and Lie in an Extra-Moral Sense' in D. Breazeale (ed. and tr.), *Philosophy and Truth: Selections from Nietzsche's Notebooks of the Early 1870's* (Atlantic Highlands, NJ: Humanities Press, 1979), p. 88.

49   Black, *Models and Metaphors*, pp. 236-237.

all cognitive processes by which a domain is viewed in terms of another domain. Robbins advocates an equally broad view of the metaphor, claiming that "many terms have been used to label the subsidiaries, the "known," that we bring to each new experience to give it meaning: "schemata," "themata," "paradigm," "world vision," "world view," "model," "framework," and "theory" are just some of these labels. But, in the most rudimentary sense, all these things – schemata, theories, world visions, and the rest – are metaphors; like metaphors, we transfer theories and schemata, world visions and world views, paradigms and themata to experiential phenomena as our way of understanding the phenomena."[50] Nor are scientists necessarily blind to the metaphorical nature of their theoretical enterprises. The chaos theory pioneer Robert Stetson Shaw claims that "you don't see something until you have the right metaphor to let you perceive it" while for the complexity theorist Brian Arthur from the Santa Fe Institute science "is about the creation of metaphors."[51] According to the English cybernetician and psychologist Gordon Pask, cybernetics was nothing else than "the art and science of manipulating defensible metaphors."[52]

In this book discussion will focus on the four specific machinic metaphors of clockwork, engine, computer, and network that have been central to the respective technoscientific discourses of mechanism, thermodynamics, cybernetics, and chaoplexity. Each metaphor owes its particularly widespread cultural influence to its embodiment in the dominant technology of the era and its pivotal position within a broad web of theories and practices. Within scientific discourse, the metaphors served as both points of departure for speculation and as heuristics bolstering the theories that sprang from them. Indeed, for Michael Arbib and Mary Hesse, "scientific revolutions are in fact metaphoric revolutions, and theoretical explanation should be seen as metaphoric redescription of the domain of the phenomena."[53] In the military sphere, paradigmatic changes in the organisation and exercise of armed force

---

50   Robbins, *The Belief Machine*.

51   James Gleick, *Chaos: Making a New Science* (London: Vintage, 1987), p. 262. King, *Social Science and Complexity*, pp. 13-14.

52   American Society for Cybernetics, "Defining 'Cybernetics'" http://www.asc-cybernetics.org/foundations/definitions.htm

53   Lily E. Kay, *Who Wrote the Book of Life? A History of the Genetic Code* (Stanford, CA: Stanford University Press, 2000), p. 22.

have likewise been structured around these four machinic metaphors which provide conceptual lenses and models for thinking about war. We can now turn to the specific technoscientific regimes of warfare to which each of these metaphors is associated.

The Four Regimes of the Scientific Way of Warfare

The advent of modernity brought about radical transformations in the practice of warfare. For Chris Hables Gray, the beginning of modern war was marked by three crucial trends emerging in the sixteenth century: the application of rationality to war instead of tradition, the development of administrative bureaucracies, and the systematic application of science and technology.[54] In practice, these three trends were closely interwoven with rationalisation underpinning both administrative reform and the scientific project.

Certainly the recruitment of reason to military affairs had not waited for the modern world. The classicist John Onians has traced the origin of Greek mathematics to "the importance of absolute order in the military sphere which gave mathematics a dominant role in all Greek culture."[55] But the marriage of warfare and science took on a new potency in a modern era which unsurprisingly consciously modelled itself on the classical world in heralding the reaffirmation of reason as its guiding light. Unprecedented means of destruction were assembled through expanding armies and logistical structures while the full spectrum of war was increasingly brought under scientific and technocratic scrutiny.

If a scientific way of warfare emerged with the advent of modernity and has since endured and gained in influence, there have nonetheless been considerable fluctuations in the specific ideas and practices ad-

---

54   Gray, *Postmodern War*, p. 111.

55   Bernhelm Booss-Bavnbek, "Mathematics and War" (Draft Essay for Hutchinson Companion Encyclopedia of Mathematics, 2001) Erastosthenes (276 BC – 194 BC) claimed the main purpose for doing cube roots was to calculate settings for ballistae. Alex Roland, "Science, Technology, and War", *Technology and Culture*, Vol. 36, No. 2, Supplement: Snapshots of a Discipline: Selected Proceedings from the Conference on Critical Problems and Research Frontiers in the History of Technology, Madison, WI, Oct. 30-Nov. 3, 1991. (Apr. 1995), p. 95.

vanced within this continuity in the appeal to technoscientific rationality. The four regimes that compose it are characterised by the successive dominant technologies and machine metaphors (the clock, the engine, the computer, and the network) and the respective sciences they have supported (mechanism, thermodynamics, cybernetics, and chaoplexity). There now follows a brief outline of the central features of these four regimes of the scientific way of warfare.

	Mechanism	Thermodynamics	Cybernetics	Chaoplexity
Key technology	Clock	Engine	Computer	Network
Scientific concepts	Force matter in motion linearity geometry	Energy entropy probability	Information negentropy negative feedback homeostasis	Information non-linearity positive feedback self-organisation emergence
Form of warfare	close order drill rigid tactical deployments	mass mobilisation motorisation industrialisation	command and control automation	decentralisation swarming

Figure 1: The four regimes of the scientific way of warfare

1. Mechanistic Warfare and the Clock. Mechanism constituted the first major scientific discourse and in many ways set the template for the future development of science. Under mechanism, the universe became understood as an entirely mechanical system composed wholly of matter in motion under a complete and regular set of laws of nature. The core ideas behind mechanism were the laws of motion as formulated by Newton, the concomitant notions of gravity and mass, the reversibility of time, and the belief that any whole could be understood through the analysis of its individual parts. The metaphor of the world as a machine also begins here, to be carried on through different iterations under successive technoscientific discourses. The specific machine metaphor around which mechanism revolved was that of the clock, or more specifically the clockwork mechanism.

Within the mechanistic philosophy and science dominating European thought throughout the seventeenth and eighteenth centuries, clockwork acted not only as a symbol of the order, regularity and predictability of the universe and its diverse natural bodies but also as a mechanism serving scientific enquiry as both an instrument and object of study. By embodying a general concept of operation and model of organisation enmeshed in wider cultural discourses, clockwork came to represent simultaneously the unveiled order of the physical world and a prescribed ideal in human affairs. Chaos was exorcised by the invocation of divine clockwork behind all phenomena and the promise of complete predictability and control. A clockwork universe also implied a divine watchmaker who had constructed its mechanisms and set it in motion, a vision that resonated with the enlightened absolutism of the day, its faith in the rational and orderly organisation of government, and the position of the monarch as uncontested divine representative and sole seat of power.

Mechanistic warfare subscribed to the same vision, with its armies emphasising rehearsed synchronous movements and characterised by the lack of autonomy of their parts and their unflinching obedience to the pre-determined sequence of battle decided upon by their commanders. Geometry and the newly discovered laws of motion were widely applied to improve fortifications and ballistics, but in the field the tendency was towards shaping armies into giant clockwork mechanisms. In an age in which the state of firearms technology meant its effects on the battlefield were maximised through coordinated volleys, and with the possibility of communications highly restricted once engagement with the enemy had begun, troops were heavily drilled into marching in step according to rigid tactical deployments and performing synchronised firing and reloading cycles at the highest possible tempo.

Mechanistic warfare attempted to maintain order and ward off chaos through a pre-programmed and centralised routine devoid of any capacity for reactivity to the actions of the opposing army. With virtually all initiative removed from individual soldiers, success required that the commanding officers meticulously plan ahead and dictate in advance the series of manoeuvres to be carried out. Although this model was the product of lengthy development which can be traced back to the Dutch armies of Maurice of Nassau at the turn of the seventeenth century, Frederick the Great's Prussian army remain its paradigmatic embodiment.

2. Thermodynamic Warfare and the Engine. With thermodynamics and the engine, science gained an understanding of the energy that drove the previously studied mechanisms of motion. As the study of heat derived from the engineering prowess that produced the steam engine, nineteenth-century thermodynamics revolutionised the scientific world-view through the discovery of both the convertibility of all forms of energy and its inevitable dissipation into randomness through entropy. No longer appearing reversible but acquiring direction, time was said to have founds its arrow, one leading to the inevitable heat death of the universe in an inexorable progression from order to chaos.

The thermodynamic world was one of instability and change in which the cultivated stability of the *ancien régime* was rapidly swept away by revolutionary and nationalistic fervour. But if time found its arrow, it was not always from order to chaos. Indeed ideologies of progress also proclaimed a direction to history at the end of which lay a liberal, socialist, or national paradise. From the chaos of the age, a final and immutable order would emerge, even if more disorder would first be required in the form of war or revolution, those great 'engines' of history. Narratives of optimistic progress and fearful decline alternated in the cultural imagination of the nineteenth- and early twentieth-century European. But if there were conflicting accounts of the direction time was taking, what remained undisputed was the new impermanence of the world and the uncertainty it brought with it. As the founder of "scientific socialism" Karl Marx famously put it, "all that is solid melts into the air" in the foundry of the new industrial world. The engine, the device that put to work the sources of motive power and was central to industrialisation, replaced clockwork as the dominant machine metaphor and the theoretical and practical nexus for the new scientific worldview.

Thermodynamic warfare saw the channelling into war of ever-greater flows of energy, whether it was the motorised energy propelling vehicles on land, sea and in the air, the ballistic energy of increasingly destructive weapons, the industrial energies driving economies mobilised for total war, or the moral energies unleashed by the nationalistic ardour of conscripts and the home front. Beginning with the feverish élan of the French Revolution and the Napoleonic wars of conquest, thermodynamic warfare culminated in the ultimate paroxysm of the the Second World War and the detonation of the atom bomb. If the logistical requirements of industrial warfare brought entire economies under unprecedented centralised control, the chaos of the battlefield imposed some tactical decentralisation, notably through the German army's *Auftragstaktik*, the mission-oriented tactics successfully experimented with by stormtrooper units during the First World War and subsequently developed into *Blitzkrieg*.

Thermodynamic thought also expressed itself in the writings of Carl von Clausewitz who recognised the essentially dynamic and irreducibly unpredictable nature of war, and theorised the inevitable friction and fog inherent in military operations. Chaos was here understood as inherent to warfare, a constant threat to the best laid plans, which military commanders should recognise and adapt to rather than engage in futile attempts to banish.

3. Cybernetic Warfare and the Computer. As the intensity and breadth of the battlefield grew along with its logistical requirements, communication technologies became necessary to achieve the required coordination of increasingly large and intricate military systems. The harnessing of electromagnetic forces for telecommunication purposes proceeded with telegraphy and telephony, stimulating growing scientific interest in the concept of information. Cybernetics emerged from the unprecedented technological and industrial effort of World War II, in particular the work on the automation of anti-aircraft defences. The self-proclaimed "science of communications and control" promised to manage chaos and disruption through self-regulating mechanisms of information feedback. By being defined in terms of negative entropy (negentropy), information became conceptualised as the source of all order. The computer, another product of the war effort, became the new dominant technology and abstract model through which the world came to be understood chiefly in terms of information-processing.

The drive for complete predictability and centralised control over armed conflict was renewed under cybernetic warfare with the deployment of computing and servomechanistic technologies and the application of the analytical tools of operations research and systems analysis. The Cold War and the permanent threat of nuclear annihilation required ever greater levels of automation and centralisation of the war machine and cybernetic technology's promise of stability in the face of perturbation appeared best suited to the containment and management of a conflict of potentially apocalyptic proportions. Vast command and control architectures were established to organise the global projection of armed force and the rapid mobilisation of military systems within the shrinking window of opportunity afforded by nuclear weaponry. Scientific methodology was applied to warfare more systematically than ever, with operations research and systems analysis comprehensively deployed to solve tactical and strategic problems. In its most pristine form, cybernetic warfare fuelled fantasies of omniscience and omnipotence on the battlefield which endure to this day despite its catastrophic failure in the jungles of Viernam.

4. Chaoplexic Warfare and the Network. From the mid-1970s onwards, the cybernetic regime came under increasing challenge from the military reversal for US forces in Vietnam, geopolitical transformation following the end of the Cold War, and novel scientific developments which grew out of the original corpus of cybernetics. The increasing application of computers to the study of scientific problems, the rediscovery of non-linear mathematics, and an extension of the cybernetic analysis of systems to questions of self-production and self-organisation constituted new scientific approaches which crystallised in the theories of chaos and complexity (referred to together as *chaoplexity*) in the 1980s. Information remains the central concept, and in this sense chaoplexity is an outgrowth of cybernetics and information theory, but the focus on change, evolution, and positive feedback breaks with the concern for stability of the cybernetic pioneers. While some of the certainties and predictability of the previous scientific theories and methodologies have been terminally undermined, a hidden order has been discovered behind chaos which is thereby no longer conceived as only an evil to avert but as order's very condition of possibility. The key notions here are those of non-linearity, self-organisation, and emergence, and the central metaphor is that of the network, the distributed model of information exchange perhaps best embodied by the Internet.

As the Cold War has receded, a monolithic threat viewed through the lens of bi-polarity has given way to a globalised world in which risks are diffuse and amorphous, requiring new approaches to security. The spectacular failure of cybernetic warfare in Vietnam when faced with a diffuse and decentralised enemy triggered a long debate on the need for a reconceptualisation of the organisation and exercise of military force. If the first incarnations of the "Revolution in Military Affairs" seemed only to offer further extensions of the original cybernetic paradigm, a growing influence of the ideas of chaos, complexity, and the role of networks has become evident in recent years, leading to the adoption of the doctrine of network-centric warfare by the Pentagon in the late 1990s. Large parts of the doctrine's theoretical body draw explicitly or implicitly on ideas of complexity and self-organisation, notably its notions of self-synchronisation and swarming. Despite this it is not yet possible truly to speak of chaoplexic warfare as network-centric warfare appears still to rest on many of the assumptions of cybernetic warfare and displays some serious theoretical and operational shortcomings. Nevertheless, the impetus towards more decentralised and autonomous forms of military organisation is clearly visible, no doubt accelerated by the successes of the insurgencies and terrorist networks that have adopted similar modes of operation.

2

Mechanistic Warfare and the Clockwork Universe

The clock is the first automatic machine applied to practical purposes. The whole theory of the production of regular motion was developed through it.

Karl Marx, 1863 letter to Engels[1]

An army is the instrument with which every species of military action is performed: like all machines it is composed of various parts, and its perfection will depend, first, on that of its several parts; and second, on the manner in which they are arranged; so that the whole may have the following properties, viz. strength, agility, and universality; if these are properly combined, the machine is perfect.

Henry Lloyd[2]

Mechanism, the philosophy and science dominating European thought throughout the seventeenth and eighteenth centuries and which characterised the first technoscientific regime of warfare, was crucially articulated around clockwork technology. While the clockwork mechanism itself served scientific enquiry as both a tool and an object of study, the clockwork metaphor came to represent the order, regularity, and

---

1   Christopher Coker, *The Future of War: The Re-Enchantment of War in the Twenty-First Century* (Oxford: Blackwell, 2004), p. 25.

2   Patrick J. Speelman (ed.), *War, Society and Enlightenment: The Works of General Lloyd* (Leiden: Brill, 2005), p. 385.

predictability science sought to uncover in the workings of the universe. What men took to be a fundamental truth about the nature of the world simultaneously became a powerful model for the organisation of human affairs. Emulation of the virtues of clockwork in military affairs was perhaps never more obvious than in the organisation and doctrine of Frederick the Great's Prussian army. However, before broaching mechanistic warfare itself and relating the machine metaphor to its contemporary form of warfare, we have to address the genesis of clockwork technology, its interplay with scientific theory and method, and its development into a metaphorical figure of Western discourse.

From Mechanical Clock to Clockwork Metaphor

While time-keeping devices such as the sundial and water clock have existed for millenia, their mechanical incarnation appeared in Europe only in the late thirteenth century.[3] Combining the ancient Greek technology of toothed wheels and gear trains, a system of weights, and the crucial addition of an escapement mechanism allowing a steady motion of strictly constant velocity, the clockwork mechanism brought about a revolution in horology and the design of automata.

Mechanical clocks remained expensive and bulky in the first two centuries that followed their invention but they nevertheless spread rapidly across Europe. With an initial emphasis put on the production of tower clocks for public buildings, mechanical timekeepers served major social functions such as regulating the opening and closing of markets in many municipalities from the fourteenth and fifteenth century onwards. The development of spring-based mechanisms in the late fifteenth century significantly improved the reliability and portability of clockwork devices and contributed to their further dissemination throughout Europe. The widespread diffusion of the mechanical clock transformed social life, divorcing it from the natural cycles of day and night and imposing a division of time into constant and regular units. Clocks enabled a greater synchronisation of social activities, with punc-

---

3   Sundials and water clocks can be traced as far back as ancient Egypt. However, until the mechanical clock, time keeping was imprecise and tributary to meteorological conditions (the availability of the sun or of temperatures above freezing).

tuality elevated to a social virtue, most notably in European courtly life of the seventeenth and eighteenth centuries. This new universal rhythm would play a major role in ordering emerging industrial societies since, as David Landes points out, "the clock is not merely a means of keeping track of the hours, but of synchronising the actions of men."[4]

While clockmaking was essentially the province of skilled artisans, the development of time-keeping devices soon became entwined with the emerging scientific method. In 1657, Christiaan Huygens, the discoverer of the wave behaviour of light, invented the first successful pendulum clock, markedly increasing the accuracy of timekeeping. This and subsequent increases in precision were of huge scientific importance as without them the study of physics as it developed in the following centuries would have simply been impossible. Furthermore, clocks were not merely another useful experimental apparatus for scientists but were also of critical conceptual significance since, as Lewis Mumford correctly observes, they "dissociated time from human events and helped create the belief in an independent world of mathematically measurable sequences: the special world of science."[5] By providing this discrete mathematical measure of time, clocks affected the way patterns of social activity, and particularly those of production, could be thought of and acted upon. It was now possible to carry out all sorts of operations upon time itself according to ever more fine and precise segmentations – to add, subtract or insert it into any arithmetical calculation, to compare and contrast it, to price, sell, and purchase it, to allocate and ration it among individuals, or to save it through particular devices, production techniques, or organisational arrangements. To this day, the rationalisation of the division of labour characteristic of the modern era relies heavily upon the objective and constant measurement of time kept by the mechanical clock.[6]

---

4   David Landes, *Revolution in Time: Clocks and the Making of the Modern World* (Cambridge, MA: Harvard University Press, 1983), p. xix.

5   Lewis Mumford, *Technics and Civilization* (New York: Harcourt, Brace and Co., 1934), p. 15.

6   A further practical application of mechanical timepieces was the solution provided to the problem of identifying the longitudinal position of a ship during navigation. Indeed, while measurement of the altitude of Polaris or that of the sun at local noon above the horizon provided an easy and reliable indication of latitude, purely astronomical methods for longitude were far more mathemati-

If mechanical time-keeping played a crucial role in the foundation of the scientific outlook, the clockwork *mechanism* itself had an equally far-reaching cultural effect as a metaphor for the motions of celestial and natural bodies. Indeed, as the clockmaking craft developed, timekeeping was often secondary to the display of elaborate mechanisms that attempted to mirror the different aspects of the natural world. Chief among these was the design of complex astronomical devices that indicated the motion of planetary bodies, such as the famous astronomical clock of Strasbourg, first constructed in 1354 and then rebuilt in 1574. The Strasbourg clock also included a rooster automaton, imitation of life being the other chief use of clockwork mechanisms. Automated reproduction of music was also popular with numerous devices mimicking the actions of a human instrumentalist produced.

The cultural influence of automata grew as clockwork mechanisms became more complex, to the extent that automata and clocks were essentially considered as a single type of device. As Otto Mayr tells us, "in dictionaries from the sixteenth to eighteenth centuries, the automaton (a machine that moved independently on the strength of both a power supply and a plan of action, or program, of its own) was the higher, general category; the clock was merely a particular variety of automaton."[7] We can infer from this that it was the clockwork mechanism itself, above the specific uses to which it was put, which impressed itself most on the minds of contemporaries, and particularly on those of the intellectual class that drove the Scientific Revolution that culminated in the

---

cally cumbersome and imprecise due to the complication introduced by the rotation of the earth. A chronometer indicating the precise time at a given location whose longitude was known could be used as a reference point to calculate present longitude on the basis of the local high noon. Producing a mechanical clock that could keep time with a high degree of precision in the face of tumultuous motion and varying conditions of temperature, atmospheric pressure, and humidity at sea proved a major engineering challenge which such luminaries as Newton and Huygens doubted could be met but was eventually solved in 1761 by the English clockmaker John Harrison. The resulting improvement in the precision of celestial navigation played no small part in enabling growth in global trade and imperial expansion in the nineteenth century, both of which were heavily reliant on seafaring.

7   Otto Mayr, *Authority, Liberty and Automatic Machinery in Early Modern Europe* (Baltimore, MD and London: John Hopkins University Press, 1986), p. 21.

development of Newtonian mechanics.[8] Contemporary references to "machines" evoked first and foremost clockwork as the most stunning technical achievement of the times. In effect, the clockwork denomination went from simply designating a specific object (the clock) to what DeLanda has called an "abstract machine" – a general concept of operation or model of organisation.[9] This conceptual shift would allow the clockwork metaphor to blossom until it formed a centrepiece of the emerging philosophical and scientific worldview of mechanism.

The Clockwork Universe: The Ascendancy of the Mechanistic Worldview

The clockwork "abstract machine" is ever-present in the European scientific literature of the sixteenth to early eighteenth centuries with its metaphorical effects resonating through scientific and philosophical discourses. First, it served as an instrument of demystification by demonstrating how apparently inexplicable motion could be accounted for by a dissimulated assemblage of cogs, weights and springs rather than by a supernatural and/or unknowable force. It also suggested that an understanding of natural phenomena could be best deduced by breaking it up into smaller parts, the study and observation of which would illuminate the entire process, a break from the holistic approach of the Aristotelian tradition. This brought to the fore the notion of cause and

---

8   The Scientific Revolution refers to the establishment of modern scientific method (principally mathematisation, mechanisation, and empiricism) and the major theoretical developments that occurred from the discoveries of Kepler and Galileo in the late sixteenth century to the publication of Newton's *Principia* (1687). The boundaries of this "revolution" are disputed, with some historians dating its beginnings to Copernicus's work on a heliocentric model of the solar system (1543) or extending it into the eighteenth century, while others even question its existence, generally on the grounds that it constituted an evolution rather than a revolution. Regardless of the finer points of this debate, it is clear that a powerful change in the scientific worldview occurred over this period in which the qualitative deductive Aristotelian conception of science, that had so dominated the later Middle Ages in its scholastic form, was replaced by a quantitative and empiricist inductive approach that still forms the basis of our present-day understandings of science.

9   DeLanda, *War in the Age of Intelligent Machines*, p. 139.

effect in a new and powerful way, Hobbes presenting science as nothing else than "the knowledge of consequences, and dependence of one fact upon another."[10] Alongside the aforementioned constitution of a mechanical time divorced from human perceptions of it, these shifts in the dominant conceptual frameworks suggest that clockwork was in fact the foundational metaphor of modern science.

These ideas and discursive practices were all central to the development of the "mechanistic" approach that rose to prominence in the seventeenth and eighteenth centuries. In essence, mechanism posited that the universe is best understood as a completely mechanical system composed entirely of matter in motion under a complete and regular system of laws of nature. For Karl Deutsch, the mechanistic model also:

implied the notion of the whole which was completely equal to the sum of its parts; which could be run in reverse; and which could behave in exactly identical fashion no matter how often these parts were disassembled and put together again, and irrespective of the sequence in which the reassembly would take place.[11]

Parallels can be drawn between the above properties of regularity, reversible motion, ease of disassembly and reassembly, and those of clockwork mechanisms.

Mechanism was as much a methodology as a set of ontological statements. It was postulated that the best method of scientific enquiry was to dissaggregate the phenomena under scrutiny into individual parts or sequences of events that could be reliably distinguished, measured, and compared using the experimental apparatus of the day. These batches of knowledge could then be related to each other to detect regularities, formulate causal links, and extract a calculable coherence of forces expressed by way of geometrical representations and algebraic functions. This practice of breaking down any problem into component parts which could be more effectively tackled individually before being reassembled is also common to that of the modern division of labour in which production in broken down into optimal stages in which individuals specialise, granting greater efficiency to the overall process. We should therefore perhaps not be surprised that it is in the manufacture

---

10   James King, *Science and Rationalism in the Government of Louis XIV* (Baltimore, MD: John Hopkins Press, 1949), p. 17.

11   Stephen David Bryen, *The Application of Cybernetic Analysis to the Study of International Politics* (The Hague: Martinus Nijhoff, 1971), p. 5.

of clockwork, the most advanced craftsmanship of the time, that the division of labour was then applied most thoroughly. The seventeenth-century Swiss horologist Ferdinand Berthoud listed no less than sixteen different sorts of workmen involved in producing clocks, while twenty-one where required for watches.[12]

English natural philosopher Robert Boyle explicitly linked clockwork to mechanist thought in 1665:

> [The mechanist] hypothesis, supposing the whole universe (the soul of man excepted) to be but a great Automaton, or self-moving engine, wherein all things are performed by the bare motion (or rest), the size, the shape, and the situation, or texture of the parts of the universal matter it consists of [...] so that the world being but, as it were, a great piece of clockwork, the naturalist, as such, is but a mechanician; however the parts of the engine, he considers, be some of them larger, and some of them much minuter, than those of clocks or watches.[13]

Thus the clockwork mechanism functioned within the mechanistic worldview as a metaphor for all physical, and by extension social, reality, articulating statements about the movement and composition of celestial and natural bodies as well as social constructs such as the state or army. It is to these more specific, yet interconnected, metaphors that we must now turn, starting with the revolution in astronomy which culminated in Newton's grand synthesis.

The Clockwork Heavens: Newtonian Mechanics and the Clockmaker God

In the burgeoning scientific community of the late Middle Ages and early modern era, the clockwork metaphor occupied a central position in the scholarly debates over the movements of the heavens. The motion and regularity of clockwork mechanisms, although highly prone

---

12 Daniel J. Boorstin, *The Discoverers: A History of Man's Search to Know his World and Himself* (Hamondsworth, Middlesex: Penguin, 1986), p. 66. According to Deleuze and Guattari, "the way in which a science, or a conception of science, participates in the organisation of the social field, and in particular induces a division of labour, is part of that science itself." Deleuze and Guattari, *A Thousand Plateaus*, p. 368-9.

13 Mayr, *Authority, Liberty and Automatic Machinery in Early Modern Europe*, p. 56.

to breaking down in their earlier incarnations, were from very early on compared to that of celestial bodies. Astronomical devices were among the first applications of clockwork and Cardwell even suggests that attempts to reproduce the motion of the heavens may have led to the very invention of clockwork, prior to the design of any mechanical time-keeping device.[14] Certainly, as early as 1377, Nicolas Oresme observed that "the situation is much like that of a man making a clock and letting it run and continue its motion by itself. In this manner did God allow the heavens to be moved continually [...] according to the established order."[15] The image of God as the ultimate Clockmaker, the designer of a perfect mechanism that would run its divinely-appointed course until the end of time, was thereafter a recurrent motif in Western culture in the following centuries, a clear case of mutually reinforcing discursive resonance between a theological argument pertaining to the creation and ordering of the world and a mechanical metaphor for the movement of the heavens.

In the first half of the sixteenth century, Copernicus greatly simplified the motion of celestial bodies with his heliocentric theory, placing the Sun at the centre of the known universe and overturning the accepted Ptolemaic geocentric system which had Earth at its centre. There was no significant concomitant increase in the precision of astronomical predictions however, but the new system's superior aesthetic was seductive. Johannes Kepler soon added a new mathematical rigour and elegance to the theory, his avowed goal being "to show that the heavenly machine is not a kind of divine, live being, but a kind of clockwork, insofar as nearly all the manifold motions are caused by a most simple, magnetic, and material force, just as all motions of the clock are caused by a simple weight."[16] While Galileo's telescopic observations confirmed the validity of the heliocentric hypothesis, a unifying theory of earthly and celestial motion to replace the discredited Aristotelian physics was still lacking. This crowning achievement of the Scientific Revolution was to be the work of Isaac Newton.

---

14   D.S.L. Cardwell, *Turning Points in Western Technology: A Study of Technology, Science and History* (New York: Neale Watson Academic Publications, 1974), p. 16.

15   David Bolter, *Turing's Man: Western Culture in the Computer Age* (London: Duckworth, 1984), p. 27.

16   Arthur Koestler, *The Sleepwalkers* (London: Arkana Books, 1989), p. 345.

Newton expounded his conception of the universe and the laws governing it in his *Principia Mathematica*, published in 1687 and destined to become the scientific text that would set the standard for all those that would follow. According to Newton, the natural world functioned in a completely rational and predictable way which could be described solely through the language of mathematics and geometry. The motion of all terrestrial and celestial bodies was explained by the physical attraction exerted on each other, dubbed *gravitas* (gravity) and whose force is a function of their respective masses and of the distance between them. Although Newton himself never explicitly used the clockwork metaphor in his work on the motion of physical bodies, his account of regular and ordered motion of planets within a single gravitational system bolstered the popular notion of a "clockwork universe."[17]

Newton also found that the acceleration exerted by gravity on bodies is identical to that experienced by bodies set in motion by other forces, so that the rate of change in the momentum of an object is directly proportional to the amount of force acting upon it in the direction in which the force is being applied.[18] He had thus seemingly uncovered the single principle behind the movements of all physical bodies and had formulated this principle into a mathematical relationship. The world thereby became understood as matter in motion according to fixed laws that could be expressed mathematically.

---

17   Pre-eminent mechanists such as Descartes objected virulently to the principle of "action at a distance" required by the concept of gravity, to which they preferred an explanation relying on the transmission of forces through the contact of particles and surfaces in the manner of cogwheels on one another, thereby defending a more faithful application of the clockwork metaphor.

18   Newton's Second Law of Gravity from the *Principia Mathematica* (1792 translation from Latin): "The alteration of motion is ever proportional to the motive force impressed; and is made in the direction of the right line in which that force is impressed. If a force generates a motion, a double force will generate double the motion, a triple force triple the motion, whether that force be impressed altogether and at once, or gradually and successively. And this motion (being always directed the same way with the generating force), if the body moved before, is added to or subtracted from the former motion, according as they directly conspire with or are directly contrary to each other; or obliquely joined, when they are oblique, so as to produce a new motion compounded from the determination of both."

A further implication of Newton's findings was that, equipped with the knowledge of the fundamental laws governing it, it was possible (at least theoretically) to predict completely the future and past of all physical systems. Indeed, if a system's state at any given moment is known with precision, then the past and future of the system can be predicted with absolute certainty. The mathematician and astronomer Pierre-Simon Laplace later mused about the implications when the entire universe is considered as a single system:

We may regard the present state of the universe as the effect of the past and the cause of the future. Given for one instant an intelligence which could comprehend all the forces by which nature is animated and the respective positions of the beings which compose it, if moreover this intelligence were vast enough to submit these data to analysis, it would embrace in the same formula both the movements of the largest bodies in the universe and those of the lightest atom: to it nothing would be uncertain, and the future as the past would be present to its eyes.[19]

The Newtonian universe was therefore thoroughly deterministic, viewing all events as the necessary results of a sequence of causes and reducible to the transmission of a single and invariant motive force. Such processes were also necessarily reversible: the original state of any system could be restored simply by applying the reverse of any dynamic changes it had gone through.

The laws of motion were idealised in that they did not account for friction, the force which opposes the relative motion of two surfaces in contact and prevents motion from being fully transmitted from one body to the other. While not ignored by classical mechanics, friction was discounted and excluded from Newton's laws of motion, downgraded to a "noise" which obscured the fundamental pattern. A main reason for this was one of practicality since one of the great advantages of the laws as formulated by Newton was their linearity. In mathematical terms, linear systems are marked by proportionality (changes in system output are proportional to changes in system input) and additivity (the whole is equal to the sum of its parts). Linear functions are simple to solve as they can be broken up into individual parts which can be solved separately and their solutions added up. In contrast, non-linear systems are characterised by the absence of proportionality and/or additivity.

---

19   Pierre Simon de Laplace, "Theorie Analytique des Probabilités", *Oeuvres Complètes de Laplace*, Vol. VII (Paris: Gauthier-Villars, 1820).

Inclusion of the variable and non-linear phenomenon of friction would have prevented the formulation of universal and easily applicable laws of motion. However, for many practical purposes and common speeds and accelerations of motion, the effects of friction were small enough to ignore. When required, a coefficient of friction could be included in calculations but could only be experimentally determined and remained an unsightly addendum to the idealised laws of motion. It is only with the development of thermodynamics that friction and the irreversible energetic losses that result from it would move to the centre stage of the scientific worldview.[20]

In establishing a theory of vast explanatory power resting on a simple fundamental principle from which all related phenomena could be deduced, Newtonian mechanics became a model for all scientists seeking to create an elegant system accounting for the behaviour of the observable world. Indeed Diderot's *Encyclopédie* encapsulated best the aspirations of those seeking to emulate Newton in its article on "system", with an exposition which relied once again on the clockwork metaphor:

System is nothing more than the disposition of the different parts of an art or a science into a state where they all mutually support each other and where the last ones are explained through the first. Those that account for the others are called principles, and the system is all the more perfect as the principles are fewer in number: it is even desirable that they should be reduced to a single one. For, just as there is one main spring in a clock upon which all others

---

20   While Newton's laws of motion are indeed linear, the systems of bodies in motion that can be constructed with them are not necessarily so. One- and two-body problems can be effectively solved as linear systems and these included all the scientific triumphs of the age, such as the calculation of the motion of celestial bodies (considered as a two-body problem in which two masses such as the earth and the moon exert gravitational attraction on one another) or the progress in ballistics (considered a one-body problem since the differentials in mass between a projectile and the earth mean the former's gravitational pull on the latter can be safely ignored). However, problems composed of three or more bodies pose largely insuperable difficulties as non-linear effects prevent decomposition of the system and the formulation of a general analytic solution. Henri Poincaré's consideration of the three-body problem in the late nineteenth century is often seen as an early insight into what would become chaos theory (see chapter 6). While an awareness of non-linearity may have existed among some mathematicians of the seventeenth and eighteenth centuries, attention was naturally focused on the problems that could be solved with the result that the study of non-linearity was largely neglected.

depend, there is also in all systems one first principle to which are subordinated the different parts that make it up.[21]

The search for such systems has remained a constant for scientists ever since Newton's formidable achievements.

The Clockwork Body and Soul: Descartes, La Mettrie and Mechanistic Physiology

Not restricted to the study of celestial bodies, the clockwork metaphor was present also in the scientific enquiry into living bodies as part of the search for universal laws governing the physical world. René Descartes, perhaps the most influential philosopher of the seventeenth century, is here a crucial figure. Descartes employed analogies between nature and clockwork frequently and extensively: "it is certain that there are no rules in Mechanics which do not hold good in Physics [...] for it is no less natural for a clock, made of the requisite number of wheels, to indicate the hours, than for a tree which has sprung from this or that seed, to produce a particular fruit."[22]

Descartes manifested a particular fascination for automata, even imagining some of his own (although there is no evidence any of them were realised), and he referred repeatedly to them when writing about the motion of animals. He was more reluctant to extend this analogy to human beings, presumably to avoid offending the religious sensibilities of the day and to satisfy his own religious qualms, and when he did so, it was in an indirect fashion. In his *Meditations*, he insisted that simple observation could not *disprove* that humans might be mechanical automata. A few years later, he would argue in *Principia Philosophiae* that "we see clocks, artificial fountains, mills and other similar machines which, though merely man-made, have nonetheless the power to move by themselves in several different ways [...] I do no recognise any difference between the machines made by craftsmen and the various bodies

---

21   «Système», *Encyclopédie, ou Dictionnaire Raisonné des Sciences, des Arts et des Métiers*.

22   Samuel Macy, *Clocks and the Cosmos: Time in Western Life and Thought* (Hamden, CT: Archon Books, 1980), p. 80.

that nature composes alone."[23] Ultimately, his solution was what became known as Cartesian dualism: man was distinguished from animals in being composed of both body and soul, the latter being the realm of spiritual authority and not within the remit of scientific enquiry. Thus Descartes described the human body in rigorously mechanistic terms, even if he avoided direct analogies with clockwork devices. This did not prevent his works being posthumously placed on the Roman Catholic Church's Index of Prohibited Books in 1667 on the grounds of their alleged atheistic bent.

Despite this, Descartes continued to exert considerable influence after his death and although the clockwork metaphor was used sparingly in relation to human beings thereafter, it can still be found in the writings of Blaise Pascal, Baruch Spinoza, and Robert Boyle.[24] Giovanni Borrelli proposed a mathematical and mechanistic description of the operation of the muscular and skeletal system of living beings in terms of pulleys and levers in his *De Motu Animalium* (1680). Gottfried Leibniz went so far as to refer to the human soul as "a kind of spiritual automaton", specifying in a rather cryptic manner that "the operation of spiritual automata, that is of souls, is not mechanical, but it contains in the highest degree all that is beautiful in mechanism."[25]

In the eighteenth-century, French philosopher and physician Julien Offray de La Mettrie went even further, claiming that the soul was a physical phenomena and not the property of an immaterial realm distinct from the body. La Mettrie used the clockwork metaphor extensively in his major work *L'Homme Machine*, arguing that "the human body is a watch." However, his most provocative statement was undoubtedly that:

Since all the faculties of the soul depend to such a degree on the proper organisation of the brain and of the whole body, that apparently they are but this organisation itself, the soul is clearly an enlightened machine. For finally, even if man alone had received a share of natural law, would he be any less a machine for that? A few more wheels, a few more springs than in the most

---

23   Capra, *The Web of Life*, p. 67.

24   Mayr, *Authority, Liberty and Automatic Machinery in Early Modern Europe*, pp. 67-68.

25   G.W. Leibniz, *Theodicy - Essays on the Goodness of God, the Freedom of Man and the Origin of Evil* – trans. E.M. Huggard (Peru, IL: Open Court Publishing Company, 1985), p. 365.

perfect animals, the brain proportionally nearer the heart and for this very reason receiving more blood – any one of a number of unknown causes might always produce this delicate conscience so easily wounded, this remorse which is no more foreign to matter than to thought, and in a word all the differences that are supposed to exist here. Could the organism then suffice for everything? Once more, yes; since thought visibly develops with our organs, why should not the matter of which they are composed be susceptible of remorse also, when once it has acquired, with time, the faculty of feeling?[26]

In that single passage, La Mettrie postulated the primacy of mechanistic physical embodiment over the immortal soul while also implying that what ultimately separated humans from animals were merely modest biological differences. Unsurprisingly, his defence that he did not "mean to call in question the existence of a supreme being; on the contrary it seems [...] that the greatest degree of probability is in favour of this belief" did little to stave off accusations of atheistic materialism. The condemnation of the Church forced him to leave France and then Holland to live in Berlin under the protection of Frederick the Great, the man who would best exemplify the ideals of the clockwork state and army.

The Clockwork State: Enlightened Absolutism

The clockwork metaphor suggested a world of harmony, order, and predictability with motion originating from a single impulse and transmitted perfectly by all the "wheels" and "gears" of the underlying mechanism. This motif naturally resonated most strongly with the emerging discourse of enlightened absolutism and its ideal of a rational and ordered system of government in which an all-powerful monarch determined the impulses to be given to the obedient machinery of state.

Thomas Hobbes, the most prominent theorist of absolutism and a committed mechanist, is known primarily for comparing the state to the human body but in the opening paragraph of *Leviathan* we find this image conflated with that of clockwork:

Nature (the art whereby God hath made and governs the world) is by the art of man, as in many other things, so in this also imitated, that it can make an artificial animal. For seeing life is but a motion of limbs, the beginning whereof is in some principal part within, why may we not say that all automata (engines that move

---

26   Julien Offray de La Mettrie, *L'Homme Machine* (1748).

themselves by springs and wheels as doth a watch) have an artificial life? For what is the heart, but a spring; and the nerves, but so many strings; and the joints, but so many wheels, giving motion to the whole body, such as was intended by the Artificer? Art goes yet further, imitating that rational and most excellent work of Nature, Man. For by art is created that great Leviathan called a Common-Wealth, or State (in Latin, Civitas), which is but an artificial man, though of greater stature and strength than the natural, for whose protection and defence it was intended; and in which the sovereignty is an artificial soul, as giving life and motion to the whole body.[27]

In seeking to grant divine sanction to his conception of the state, Hobbes is not simply arguing that art is the imitation of nature; he is also blurring the distinction between the natural and the artificial since God himself is an "Artificer". The clockwork metaphor serves here both to underlie the artifice of human life and to assert the fundamental truth about nature captured by clockwork. Hobbes thereby not only bolsters his own metaphor of the state as body but also ties in the notion of the Leviathan with a mechanistic understanding of the world in which its different totalities (nature/man/clock/state) are set in motion by a single source of impulse, "the beginning whereof is in some principal part within" (God/soul/watchmaker/ sovereign).[28]

Louis XIV was arguably the paragon of absolutism, to whom is commonly attributed the perhaps apocryphal phrase: "l'état, c'est moi" (Frederick II would make the more modest claim of being the "servant of the state"). The designated virtues of order and regularity were actively sought within the French government with reform achieved primarily through the instruments of law and *règlements*. Statistical and social surveys became an institutionalised practice of government, efforts were made to harmonise legislation across the territories, and the state bureaucracy was expanded and reformed to centralise power and weaken traditional allegiances other

---

27 Thomas Hobbes, *Leviathan* (Oxford University Press, 1998), p. 7.

28 The methodology employed by Hobbes for his writings on politics was explicitly mechanistic as the following passage excerpted from the preface to *De Cive* (1651) illustrates: "Everything is best understood by its constitutive causes; for as in a watch, or some such small engine, the matter, figure, and motion of the wheels cannot well be known except it be taken asunder and viewed in parts; so to make a more curious search into the rights of states and duties of subjects, it is necessary, I say, not to take them asunder, but yet that they be so considered as if they were dissolved."

than that to the king.[29] This vision of the state endured beyond the lifetime of Louis XIV; the general and member of the French academy, Jacques-Antoine-Hippolyte de Guibert, writing in 1772 observed that: "discipline must be made national. The state I depict will have simple, reliable, easily controlled administration. It will resemble those vast machines which by quite uncomplicated means produce great effects."[30] For some Enlightenment thinkers (but certainly not all), the *esprit de systéme* and *esprit géometrique* were instruments of despotism, notably illustrated by the fact that Maréchal Vauban, responsible for the some of the most remarkable innovations in the application of geometry to the design of fortifications, was also behind plans for the equal taxation of the produce of all land in France.[31]

Louis XIV's court life was notoriously regimented with his days following rigid timetables and etiquette and with punctuality elevated to the highest of virtues, prompting the duke of Saint-Simon to say of the monarch that "with an almanac and a watch one could tell, three hundred leagues away, what he was doing." Indeed, even when travelling, both clockmakers and large numbers of clocks would accompany the royal cortege. The king's fondness for order and a linear aesthetic was also reflected in the pure geometric forms of the palace garden in Versailles. While he viewed French excellence in philosophy and science as a symbol of prestige in Europe, establishing national academies and patronage for its promotion, he was personally of a limited intellectual disposition and quick to censor any work that appeared incompatible with absolute monarchy. If Louis XIV was therefore a fine representative of absolutism, his desire for order and stability echoing the clockwork metaphor, the title of enlightened monarch is most appropriate for Frederick II of Prussia, the Philosopher King.

Aside from the aforementioned La Mettrie, to whom he granted patronage when he was forced into exile and even composed the official eulogy, Frederick the Great surrounded himself with many of the leading rationalist and mechanistically inclined philosophers of his time, such as D'Alembert, Voltaire, Euler, Maupertuis and Algarotti. The Prussian mon-

---

29   King, *Science and Rationalism in the Government of Louis XIV*, pp. 312-313.

30   Foucault, *Surveiller et Punir*, p. 198. The term used by Guibert in French for "means" is "ressorts" which is also the word for "springs."

31   David D. Bien, "Military Education in 18th Century France; Technical and Non-Technical Determinants" in Wright and Paszek (eds), *Science, Technology and Warfare*, p. 57.

arch undoubtedly shared many of the mechanistic ideas of these illustrious contemporaries and prided himself for his philosophical leanings. Writing in 1750 on the role of laws in the state, Frederick's mechanist beliefs are evident in his vision of the ideal state:

A body of perfect laws should be the crowning achievement of the human spirit as regards the politics of government: one would observe there a unity of design and of rules so exact and so well proportioned that a state conducted by such laws would resemble a watch all of whose springs have been made for the same purpose; [...] everything would be anticipated, everything would be coordinated, and nothing would be subject to mishap.[32]

Johann Heinrich Gottlieb von Justi, the contemporary Prussian political economist, expressed best the role of the sovereign within mechanised government: "a well-constituted state must perfectly resemble a machine where all the wheels and gears fit each other with the utmost precision; and the ruler must be the engineer, the first driving spring or the soul [...] that sets everything in motion."[33]

In both the reigns of Louis XIV and Frederick II, as well as to a lesser extent those of Joseph II of Austria and Catherine II of Russia, far-reaching rationalisation and centralisation of the state were carried out, accompanied by an expanding bureaucracy, the "wheels and gears" of government. This mechanising trend would perhaps be nowhere clearer than in the changes brought about in warfare, a social activity in which order and discipline were most naturally valued. It is with Frederick II's army, the last great war machine before the advent of the French imperial *Grande Armée*, that the clockwork model can be observed most clearly in military affairs.

Mechanistic Warfare: Frederick the Great's Clockwork Army

Throughout the seventeenth and eighteenth centuries, the conduct of war increasingly came under scientific scrutiny, a trend that has only intensified since. In some cases, practical problems that arose in war stimulated scientific discoveries; in other cases, it was the successes of the physical sciences that inspired the quest for the discovery of equiva-

---

32   Mayr, *Authority, Liberty and Automatic Machinery in Early Modern Europe*, p. 108.

33   Ibid., p. 111.

lent universal laws. As Azar Gat notes, "the ideal of Newtonian science excited the military thinkers of the Enlightenment and gave rise to an ever-present yearning to infuse the study of war with the maximum mathematical precision and certainty possible."[34]

Certainly, bombardment and fortification became increasingly guided by geometrical principles and the developing science of ballistics. Ballistic knowledge (notably of the parabolic trajectory of projectiles) was greatly enhanced through Galileo's discovery of the principle of inertia, the law of freely falling bodies, and the principle of the composition of velocities, which he partly came to through his study of military problems.[35] Paul Virilio explicitly connects the subsequent progress made in ballistics to that of the astronomical sciences, as well as to a whole range of mathematical innovations from Descartes' analytical geometry and Poncelet's projective geometry to Euler's method for calculating ballistic trajectories.[36] In response to the destructive power of the cannon and the advantage it provided armies besieging cities, geometry was applied to the purpose of optimising increasingly complex polygonal fortification designs such that "safety was achieved less by tangible masses of masonry than by abstract geometrical patterns of line of fire."[37] Thus the British military theorist Henry Lloyd could say in 1766 that fortifications were "purely geometrical" and artillery "nothing but geometry."[38]

Nor was the belief that mechanistic conceptions could be applied to military affairs solely limited to ballistics and fortification. Indeed Louis

34   Azar Gat, *A History of Military Thought: From the Elightenment to the Cold War* (Oxford University Press, 2001), p. 30.

35   DeLanda, *War in the Age of Intelligent Machines*, p. 40. Mathematician and military engineer Benjamin Robins subsequently improved markedly on Galileo's calculations in the 1740s, adding a crucial understanding of air resistance. According to Steele, Robins's analysis of muzzle velocities of projectiles fired from muskets – assisted by a "ballistics pendulum" of his own invention – marked an early thermodynamic understanding of an internal combustion engine which may have played a role in the future development of the science of energy. Brett D. Steele, "Muskets and Pendulums: Benjamin Robins, Leonhard Euler, and the Ballistics Revolution", *Technology and Culture*, Vol. 35, No. 2. (Apr. 1994), pp. 348-382.

36   Paul Virilio, *The Lost Dimension* (New York: Semiotext(e), 1991), p. 46.

37   Thomas P. Hughes, "Commentary" in Wright and Paszek (eds), *Science, Technology and Warfare*, p. 71.

38   Gat, *A History of Military Thought*, p. 72.

Pierre de Chastenet, Count of Puységur, claimed that the field of military tactics "is easily reduced to sure rules, because it is entirely geometrical like fortifications."[39] According to Lynn, it was Diderot's epochal *Encyclopédie* which "enshrined the conviction that geometry linked fortress design, siege warfare, and battle tactics" when it listed military architecture and tactics as a form of "Elementary Geometry" under the entry on "Science of Nature."[40] The aforementioned Henry Lloyd was also drawing from Newtonian mechanics when he asserted that mathematical principles extended to battle formations since "the impulse that bodies, animate or inanimate, make on each other [...] is in proportion to mass and velocity."[41]

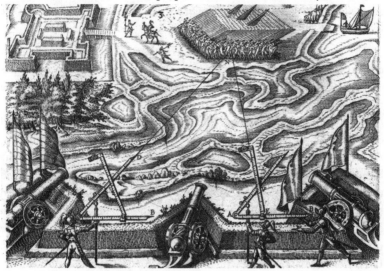

Figure 2: Geometric warfare[42]

---

39   John A. Lynn, *Battle: A History of Cobat and Culture* (Boulder, CO: Westview Press, 2003), p. 126.

40   Ibid., pp. 120-121. See also John A. Lynn, "The Treatment of Military Subjects in Diderot's Encyclopédie", *The Journal of Military History*, Vol. 65, No. 1. (Jan., 2001), pp. 131-165. Lynn also points to Pierre Lenfant's painting of 1761 commemorating the French victory at the battle of Fontenoy in 1744 as the embodiment of the ideals of 'linear warfare' in its depiction of the battle as elegantly ordered with the arrangement of troops obeying perfect geometrical regularity even in the heat of combat. (*Battle*, p. 114).

41   Gat, *A History of Military Thought*, p. 72.

42   Benjamin Bramer, *Bericht zu M. Jobsten Burgi Seligen Geometrischen Triangular Instruments* (Kassel, 1648).

As the Enlightenment and the Scientific Revolution took hold, reason and scientific method were recruited for the study and organisation of all fields of natural phenomenon and human activity, including a quest for the discovery of the fundamental laws governing warfare. In his *Essai Général de Tactique* (1770), General Guibert deplored the fact that military science was yet to match the accomplishments of the Newtons and D'Alemberts and thereby sought to determine tactics which:

would constitute a science at every period of time, in every place, and among every species of arms; that is to say, if ever by some revolution among the nature of arms which it is not possible to foresee, the order of depth should again be adapted, there would be no necessity in putting the same [tactics] in practice to change either manoeuvre or constitution.[43]

The question of formations and tactics was all the more paramount due to the considerable transformations in the organisation of armies experienced in this period. Improvements in firearm technologies made musket-equipped infantry the core unit of any army, with mobile artillery providing support. With the adoption of the bayonet at the end of the seventeenth century, pikemen were rendered largely dispensable. As for the cavalry, its medieval glory days long gone, it remained as the bastion of the aristocracy but its influence on the battlefield was limited to opportunistic charges once an opposing infantry formation had been broken by hostile fire. With chivalry now an archaic concept to which only lip service was occasionally paid, eighteenth-century armies were predominantly composed of mercenaries and professional soldiers. Desertion was an ever-present threat which commanders were acutely aware of. Combined with the limited command and control technologies of the age in increasingly noisy and smoke-filled battlefields and involving growing numbers of troops, this imposed severe limits on potential tactical flexibility.

Frederick the Great's solution to this problem was to reduce individual initiative to a minimum, insisting in his own writings that military effectiveness "depended on strict discipline, unconditional obedience, prompt execution of orders", and that the common soldier should fear his officer more than the enemy.[44] Van Creveld observes that

---

43   Gat, *A History of Military Thought*, p. 50.

44   Dennis Showalter, *The Wars of Frederick the Great* (London and New York: Addison Wesley Longman, 1997), p. 330.

the Prussian king "was among the first modern commanders to try to command all of his army all of the time, but this could only be achieved by turning it into a mindless, lifeless machine."[45] Here is perhaps the clearest attempt to model an army on the regularity and predictability of clockwork with every cog playing a pre-determined role fixed by the original conveyer of motion. While such an army would be unable to respond dynamically to events on the battlefield, this would nonetheless allow Frederick to experiment with a number of complex, though rigid, tactical deployments. The result was a formidable military machine superior to anything rival states could field at the time and which became a model army which contemporaries sought to emulate, even to the point of replicating the Prussian uniform in some cases. Notwithstanding Frederick's own input, in many ways it was also the culmination of two centuries of military transformation across Europe that had seen the establishment of professional standing armies, the widespread use of drilling, and the development of gunpowder and firearms.

The introduction of systematic drills covering the handling of firearms, basic body positions and marching in ranks can be dated back to the Dutch army of Maurice of Nassau, Prince of Orange, subsequently emulated and improved upon to great effect by Gustavus Adolphus of Sweden in the first half of the seventeenth century.[46] The introduction of firearms meant that the importance of individual physical prowess declined to the benefit of trained professional skill and, at a time where musket technology did not allow for precision targeting, their effective use required speed, regularity, and volume in numbers. Maurice of Nassau discovered in the 1590s that by breaking down the process of loading and firing matchlock muskets into a sequence of individual moves, soldiers could be taught to execute them in a synchronised fashion in response to shouted commands. In 1607, Jacob de Gheyn published the highly influential *Wapenhandlighe* ("The Exercise of Arms"), one of the earliest manual of arms which went through several editions and was

---

45   Van Creveld, *Command in War*, p. 45.

46   Geoffrey Parker, The Military Revolution – Military Innovation and the Rise of the West, 1500-1800 (Cambridge University Press, 1996), pp. 18-24; Theo Farrell and Terry Terriff (eds), *The Sources of Military Change: Culture, Politics, Technology* (Boulder, CO: Lynne Rienner, 2002), pp. 73-74; Michael Roberts, "The Military Revolution, 1560-1660" in Michael Roberts, *Essays in Swedish History* (London: Camelot Press, 1967), pp. 195-225.

translated in English, French, German and Danish. *Wapenhandlighe* acted as an "integrated instructional device", breaking down the use of any given weapon into a series of distinct component steps which where arranged in a numbered, logical sequence and each associated with an individual verbal command. The sequence of steps formed a complete cycle to be repeated as many times as required.[47]

In the Prussian army of the eighteenth century, this practice was further refined and extended, the military manual of 1726 specifying 76 stages in the loading and firing of a musket compared to "only" 42 stages in the *Wapenhandlighe* of a century earlier.[48] Each of these stages, analogous to individual cogs in the operation of a mechanical process, could be isolated and improved upon in terms of speed and efficiency to contribute to the overall performance of the process. Frederick was known to monitor the performance of firing exercises with his watch, with elite troops able to fire as many as seven blank rounds a minute (although in battle conditions this dropped to three live rounds at most). His lieutenant-general, Friedrich Christoph von Saldern, in charge of troop discipline, is also reported to have used a stop watch during marching exercises to determine the exact number of steps per minute and the length of each step.[49] Clockwork here offered simultaneously a conceptual model for the decomposition of actions into separate discrete movements to be individually perfected as well as an

---

47   M.D. Feld, "Middle-Class Society and the Rise of Military Professionalism: The Dutch Army 1589-1609", *Armed Forces and Society*, Vol. 1 , No. 4, 1975, p. 424. Feld further observes that the new drilling practices also acted as a testing device allowing for the "application of what was being taught [to] be immediately demonstrated and evaluated." Aptitude for combat was therefore no longer an opaque quality only to be revealed in battle since it could now be measured by the individual's ability to reproduce at the required speed a sequence of moves triggered by verbal commands, a performance which could be continuously supervised and assessed during drill exercises. This new yardstick of military competence did not only concern subordinate soldiers since commanding officers could now also be judged in terms of their ability to marshal their troops accordingly.

48   Parker, *The Military Revolution*, p. 22.

49   Maryl Flesher, "Repetitive Order and the Human Walking Apparatus: Prussian Military Science versus the Webers' Locomotion Research", *Annals of Science*, Vol. 54, No. 5, 1997, p. 468.

objective measure of time by which the rapidity and regularity of such movements could be gauged.

In addition to systematisation in the handling of firearms, equally crucial to their effective use in battle was the introduction of linear tactics and the countermarch at the turn of the sixteenth century. Soldiers equipped with firearms would be arranged in successive ranks, several lines deep. Upon the delivery of fire by the first rank, it would turn and march to the rear where it would start reloading while the next rank discharged its own weapons. The manoeuvre would then be repeated by the next ranks so that by the time the original first rank returned to the frontline it would be fully loaded and able to fire immediately. [50] In this manner, continuous volleys of fire could be ensured and the shock effect of firearms maximised. The individual loading and firing cycle of each soldier (or rank of soldiers) was therefore itself inserted into another cycle of manoeuvres which rotated ranks sequentially – a hierarchy of cogs in a great clockwork army.

Over the course of the 150 years following its introduction under Maurice of Nassau, the practice of drilling spread throughout European armies, reaching its acme under Frederick the Great. The number of ranks of musketeers necessary for sustained volleys of fire was reduced to three in Frederick's army, compared with the ten required under Maurice of Nassau. Cadenced marching, the synchronisation of the step of all men marching together, which had been lost since Roman times, was reintroduced to Prussian drill by Frederick William I in the 1730s, and subsequently utilised systematically for tactical purposes by his son. [51] By the end of the Frederick II's reign, a steady pace of 75 steps per minute had become the standard employed for movement at drill, on the march, in the field, off duty and even when carrying loads. Two French military officers, Toulongeon and Hullin, visiting Prussia in 1786, remarked that "the measure of this pace is imprinted in the soldier's brain, and his legs have been so accustomed to working at this speed that they seem to act by clockwork."[52] The Prussian soldier

---

50   M.D. Feld, "Middle-Class Society and the Rise of Military Professionalism: The Dutch Army 1589-1609", *Armed Forces and Society* Vol. 1 , No. 4, 1975, p. 425.

51   Showalter, *The Wars of the Frederick the Great*, pp. 109-110.

52   Christopher Duffy, *The Army of Frederick the Great* (Vancouver: David and Charles, 1974), p. 83.

was effectively "mechanised" in the process of drilling, his movements systematically dictated and rehearsed until they became instinctive.

This constant emphasis on speed during drill may however have been counter-productive at times, the Prussian officer von Gaudi complaining that "with this damned 'minute fire' the men become exhausted and incapable of doing anything more after loosing off a few of these over-hasty salvoes. You could push them over with your little finger."[53] Showalter has also commented that, in the latter part of Frederick's reign, "drill movements, always precise and demanding, became exacting to the point of impossibility even for experienced men."[54] Regardless of its excesses, the Prussian obsession with drilling produced highly trained and obedient troops who could perform complex and innovative tactical manoeuvres such as the oblique order and deliver fire faster than any of their contemporaries despite the poor quality of Prussian muskets.

The cardinal importance of drill and its associated disciplinary techniques for what has been often referred to as the "military revolution" of the early modern era can hardly be overestimated. Indeed Max Weber argued that "gun powder and all the war techniques associated with it became significant only with the existence of discipline."[55] Furthermore, the widespread deployment of the new disciplinary practices within the European armies of the seventeenth and eighteenth centuries served several other functions besides maximising the efficiency of troops on the battlefield. Over this period, the centralisation of political power within the emerging modern state was accompanied by the erection of increasingly large standing armies in place of autonomous bands of mercenaries of dubious loyalty. Drill and the associated surveillance of troops helped ensure political obedience and greater reliability of the military instrument for purposes of both internal rule and the settling of disputes with other states. The frequency of drilling exercises also had the advantage of reducing the idleness of troops whose time was mostly spent in anticipation of encounters with the enemy rather than in battle, contributing to an *esprit de corps* and enforcing orderly conduct, as

---

53   Ibid., p. 89.

54   Showalter, *The Wars of the Frederick the Great*, p. 332.

55   Max Weber, "The Meaning of Discipline" in H.H. Gerth and C. Wright Mills (eds), *From Max Weber: Essays in Sociology* (London: Kegan Paul, Trench, Trubner and Co., 1947), p. 257.

much within military units as with regard to the behaviour of troops in relation to local populations traditionally fearful of their depredations. Finally, public military exercises served a symbolic and ritualistic function, embodying the mechanistic vision of army and state. The clockwork appearance of the Prussian army, most observable in the controlled conditions of the biannual military reviews Frederick was so fond of and in which up to 40,000 troops could be present, was not lost on contemporary commentators. On his only visit to Berlin in 1778, Goethe wrote that "from the huge clockwork that unrolls before you, from the movement of the troops, you can deduce the hidden wheels, especially that big old [program] drum, signed F[redericus] R[ex], with its thousand pins which generate these tunes, one after another."[56]

Frederick's army was akin to a giant clockwork mechanism in which bodies and technologies were combined to produce a "war machine" that embodied all the virtues of its model: precision, predictability and order. The Prussian army represented the pinnacle of a mechanistic understanding of warfare in which, according to Harald Kleinschmidt:

commanders were expected to execute minutely the general rules of the war game in detail and into which the common soldiers were to be integrated as if they were parts of a neatly composed machine. The machine was regarded as a well-organised man-made assembly of smoothly cohering parts, whose order was perfectly in line with the principles of organisation followed by "nature."[57]

Naturally, actual combat conditions saw the war machine operating with much less order than its model, sometimes even being prone to break down spectacularly, but the considerable military successes achieved by Frederick the Great during his reign are clear evidence of its effectiveness and resilience. While tactical adjustments were practically

---

56   Mayr, *Authority, Liberty and Automatic Machinery in Early Modern Europe*, p. 109. Foucault further underlines the diagrammatic importance of clockwork mechanisms in noting that "the celebrated automata [...] were not only a way of illustrating an organism, they were also political puppets, small-scale models of power: Frederick II, the meticulous king of small machines, well-trained regiments and long exercises, was obsessed with them." Foucault, *Surveiller et Punir*, pp. 160-161.

57   Harald Kleinschmidt, "Using the Gun: Manual Drill and the Proliferation of Portable Firearms", *The Journal of Military History*, Vol. 63, No. 3. (July, 1999), p. 612.

impossible once battle had been initiated, uncertainty was minimised by automating the actions of soldiers according to a centralised predetermined plan. McNeill notes that it is through the intensive drilling of troops that "the individual movements of soldiers when firing and marching as well as the movements of battalion across the battlefield could be controlled and predicted as never before."[58] Mechanistic warfare's solution to the threat of chaos on the battlefield was thus to preordain the actions of every soldier in accordance with an overarching organisational plan which shaped the army, at least in theory, into an extension of the sovereign's will as the impulsion setting in motion an idealised clockwork mechanism.

Conclusion

Organised around the figure of clockwork, mechanism constituted the first cohesive body of scientific ideas and practices in the modern world. Its cultural resonance was far-reaching, impacting multiple areas of knowledge and social activity and offering the promise of an enlightened and permanently ordered world. Mechanistic warfare briefly appeared to provide a superior answer to the perennial uncertainties of battle and limitations to the exertion of the commander's will, introducing many disciplinary techniques which are still in use to this day. But just as it seemed to have found its purest expression in the army of Frederick the Great, the first regime of the scientific way of warfare faced growing criticism for its alleged excessive rigidity and calls for a more dynamic understanding of conflict. The failings of mechanistic warfare were to be dramatically demonstrated when the French revolutionary and subsequent imperial armies burst onto the scene and repeatedly annihilated the formerly fearsome Prussian military. The carefully cultivated order of the *ancien régime* was irreversibly swept away in the birth pangs of a new world marked by industrial and political upheaval. Along with it came new technologies and sciences, chief among which were the engine and thermodynamics, the science of energy.

---

58   McNeill, *Pursuit of Power*, p. 130.

3
Thermodynamic Warfare and the Science of Energy

For classical mechanics the symbol of nature was the clock; for the Industrial Age, it became a reservoir of energy that is always threatened with exhaustion. The world is burning like a furnace; energy, although being conserved, also is being dissipated.

Ilya Prigogine and Isabelle Stengers[1]

The artillery of our division are excellent shots, the first impact arriving on the dot. The howling approach of the iron blocks grows increasingly dense and polyphonic, simply for the purpose of drowning the other side in a steadily swelling tide of vicious, raging and numbing sounds. Landmines draw their beaded arcs of sparks above us and shatter in volcanic explosions. White signal rockets flood the twinkling clouds of smoke, gases and dust, which simmer with a glaring light, like a boiling lake over the fields. Multicoloured rockets hang over the trenches, bursting into little stars and suddenly expiring like the coloured signals in a giant marshalling yard. All machine guns in the second and third lines are highly active. The hiss of their countless blurred shots forms the grim background, which fills the minute gaps in the sound of the heavy guns.

Ernst Jünger[2]

---

1   Prigogine and Stengers, *Order out of Chaos*, p. 111.

2   Ernst Jünger, *Der Kampf als Inneres Erlebnis* (Berlin: E. S. Mittler and Sohn, 1922).

The thermodynamic era was one of instability and change, a period of rapid and turbulent socio-cultural transformation whose paradigmatic technology was undoubtedly the engine. For Sadi Carnot, the forefather of thermodynamics, writing in 1824, the engine seemed "destined to produce a great revolution in the civilised world":

Already the steam-engine works our mines, impels our ships, excavates our ports and our rivers, forges iron, fashions wood, grinds grain, spins and weaves our cloths, transports the heaviest burdens, etc. It appears that it must some day serve as a universal motor, and be substituted for animal power, water-falls, and air currents.[3]

For Carnot and other inquisitive minds, such a revolutionary technology impelled science to uncover the physical laws governing it and this was achieved in the course of the nineteenth century, transforming the entire scientific worldview in the process. In 1908, Joseph Larmor, who held the Lucasian Chair of Mathematics at Cambridge once occupied by Newton, could proclaim that thermodynamics "has not only furnished a standard of industrial values which has enabled mechanical power [...] to be measured with scientific precision as a commercial asset; it has also in its other aspect of the continual dissipation of mechanical energy, created the doctrine of inorganic evolution and changed our conception of the material universe."[4] As with clockwork, the engine was both a technological artefact that spread throughout the social body and a central metaphorical and heuristic figure within a new scientific worldview. Along with it there emerged a new regime of the scientific way of warfare in which the mobilisation, concentration, and discharging of energy – whether material, physical or moral – became paramount. At times, this led to an even more all-encompassing use of the inflexible programmatic approaches that were characteristic of mechanistic warfare. At others, it was accompanied by a more dynamic understanding of warfare that required decentralisation and greater responsiveness to the contingencies of battle, as expressed in the writings of Clausewitz.

---

3   Sadi Carnot, *Reflections on the Motive Power of Fire and on Machines Fitted to Develop that Power* (1824).

4   Smith, *The Science of Energy*, p. 14.

The Engine: the Industrialisation and Motorisation of Society

While clockwork mechanisms could transmit motion steadily and efficiently, they still relied on an external source of power: energy generated by the force of gravity (as with the weight-driven clock), the muscular power of man and animal (be it directly transferred or stored as with the spring), or by the natural elements of wind and running water. The eighteenth century would see the early development of a dynamic technology that could drive *itself* by unlocking and harnessing intimate sources of power and converting them into mechanical work.

Steam-powered devices were built as early as the turn of the Christian era and even perhaps as far back as Ancient Egypt, but were little more than experimental or ornamental objects until the end of the seventeenth century. Building on von Guericke's scientific research on atmospheric pressure, Thomas Savery patented in 1698 the first steam-powered machine to pump water out of coal mines. A partnership with Thomas Newcomen led to a commercially viable machine in 1712 with the addition of piston and cylinder. It is estimated that over a thousand of these "atmospheric steam engines" were built by the end of the century but their cost-efficiency was very poor and they were not employed outside the mining industry where coal, the engine's fuel, was abundant. Realising in 1765 that the Newcomen steam engine was wasting nearly three-quarters of the steam energy in heating the piston and chamber, James Watt significantly improved its design over the following years, thereby rendering it much more efficient and economical.

By the beginning of the nineteenth century, the steam engine had become a vital technology in industrialising Britain and was no longer limited to pumping water out of mines; it was also driving mills and powering the nation's burgeoning factories. The steam engine was employed not only in a revolution in the means of production; it would also herald an equally momentous revolution in transportation, with the first application of its motive power to maritime transport in 1788 and the construction of the first railway in 1825. The rapid spread of railroads provided an expanding transport infrastructure which further stimulated economic development and social transformation. The steam-powered locomotive was as potent a symbol of the thrust of modernisation as any, annihilating distances, transporting goods, bodies, and ideas over great distances and was undoubtedly an impressive sight for those unfamiliar with it. States enthusiastically embraced railways, to the extent that some countries, such as Spain, were so enraptured with their "railway dream" that they neglected the development of the industries that would provide the freight for the railroads to carry.[5]

Marked by a dramatic transformation in the modes of economic production, demographic explosion, rapid urbanisation, and the emergence of a new proletarian class, the nineteenth century was a time of great socio-economic upheaval in the rapidly industrialising world. By removing human dependency on wind and water streams as sources of energy, the engine enabled the widespread automation of processes previously executed by hand. Through division of labour and the assembly line, the workforce was deployed in such a manner as to allow the smoothest possible operation of machines. As a result, the work rate was now imposed by mechanical devices onto the worker, reversing the relationship of the labourer to his tools. This new organisation of production was rationalised in the "scientific management" of Taylorism at the turn of the twentieth century and its productive capacity further increased with the motorisation of the assembly line introduced by Ford in 1913.

Although primitive devices existed as early as 1807, it was not until the second half of nineteenth century that practical internal combustion engines appeared, in no small part due to the theoretical advances of thermodynamics discussed below. In 1859, Jean-Joseph Lenoir first demonstrated an electric spark internal combustion engine using a combination of compressed air and coal gas as its energy source, applying it to sea and land transport in the following decade. By 1883, Daimler and Maybach had a successful combustion engine using liquid fuel running, followed within a few years by the construction of the first automobiles by Daimler and Benz. Over the next fifty years, combustion engines were widely applied to land, air and sea transport as well as industry, signalling a shift from coal to petroleum fossil fuels as the main source of energy. As for the electric motor, it was born when Michael Faraday discovered electromagnetism in 1821. Subsequent development of large-scale electricity-generating systems in the late-nineteenth and early-twentieth centuries led to numerous practical domestic and industrial applications for electric motors.

---

5   Pacey, *Technology in World Civilization*, p. 141.

Despite their growing importance by the 1820s, the Watt steam engine and its successive incarnations were the product of only an approximate understanding of atmospheric phenomena and decades of experimentation. A comprehensive scientific understanding of the physical processes involved was still lacking. The first breakthrough would be found in the work of the French military engineer Sadi Carnot, giving birth to the science of energy known as thermodynamics.

Thermodynamics: the Universe as a Heat Engine

While clockwork mechanisms merely transmit motion along a preordained path, heat engines generate their own energy and therefore motion. As Prigogine and Stengers put it, "the mechanical work produced must be seen as the result of a true process of transformation and not only as transmission of movement."[6] Scientific enquiry naturally turned to the study of these processes of transformation, leading to the formulation of the fundamental natural laws of energy, thereby establishing the science of thermodynamics and revolutionising all aspects of the scientific worldview. By 1875, the new science had gained such a prominent status that the Britannica entry for "energy" could proclaim that "a complete account of our knowledge of energy and its transformations would require an exhaustive treatise on every branch of physical science, for natural philosophy [physics] is simply the science of energy."[7]

In 1824, the engineer Sadi Carnot published his famous treatise, *Reflections on the Motive Power of Fire and on Machines Fitted to Develop that Power*, in which he set out the physical principles behind the operation of the heat engine. Carnot had sought to answer the much-debated question of "whether the motive power of heat is unbounded, whether the possible improvements in steam-engines have an assignable limit – a limit which the nature of things will not allow to be passed by any means whatever – or whether, on the contrary, these improvements may be carried on indefinitely."[8] He thereby discovered that heat flowed from warmer to cooler areas (from the hot boiler to the cool condenser

---

6   Prigogine and Stengers, *Order out of Chaos*, p. 106.

7   Smith, *The Science of Energy*, p. 2.

8   Carnot, *Reflections on the Motive Power of Fire*.

in a steam engine) and that wherever there is a difference in temperature, there is the potential for the production of motive power. Thus the greater the differential between temperature reservoirs, the more work can be extracted from it. While Carnot theorised the operation of a perfect engine in which available heat was fully converted into the equivalent motive power, he also realised that this constituted a limit which could be approached but never attained and that consequently heat would necessarily always be wasted.[9]

Carnot's work would permit the mathematical calculation of the maximum amount of work (or motive power) that any given engine could produce but the wider implications of his theory were much more profound. His discovery of the physical laws upon which the operation of the steam engine relied required its conceptualisation as an abstract machine. Carnot insisted, in what can be seen as the founding statement of the science of thermodynamics, that:

In order to consider in the most general way the principle of the production of motion by heat, it must be considered independently of any mechanism or any particular agent. It is necessary to establish principles applicable not only to steam engines but to all imaginable heat engines, whatever the working substance and whatever the method by which it is operated.[10]

With this formulation, Carnot allowed for the engine to be understood as an abstract mechanism, a diagrammatic organisation detached from any single material embodiment and now ripe for conceptual and metaphorical migration. In 1854, the scientist William Rankine was merely following in these footsteps in defining a "thermo-dynamic engine" as "any body, or assemblage of bodies, which produces mechanical power from heat."[11] For DeLanda, the abstract mechanism of the engine can be seen to consist of three separate components: "a reservoir (of steam, for example), a form of exploitable difference (the heat/cold

---

9   Sadi's father, the French revolutionary General Lazare Carnot, had previously studied the efficiency of mechanical machines and some of his son's later ideas can be traced back to those original insights. In his 1786 *Essai sur les Machines en Général*, Lazare had concluded that there was always a necessary loss of "movement of activity" (i.e. of useful work) in any mechanical transmission of motion.

10   Hans Christian von Baeyer, *Information: The New Language of Science* (London: Weidenfeld and Nicolson, 2003), p. 153.

11   Smith, *The Science of Energy*, p. 155.

difference) and a diagram or program for the efficient exploitation of (thermal) differences."[12] In a steam engine it is the differences in pressure of the air according to its temperature that are used to set a piston in motion, whereas electric engines exploit the differences in polarity in the electromagnetic field to convert electrical energy from a battery (or other electrical reservoir) into mechanical energy.

With Carnot the entire known physical world became liable to being understood through the dynamics of the heat engine as well as being tapped as an energetic resource for human needs:

It is to heat that we must attribute the great and striking movements on the earth. It causes the agitations of the atmosphere, the rise of clouds, the fall of rain and other forms of precipitation, the water currents which channel the surface of the globe, and of which man has thus far employed but a small portion; finally earthquakes and volcanic eruptions are also caused by heat. It is from this immense natural reservoir that we can draw the motive power necessary to our purposes. Nature, in providing us with combustibles on all sides, has given us the power to produce, at all times and in all places, heat and the impelling power which is the result of it. To develop this power, to appropriate it to our uses, is the object of heat engines.[13]

If thermodynamics would thus participate in further extending human mastery over the natural world, the new scientific worldview which grew out of Carnot's work departed significantly from the mechanistic vision of a pristinely ordered clockwork universe transmitting motion perfectly between the material parts that composed it.

In subsequent decades there occurred several crucial developments in the construction of this worldview. James Joule discovered in the 1840s that energy could be converted from one form to another, heat being only one of them. From this was postulated the first law of thermodynamics and the principle of the conservation of energy. It stated that the total amount of energy in the universe was a constant but which could take a variety of convertible forms, whether chemical, electrical, kinetic, or other. Rudolf Clausius and William Thomson confirmed in the 1850s what had been hinted at in Carnot's writings and came to be known as the second law of thermodynamics: that within a closed system the amount of useable energy decreases as it is employed. En-

---

12   DeLanda, *War in the Age of Intelligent Machines*, p. 141.

13   Carnot, *Reflections on the Motive Power of Fire*.

tropy is the measure of this phenomenon, namely that of the level of disorder (i.e. unusable energy lost to dissipation or friction) within a system. Another way of formulating it is to say that energy naturally flows only from being concentrated in one place to becoming diffused or dispersed, i.e. from hot to cold, and *never* the reverse. Hence the exploitable differences which could be converted into work within a closed system will be eventually irretrievably lost.

The ultimate implications of the second law could not be more dramatic: if the universe is taken as a closed system, then it must necessarily be experiencing increasing and irreversible entropy. In other words, as all the thermodynamic differences to which physical activity is attributed are being progressively annihilated, the universe is winding down into the state of an entirely lifeless and motionless void marking "heat death." The second law of thermodynamics thus became known as "time's arrow" as it stated a clear direction to physical processes: from order to disorder. This was a huge blow to the stable, reversible clockwork universe of perpetual motion that the mechanist worldview supported. The dissipation of energy implied non-reversible processes, in contrast with all previously established physical laws. It suggested direction, degradation and end to all the phenomena of the physical universe.

In the place of the stable and linear motion of clockwork, steam and fire also brought to the fore the notions of randomness and unpredictability.[14] In the science of the day, this manifested itself by a shift from a world of mathematical regularity and precision expressed through geometry to a stochastic world in which the mathematics of probability played a growing role. In the second half of the nineteenth century, Ludwig Boltzmann related the probabilistic behaviour of material particles such as molecules with the phenomenon of rising entropy in closed systems, formulating for the first time a physical law in statistical terms and founding the hugely influential disciplines of statistical physics.[15]

---

14 Steam engines tended to be unstable, requiring a careful balance of pressure to maintain a constant speed (and, more critically, to avoid an explosion). This led to the invention of the centrifugal Watt governor, the first feedback control mechanism, allowing the automatic regulation of engine speed. The founders of the science of cybernetics would later hail the Watt governor as one of the finest early embodiments of the self-regulating servomechanism (see next chapter).

15 According to Boltzmann's theories, the state of maximum entropy or disorder postulated by the second law of thermodynamics is only the probabilistic out-

Michel Serres sees in the paintings of Joseph Turner the "translation" of Carnot, that is, the influence of thermodynamic notions. Contrasting with the use of "lines, points and circles" in the technique of George Garrard (the development of geometry having permitted the discovery of classical perspective projection in art), Serres points at the randomness and fragmentation of shape in scenes dominated by clouds, fire, smoke and fog: "the perception of the stochastic replaces the drawing of form."[16] Turner is most famous for his dramatic portrayals of the turbulence and power of nature, but, like many contemporaries, he was also fascinated by the wrenching transformation of the Industrial Revolution. He painted the railroad in *Rain, Steam, and Speed*, ironworking in *Dudley*, textile mills in *Leeds*, and coal production in *Keelmen Heaving in Coals by Night*, seeking to reproduce motion and randomness in his art rather than the immaculate stillness of classical painting.

In the 1860s, William Thomson (later known as Lord Kelvin) and Peter Guthrie Tait published a highly influential treatise whose intention was to provide an overarching account of the state of knowledge of the physical sciences in regard of the different advances made by thermodynamics. In 1868 the *Scotsman* newspaper reviewed the resulting *Treatise on Natural Philosophy*:

The world of which they give the Natural Philosophy is not the abstract world of Cambridge examination papers – in which matter is perfectly homogenous, pulleys perfectly smooth, strings perfectly elastic, liquids perfectly incompressible – but it is the concrete world of the senses, which approximates to, but always falls short alike of the ideal of the mathematical as of the poetic imagination [...] Nowhere is there actual rest; nowhere is there perfect smoothness; nowhere motion without friction.[17]

Energy dissipation and entropy undermined the eighteenth-century vision of frictionless and reversible mechanisms and its promise of absolute control and predictability. As Prigogine and Stengers observe, "un-

---

come of the motion of particles in a closed system. It is therefore theoretically possible for total entropy in such a system to decrease but the probability of such an event is vanishingly small.

16   Michel Serres, *Hermes III: La Traduction* (Paris: Les Editions de Minuit, 1974), p. 237.

17   Smith, *The Science of Energy*, p. 192.

like dynamic objects, thermodynamic objects can only be *partially* controlled. Occasionally they "break loose" into spontaneous change."[18]

With the ascendancy of the engine and the industrial age, mechanical processes were not so much replaced as subsumed within the overarching laws governing the energy which drove such mechanisms. The emergence in this period of a new corpus of scientific ideas organised around the central concept of energy can be further observed in the contemporary production of knowledge in the sciences which took body and mind as their object of study.

The Human Engine: Thermodynamic Bodies and Minds

If mechanism had promulgated an understanding of the human body's animation in terms of levers, springs and cogs, thermodynamics would now inspire a vision of the body as a hot and noisy energy-consuming machine. Emphasis was put on respiration, blood circulation, and the consumption of nutrients that provided the energy for its operation. The engine came to serve the same central metaphorical function as clockwork had in a previous era with the physiologist Auguste Chauveau claiming in 1887 that "what we can state as far as the engines of the physical world are concerned can necessarily and completely be applied to organised machines, and [...] to the human machine, which we can study most easily and scientifically."[19]

Analogies between heat engines and the human body can already be found in the work of Antoine Lavoisier, often referred to as the father of modern chemistry. Following experiments conducted on guinea pigs, he wrote in 1780 that:

Respiration is thus a very slow combustion phenomenon, very similar to that of coal; it is conducted inside the lungs, not giving off light, since the fire matter is absorbed by the humidity of the organs of the lungs. Heat developed by

---

18   Prigogine and Stengers, *Order out of Chaos*, p. 120.

19   Auguste Chauveau, *La Thermodynamique et le Travail Chez les Etres Vivants* (Revue Scientifique, 1887), p. 678 quoted in Jacques Gleyse and al., "Physical Education as a Subject in France (Shool Curriculum, Policies and Discourse): The Body and the Metaphors of the Engine – Elements Used in the Analysis of a Power and Control System during the Second Industrial Revolution", *Sport, Education and Society* 1, Vol. 7 (2002), pp. 5-23.

this combustion goes into the blood vessels which pass through the lungs and which subsequently flow into the entire animal body. Thus, air that we breathe is used to conserve our bodies in two fashions: it removes from the blood fixed air, which can be very harmful when abundant; and heat which enters our lungs from this phenomenon replaces the heat lost in the atmosphere and from surrounding bodies.[20]

Bodies were thus modelled on engines with a circulation diagram in which oxygen acted as a fuel for the production of heat, replacing that which was lost from the body's activity. Further experiments enabled Lavoisier to establish that increases in oxygen consumption, pulse rate, and respiratory rate could be observed when the body was exerted, linking mechanical work to heat production. These ideas continued to gain credence throughout the scientific community in the nineteenth century.

Medical practitioners eventually came to an awareness of the importance of heat production to biological organisms, although nearly a century after Lavoisier's discoveries. Daniel Fahrenheit had invented the mercury thermometer in 1714, along with the temperature scale that carries his name, thereby creating a much-needed universal standard of heat measurement. However, clinical thermometry did not become an accepted part of medical diagnostics until the 1860s and the publication of Carl Wunderlich's research. The German physician took over a million readings from 25,000 patients, establishing a range of normal body temperature from 36.3 to 37.5°C. Since deviation from this could be indicative of disease and a malfunction of the human heat engine, thermometers thereupon become central instruments of medical diagnostic.

The thermodynamic era also yielded a greater understanding of the human metabolism and the respective roles of proteins, carbohydrates, and lipids in providing energy for the operation of the human body. Metabolism (from the Greek word for "change") refers to the manner in which the body consumes food and converts it into energy, measured in calories that are "burnt" through the exercise of the body. The nutritional term of calorie is directly borrowed from the equivalent term in physics, defined as the amount of heat necessary to raise the temperature of one gram of water by one degree celsius. Following on from the

---

20   Antoine Lavoisier and Pierre-Simon Laplace, "Mémoire sur la Chaleur" in *Mémoires de l'Académie des Sciences, Année 1780* (1862), p. 331.

first law of thermodynamics, the calorie unit allows for the quantitative measurement and convertibility of all forms of energy.

The first half of the nineteenth century saw the beginning of a shift in physiology away from a focus on stance towards one on gait and locomotion. The search for idealised universal stances to which the human body should comply was increasingly challenged by calls for the identification of the most energetically efficient movements, even allowing for variability according to individual morphology – "an entirely different problem than that of a body moving forward in a naturally responsive way and thus most efficiently in a dynamic field of forces is that of conforming to pre-patterned group actions requiring unnatural, maximal muscular effort."[21] In an implicit critique of the uniform step typical of Prussian drill, Wilhelm and Eduard Weber argued in the 1830s that such a gait was "not expedient" since a repetitive cadence could be obtained with less energetic expenditure by relying on the body's naturally self-regulated movements.[22]

The evolution of gymnastics as part of the school curriculum in France further illustrates this shift towards an energetic model. Until the 1880s, gymnastics were essentially mechanistic with a focus on ground-based and segmented movements similar to the previously discussed drilling of the Prussian army – an unsurprising fact given that teachers generally received their training during military service. Physiologists and chronophotographers Etienne-Jules Marey and Georges Demenÿ, among others, began to push for a new approach, emphasising the similarities between heat engine and body:

Our blood contains hydrocarbons similar to the oil burnt in our lamps, the coal burnt in our fires. It also contains oxygen which, as it combines with the former elements, causes their combustion, providing a source of heat and energy. Muscular contraction and movement are the result of this physiological process. Will power provokes movement just as an electric spark will provoke an explosion in an unstable volatile matter.[23]

Subsequently, movement in gymnastics (soon renamed physical education), while not abandoning completely mechanistic conceptions,

---

21   Flesher, "Repetitive Order and the Human Walking Apparatus", p. 476.

22   Ibid., pp. 475-476.

23   Georges Demenÿ, *Les Bases Scientifiques de l'Education Physique* (Paris: Alcan, 1902), p. 12.

paid much greater attention to the energetic notions of input and output, with a view to optimising those processes and avoiding "overheating." The military aspects of gymnastics were largely expurgated from training manuals while the dynamic exercise of sports and games played a greater role.[24]

We can also find thermodynamic influences at work in Sigmund Freud's theory of the mind which referred in 1895 to psychical energy as bound (order) and unbound (disorder).[25] In effect, Freud's model of the mind echoes the abstract diagram of the engine with a circulation diagram between conscious and unconscious. A decrease in the energy of one area results in an equivalent increase in the energy of the other (the first law of thermodynamics) with a tendency for psychic energy to flow from the "hotter" area to the "cooler" area as in the resurgence of repressed urges (the second law). The notion of impulses as bursts of psychic energy also suggests a disruptive and unstable force much more akin to the worldview expounded by thermodynamics than that presented by mechanism. The concept of entropy can also be seen in the death drive's urge for complete satisfaction, effectively a total dissipation of psychic energy as a form of final equilibrium.[26]

Thermodynamic Warfare: Prometheus Unbound

In the thermodynamic age, conflict grew rapidly in scope and intensity with states committing all their military, industrial and moral energies into war. Nationalist and revolutionary ideals galvanised entire societies into armed struggles charged with metaphysical significance as war became viewed as the principal vector for the realisation of historical destiny — whether it was nationhood, empire, or socialism which was being sought. The motor introduced unprecedented vectors of speed and movement and new weapons resulted in a vertiginous increase in the means of destruction as warfare became geared towards mobilising the greatest possible resources in order to hurl them at the enemy. While

---

24   Gleyse and al., "The Body and the Metaphors of the Engine".

25   John Lechte, *Key Contemporary Concepts: From Abjection to Zeno's Paradox* (London: Sage, 2003), p. 207.

26   Ibid.

the harnessing of industrial might and the concentration of energies resulted in increasing centralisation of production and a trend towards command economies, thermodynamic warfare was also marked by a tentative recognition of the dynamic and unpredictable nature of war, resulting in a number of tactical and strategic experimentations which saw greater autonomy and flexibility being granted to the individual military units.

Criticism of the mechanistic warfare which had reached its zenith in the armies of Frederick the Great became increasing vocal following the Seven Years' War, disparaging its lack of tactical flexibility and questioning the very belief in the possibility of successfully pre-ordaining the course of a battle. Manual drill was seen as breeding excessively rigid soldiers and battle tactics that could not respond to changing circumstances. As a result, "static choreographies were modified through the introduction of dynamic elements which allowed the infantrymen to increase the mobility of their bodies, enhance the speed of their movements, and become more flexible in the execution of given orders."[27] Having suffered several recent military debacles, the French were receptive to new thinking and at the forefront of this reformist agenda. Although still a strong advocate of a scientific approach to war, Guibert developed a more dynamic and mobile conception of deployment on the battlefield, moving away from geometric conceptions of manoeuvre and granting battalions greater autonomy.[28] For Gat, Guibert was the author of ground-breaking ideas with a lasting influence on the development of the French army on the eve of the Revolution. He notably advocated "mobility, rapidity, and boldness in the conduct of operations [...]; movement in independent formations [...]; and flexible manoeuvring in open columns before deploying into the firing-line, instead of the highly complex and rigid manoeuvring of the linear formation that had been employed and perfected by the Prussians."[29]

It is under Napoleon's command that these tactical innovations would come to their full fruition in the French army. Indeed the revolutionary

---

27   Harald Kleinschmidt, "Using the Gun: Manual Drill and the Proliferation of Portable Firearms", *The Journal of Military History*, Vol. 63, No. 3. (July 1999), p. 627.

28   Lawrence, *Modernity and War*, p. 16.

29   Gat, *A History of Military Thought*, p. 54.

and Napoleonic wars were marked not by rapid technological change but by organisational and ideological transformations that radically altered the practice of warfare, as well as the meaning ascribed to it. In contrast with Frederick's attempts to control his entire army, Napoleon devolved high levels of autonomy to individual corps, allowing for the deployment of forces over a wider area and greater flexibility and inter-changeability in the position and role of respective corps. According to van Creveld, "whereas Napoleon's opponents sought to maintain control and minimise uncertainty by keeping their forces closely concentrated, Napoleon chose the opposite way, reorganising and decentralising his army in such a way as to enable its parts to operate independently for a limited period of time and consequently tolerate a higher degree of uncertainty."[30] The granting of greater autonomy to individual units was easier and less risky in an army of conscripts dedicated to the revolutionary and national cause and whose loyalty could be relied upon far more than in the pre-revolutionary armies.

Witnessing Napoleon riding past after his victory at Jena in 1806, Hegel saw in the Emperor the "world-spirit", the embodied march of History. No longer merely serving the ambitions of an aristocratic class, wars were now the "engines" of history, crucial junctures at which nations, peoples and classes revealed their true nature and purpose, fulfilling their historical destiny. Despite all the attempts by Metternich and the representatives of the Old Regime to turn back the clock in 1815, the forces unleashed by the Napoleonic wars had definitively set the world on a new trajectory.

From the second half of the nineteenth century, war was increasingly rationalised with the aid of evolutionary theory, a dynamic understanding of biology that had replaced the static taxonomy of eighteenth-century natural science.[31] In the last pages of *The Origin of Species*, Charles Darwin claimed that:

---

30   Van Creveld, *Command in War*, p. 61.

31   While thermodynamics pointed to a movement from the ordered to the chaotic and the differentiated to the homogenous with the dissipation of useable energy, the theory of evolution provided an account of increasing differentiation and complexity in the living world. This is not necessarily the contradiction it may at first appear to be since thermodynamics allows for pockets of decreasing entropy within an overall picture of rising entropy. Crucially, however, both theories provided a direction to physical processes, an arrow to time. Further-

From the war of nature, from famine and death, the most exalted object which we are capable of conceiving, namely the production of higher animals, directly follows. There is grandeur in this view of life, with its several powers, having been originally breathed into a few forms or into one; and that, whilst this planet has gone cycling on according to the fixed law of gravity, from so simple a beginning endless forms most beautiful and most wonderful have been, and are being, evolved.[32]

Thus, war and conflict were elevated to a fundamental physical law as universal and uncontested as Newton's theory of gravity but which replaced the immutable cyclicality of the latter with a diachronic theory of change. The very laws of nature thus dictated that war was a progressive and virtuous endeavour through which higher individual and collective life-forms would be issued.

For Karl Marx, it was above all class war which was driving history, although the success of the Bolsheviks in a defeated Russia would later prompt Leon Trotsky to proclaim that war more generally was the "locomotive of history", combining the notion of motorised acceleration with that of a teleological set of "rails" leading to the final destination of communism. Marx's view of the political conditions in nineteenth-century Europe was one in which vast forces were threatening to erupt violently at any time to sweep away the established order, forces whose unleashing he explicitly attributed to the spread of the new energy technologies:

The so-called Revolutions of 1848 were but poor incidents – small fractures and fissures in the dry crust of European society. However, they denounced the abyss. Beneath the apparently solid surface, they betrayed oceans of liquid matter, only needing expansion to rend into fragments continents of hard rock. Noisily and confusedly they proclaimed the emancipation of the Proletarian *i.e.*, the secret of the nineteenth century, and of the revolution of that century. That social revolution, it is true, was no novelty invented in 1848. Steam, electricity, and the self-acting mule were revolutionists of a rather more dangerous character than even citizens Barbès, Raspail and Blanqui.[33]

---

more, Michel Serres sees in Darwin's theories the manifestation of the 'abstract motor' with a reservoir of populations generating dynamic evolution through the exploitation of differences in survival fitness, following a mechanism of circulation of naturally selected species. DeLanda, *War in the Age of Intelligent Machines*, p. 141.

32   Pick, *War Machine*, pp. 85-6.

33   Karl Marx, Speech at the Anniversary of the People's Paper in Robert Tucker (ed.), *The Marx-Engels Reader* (New York: W.W. Norton, 1972), p. 427.

Marx inherited from Hegel dialectal thinking which emphasised the role of contradiction as the driver of a history which strove for a final resolution of this tension. In the materialist version of dialectics argued for by Marx, political upheaval was all the more inevitable as the inequality in the possession and control of the means of production between the bourgeois and proletarian classes intensified. Only a socialist society in which these differences had been annihilated could be truly pacified. Trotsky used another thermodynamic metaphor when arguing for the role of a vanguard party in effectively concentrating and putting to work proletarian energies: "without a guiding organisation the energy of the masses would dissipate like steam which is not enclosed in a piston-box. But nevertheless what moves things is not the piston or the box, but the steam."[34]

Although the post-Napoleonic settlement sought to return the European state system to an age of limited wars, this could only be achieved temporarily as the nationalist passions which had been stirred came to find in armed conflict the truest expression of the nation-state's vitality and greatness. Entire nations were soon pitted against each other, with each successive war announcing a new and unprecedented level in the mobilisation of human, economic and industrial resources. As well as extending over regions, countries and continents rather than specific locations, battles would increasingly last days, weeks and even months. The industrialisation of the means of destruction created huge problems in terms of logistics, not least for the supply of ammunitions, spare parts and fuel. While in 1870-1 over nine-tenths of the supplies consumed by the German army were food and fodder, in 1916 two-thirds of all the supplies for a British division were made of ammunition, engineering materials and other kinds of equipment.[35]

The first direct application of motor power to warfare was precisely a logistical one with railways allowing for both a rapid deployment of troops across great distances and reliable logistics that sustained large armies. Previously, armies essentially depended on the resources they

---

34   Leon Trotksy, *The History of the Russian Revolution (Volume I) – Preface.*

35   Van Creveld, *Command in War*, p. 185. Although the increase in the share of *matériel* relative to food over this period testifies to the industrialisation of war, improvements in productivity of agriculture (combined with the invention of processed food and canning) were equally critical to sustaining mass armies for several years.

could find in the territory they were occupying whereas increasingly they could and had to be supported by agriculture and industries located hundreds of kilometres away from the front. As early as 1842, Prussia planned the construction of a strategic railway network in preparation for the eventuality of a simultaneous war against France and Russia. It went on to make increasing use of railways in its spectacularly successful campaigns in Schleswig Holstein, Austria, and France between 1864 and 1870. Combined with industrial production and the early electromagnetic telecommunication technologies (a lengthier discussion of which follows below), railways participated in the constitution of the huge static war fronts of World War I, capable of sustaining enormous costs in lives and material.

For Feld, the formidable mobilisation required and the attendant logistical problems meant that war planning became the central concern of the military hierarchy: "it was the duty of the professional officer to draw up a program that would result in the most massive and rapid possible thrust of the mobilised resources in the centre of enemy resistance."[36] The minutial war by timetable which resulted from it often left generals unwilling or unable to deviate from their original plans, regardless of the actual intentions and actions of the enemy. Here the tactical centralisation and rigidity associated with mechanistic warfare were generalised to the strategic level as a result of thermodynamic warfare's drive to galvanise and project the greatest possible energy.

Improvements in firearm technology experienced throughout the nineteenth century and first half of the twentieth century, both in terms of power and accuracy, played no small role in this escalation in the releases of energy on the battlefield and brought with them their own tactical and strategic challenges. Ballistics was complemented by a new understanding of the chemistry of explosives and the physical laws of heat, with focus shifting from the reversible phenomenon of "trajectory" to the irreversible process of "explosion."[37] If up to the mid-nineteenth

---

36   M.D. Feld, "Military Professionalism in the Mass Army", *Armed Forces and Society*, Vol. 1 , No. 2, 1975, p. 204.

37   DeLanda, *War in the Age of Intelligent Machines*, p. 242. Van Creveld notes that a gun can be simply understood as an internal combustion engine acting in one direction instead of two. Automatic firearms such as eponymous machine gun developed by Hiram Maxim in 1884 are even self-powered, using either the recoil or gas from each shot to provide continuous fire in an analogous manner

century, the rifle could only be used with any significant effectiveness when employed en masse, new firearms allowed precision targeting along with an exponential rise in the rate of fire. Accompanied by the development of ever more powerful artillery, this increasingly made tight formations of advancing men unsustainable. However the military establishment was often slow to recognise this and tactical inertia led to disaster in World War I with the machine gun rendering charges across open ground all but suicidal.

Most of World War I was thus characterised by a tactical and strategic stalemate during which European nations focused all the firepower and industrial might they could muster in very concentrated areas. The resulting casualties were horrendous: 260,000 men died and a further 450,000 were injured during the Battle of Verdun alone. As World War I veteran Ernst Jünger put it, the soldier was reduced to fuel for the war machine, "just like charcoal, which is hurled under the glowing cauldron of war so as to keep the work going. 'The troops are burnt to cinders in the fire' is the elegant formula found in the manuals of the military art."[38] Jünger's words remarkably echo those of Clausewitz in his letter to Fichte in 1809, in which he insisted on the need for "mobilising the energies of every soldier to the greatest possible extent and in infusing him with the warlike feelings, so that the fire of war spreads to every component of the army instead of leaving numerous dead coals in the mass."[39]

But for Jünger, men were not only consumed by the Great War; some were also recast it in its fire. With machines of fire and metal now dominating the battlefield, survival required that men take on their attributes, the soldier reduced to "a single accentuated determined release of energy":[40]

The spirit of this *Materialschlacht* ["battle of materials"] and war of the trenches, which had been fought more ruthlessly, more wildly and more brutally than any other, produced men which the world had not seen before. It was a new

---

to the cyclical operation of a piston in a steam engine. Van Creveld, *Technology and War*, p. 82.

38   Jünger, *Der Kampf als Inneres Erlebnis*.

39   Pick, *War Machine*, p. 36.

40   Christopher Coker, *War and the Illiberal Conscience* (Boulder, CO: Westview Press, 1998), p. 54.

race, embodying energy and charged with the greatest strength. Sleek, lean and sinewy bodies with striking facial features, beneath the helmets were eyes petrified by a thousand frights. They were vanquishers, *Stahlnaturen* ["natures of steel"], tuned in with the struggle in its most abominable form. Their approach over splintered landscapes meant the last triumph of a fantastic horror. Whenever their bold troops closed in on battered positions, where pale creatures with mad eyes stared at them, unforeseen energies were set free. As jugglers of death, masters of explosives and the flame, and as glorious predators, they moved through the trenches.[41]

Like many young men of his generation, Jünger was profoundly affected by what he saw and experienced during World War I. While the unspeakable horror of the industrial battlefield had broken many men, among others such as Jünger it was a revelatory experience, fuelling futurist fantasies which would resonate in the post-war politics of traumatised European societies. Alongside the exaltation of war, fascism embraced the cult of the machine, the relentless advance of modernisation, and the perceptible increase in speed that touched all aspects of social life but were above all embodied by motorisation.[42] Hitler wrote in *Mein Kampf* of "the universal motorisation of the world, which in the next war will be overwhelmingly decisive in the struggle."[43] For Mussolini, movement was the word which summed up best the new century: "movement towards the icy solitude of the poles and towards the virgin peaks of the mountains, movement towards the stars and towards the depths of the seas... movement everywhere and acceleration in the rhythm of our lives."[44]

In his book *Fire and Movement*, Ernst Jünger identified motorisation of movement as the very means to overcome the deadlock created by projected energy weapons in World War I: "it appears absurd to us today that the warring Will nearly exclusively uses the technical apparatus at its disposition to increase firepower, whereas movement in combat is still essentially limited to primitive energy, that of the muscular strength

---

41 Jünger, *Der Kampf als Inneres Erlebnis*, p. 14.

42 For Paul Virilio, speed is inherently fascistic. If such a blanket statement is perhaps overly reductionist, he is correct is identifying an affinity which accounts for the enthusiasm of fascism for motorisation. Paul Virilio, *Speed and Politics: An Essay on Dromology* (New York: Semiotext(e), 1986).

43 Gat, *A History of Military Thought*, p. 620.

44 Ibid., p. 581.

of man and horse."[45] While the tank had arrived too late to prove decisive in World War I, it had nevertheless heralded the application of the combustion engine to armoured ground vehicles. For Deleuze and Guattari, "it was the tank that regrouped all of the operations in the speed vector and recreated a smooth space for movement by uprooting men and arms."[46] If most military practitioners were initially unsure about the value of this new weapon system, Colonel J. F. C. Fuller had no doubts about its revolutionary impact:

As the tank can use its weapons and carry its own protection when in movement, it will enable the present static fighting to be replaced by dynamic fighting; that is to say, the soldier, whether infantryman or gunner, will not have to halt in order to deliver blows, but will do so whilst in movement. This possibility must sooner or later lead to a radical recasting of tactical organisation, as radical as that which followed the introduction of gunpowder.[47]

Indeed motorisation of movement on the battlefield proceeded apace with the development of armoured ground and airborne vehicles propelled by combustion engines. The British military, in particular, was at the forefront of tank technology and radical thinking about military tactics in the first decade or so which followed World War I.[48] However it was ultimately the Wehrmacht that would make the most spectacular use of the new motorised weapon systems with the highly successful tactics deployed during the first part of World War II. *Blitzkrieg*, as these tactics came to be known, relied on the combination of aerial bombardment with motorised ground forces to achieve a high degree of surprise through mobility and speed. The Wehrmacht privileged decentralised operations (*Auftragstaktik*, also known as mission-oriented tactics) with commanders providing overall objectives and troops granted a great level of initiative to adapt to the fluidity of the battlefield. Van Creveld observes that "like Napoleon, but in charge of forces whose mobility was

---

45 Ernst Jünger, *Feuer und Bewegung* in Ernst Jünger, *Sämtliche Werke*, vol. I-IX (Stuttgart, 1980) V, p. 118.

46 Deleuze and Guattari, *A Thousand Plateaus*, p. 397.

47 J. F. C. Fuller, *The Foundations of the Science of War* (1926). http://cgsc.leavenworth.army.mil/carl/resources/csi/fuller2/fuller2.asp In the same work, Fuller proposed a "Law of the Conservation of Military Energy", a clear nod to the first law of thermodynamics.

48 J.P. Harris, *Men, Ideas and Tanks: British Military Thought and Armoured Forces, 1903-1939* (Manchester University Press, 1995).

far superior and which consequently spread over much larger spaces, the World War II panzer leader was forced to decentralise the chain of command and rely on intelligent initiative at every rank, beginning with the lowest in order to seize every opportunity and exploit it to the hilt."[49] The German army had already experimented with similar tactics in the later stages of World War I with the use of *Sturmtruppen*, elite shock troops that would infiltrate allied defences and use surprise to capture or destroy headquarters or strongpoints. Such battalions, of which Jünger was a distinguished member, employed flexible chains of command and although their successes were insufficient to win the war, they foreshadowed the organisational innovations that would follow.[50]

Finally, the new increase in mobility brought on by motorisation also resulted in the disappearance of the front as strategic bombing brought lethality to entire nations. Civilian populations were soon explicitly targeted as war became total, while science and technology were directed to the development of ever more destructive energy weapons. When nuclear weapons were dropped on Hiroshima and Nagasaki, the spectacular final act of the most destructive and lethal war in history, few could doubt anymore the prescience of the prediction made by the electrical engineer and scientist Nikola Tesla in 1900 concerning the evolution of "the war apparatus toward the greatest possible speed and maximum rate of energy-delivery."[51] The final increase in the destructiveness of war which Hiroshima and Nagasaki heralded and which was pursed *ad absurdum* with the rapid development of nuclear weaponry appeared to bring to a close the era of total war. As John Schaar put it, "we have finally made the engine that can smash all engines, the power that can destroy all power."[52]

Political and military leaders were left to ponder how to reconcile political expediency with the fearsome power they had inherited - that

49   Van Creveld, *Command in War*, p. 191.

50   While the Kaiser's army is usually credited with the innovations that restored tactical mobility on the Western front, the British army also developed shock troop formations with "mission-order" tactics in the second half of World War I. Paddy Griffith, *Battle Tactics of the Western Front: The British Army's Art of Attack, 1916-1918* (London: Yale University Press, 1996).

51   H. Bruce Franklin, *War Stars: The Superweapon and the American Imagination* (New York: Oxford University Press, 1988), p. 205.

52   Lawrence, *Modernity and War*, p. 88.

to become, in Oppenheimer's words, "destroyers of worlds." George Kennan would observe in 1961 that:

The atom has simply served to make unavoidably clear what has been true all along since the day of the introduction of the machine gun and the internal combustion engine into the techniques of warfare […] that modern warfare in the grand manner, pursued by all available means and aimed at the total destruction of the enemy's capacity to resist, is […] of such general destructiveness that it ceases to be useful as an instrument of any coherent political purpose.[53]

The application of the computer and electromagnetic telecommunication technologies to strategic and military affairs during the Cold War would largely preoccupy itself with trying to reconcile war with the existence of such terrible means of destruction, whether in preparation for a nuclear exchange or in managing conflict so that this threshold would never be passed. This new cybernetic approach will be the subject of the next two chapters. We must however first conclude our present discussion with Carl von Clausewitz and the relation of the ideas he developed in *On War* to the thermodynamic world whose birth he was witnessing and to the later scientific developments he appeared to anticipate.

Clausewitz "Translates" Thermodynamics

While Azar Gat has made a persuasive case for the influence of romanticism and its anti-rationalist impulses on the writings of Carl von Clausewitz,[54] it is nevertheless also possible to relate the Prussian officer's ideas to the thermodynamic developments in science. Notwithstanding his emphasis on genius and moral factors, those qualities most celebrated by the romantics, it would be misleading to view Clausewitz himself as anti-science or anti-reason. Indeed, although he neglected the growing importance of new energy technologies, writing as he was at a time in which technological change in military affairs was still relatively slow, Clausewitz was scientifically literate, reading mathematical treatises and attending physics lectures just as science was turning to the study of energy and advances in the theories of probability were

---

53   Gray, *Postmodern War*, p. 138.

54   Gat, *A History of Military Thought*, pp. 158-256. John Lynn has subsequently adopted and expanded much of this analysis; see Lynn, *Battle*, pp. 190-210.

being made. His major work, *On War*, still sought to provide a reasoned understanding of war but one which recognised the inherent limits of reason when grappling with such a dynamic and complex phenomenon, in the same way that thermodynamicists came to trade the mechanistic claims of complete predictability for a more stochastic understanding of the natural world. Despite his professed dislike of metaphors in military theory, Clausewitz employed a broad range of them, many of which echo thermodynamic notions. Situated in an epoch on the cusp of the science of energy, Clausewitz inherited several terms drawn from the vocabulary of mechanism (such as centre of gravity or friction) but many of the ideas he developed broke significantly with mechanistic approaches to warfare.

Clausewitz's approach must be contrasted with many of the popular contemporary military theorists, most prominently Jomini and von Bülow, who still sought to discover the eternal laws of war that had conferred victory throughout the ages. This led to the elaboration of a number of fixed rules, algebraic formulas, and geometric principles which remained very much in the spirit of mechanist conceptions of warfare in assuming proportionality, linearity, and thus predictability. While Jomini, drawing on his experience of Napoleonic warfare, advocated mobility, initiative, and aggressive conduct in military operations, his work remained heavily premised on the existence of optimal geometric lines of operation which if properly followed would ensure victory at all times and places. This attitude was even more marked in Bülow with Newtonian physics weighing heavily on his theory of military force, his use of language and arithmetic mirroring that of the law of gravitation:

The agency of military energies, like other effects or nature, becomes weaker [...] in an inverse ratio of the squares of the distance; that is to say, in this particular, of the length of the line of operations. Why should not this law, which governs all natural effects, be applicable to war, which now consists of little more than the impulsion and repulsion of physical masses? If, which I do not doubt, it is admissible in the theory of the line of operations, we may in the future easily calculate the utmost extent to which military success may be carried.[55]

---

55   Gat, *A History of Military Thought*, p. 85. Bülow concluded that with the discovery of the eternal laws of warfare "war will be no longer called an art, but a science [...] every one will then be capable of understanding and application; the art itself will be a science, or be lost in it." (Gat, p. 84).

Clausewitz rejected the mechanistic approach, indicting it for only paying "regard to activity on one side, whilst war is a constant state of reciprocal action, the effects of which are mutual."[56] We must remember that the original audience being addressed in *On War* was the Prussian military elite which had suffered humiliating defeats at the hand of Napoleon and longed for a return to its glory days. Clausewitz therefore naturally emphasised those aspects of the Prussian tradition which he considered harmful, particularly its drive for "an army made like an automaton by its rigid formations and orders of battle, which, movable only by the word of command is intended to unwind its activities like a piece of clockwork."[57] For Clausewitz, such an approach came to the detriment of an understanding of war as a dynamic process: "the shock of two hostile bodies in collision, not the action of a living power upon an inanimate mass."[58]

While the feedback process of the "reciprocal actions" by the two opposing forces will theoretically tend to the "extreme" and the "absolute", the escalation to pure unlimited war is impossible because conflict is necessarily circumscribed by its historical context and hence always by policy and its instrumental calculations.[59] Clausewitz concludes that "if the extreme is no longer to be apprehended, and no longer to be sought for, it is left to the judgement to determine the limits for the efforts to be made in place of it, and this can only be done on the data furnished by the facts of the real world by the *laws of probability*."[60] The Prussian major-general proceeds:

The absolute, the mathematical as it is called, nowhere finds any sure basis in the calculations in the art of war; [...] from the outset there is a play of possibilities, probabilities, good and bad luck, which spreads about with all the coarse and fine threads of its web, and makes war of all branches of human activity the most like a gambling game.[61]

The role of chance and the "fog of war" necessarily deny the military commander the complete predictability and control of operations that

---

56   Carl von Clausewitz, *On War* (Hertfordshire: Wordsworth, 1997), p. 86.

57   Quoted in Pick, *War Machine*, p. 37.

58   Clausewitz, *On War*, p. 8.

59   Ibid., pp. 9-10.

60   Ibid., p. 12.

61   Ibid., pp. 19-20.

mechanistic warfare strived for, therefore "war must always set itself free from the strict law of logical necessity, and seek aid from the calculation of probabilities."[62] Clausewitz's emphasis on chance is to be contrasted with eighteenth-century general Maurice de Saxe's belief that "war can be made without leaving anything to chance. And this is the highest point of perfection and skill in a general."[63]

War is thus for Clausewitz a phenomenon marked by uncertainty and capable of erupting with the suddenness of "a perfect explosion."[64] Clausewitz returns several times to this conception of war as an indeterminate release of energy: "a pulsation of violent force more or less vehement, consequently making its discharges and exhausting its powers more or less quickly."[65] Acting as a brake on the tendency of war towards the extreme, policy is "interwoven with the whole action of war, and must exercise a continuous influence on it" but only "as far as the nature of the forces liberated by it will permit."[66] Reason, in the form of policy, is crucial in order to exert some control over the use of armed conflict and *de facto* prevents its escalation to the absolute, but this control is still nonetheless limited in the face of the energies released by war.

We can also see thermodynamic notions at play in the famous concept of *friction*, the innate tendency for the accumulation of small setbacks that can result in severe breakdowns in the operation of the military machine. It might seem at first sight that the metaphorical term refers back to a mechanistic understanding of war but closer analysis does not allow for such a straightforward reading:

Everything is very simple in war, but the simplest thing is difficult. These difficulties accumulate and produce a friction which no man can imagine exactly who has not seen war. [...] The military machine, the army and all belonging

62   Ibid., p. 27.

63   Lynn, *Battle*, p. 129.

64   Clausewitz, *On War*, p. 13.

65   Ibid., p. 21. This notion of war as an indeterminate release of energy that eventually exhausts itself manifests itself also in his notion of the "culminating point of the attack" according to which any offensive diminishes in strength as it continues to advance until the point at which it can be reversed with ease by the opposition. The task of the commander therefore becomes the identification of this point, which cannot be objectively calculated or determined and is therefore the province of intuition and genius.

66   Clausewitz, *On War*, p. 21.

to it, is in fact simple, and appears on this account easy to manage. But let us reflect that no part of it is in one piece, that it is composed entirely of individuals, each of which keeps its own friction in all directions. Theoretically all sounds very well: the commander of a battalion is responsible for the execution of the order given; and as the battalion by its discipline is glued together into one piece, and the chief must be a man of acknowledged zeal, the beam turns on an iron pin with little friction. But it is not so in reality, and all that is exaggerated and false in such a conception manifests itself in war. The battalion always remains composed of a number of men, of whom, if chance so wills, the most insignificant is able to occasion delay and even irregularity.[67]

Clausewitz rejects here the linear notions of additivity and assembly of the clockwork metaphor, arguing that the military machine cannot be reduced to parts any larger than its most basic constitutive elements, human bodies. Hence, friction "is not concentrated, as in mechanics, at a few points" but rather "is everywhere brought into contact with chance, and thus incidents take place upon which it was impossible to calculate, their chief origin being chance."[68] Recall that the non-linear phenomenon of friction had been excluded from Newton's laws of motion on the grounds that its effects were so marginal for most cases that they could be safely ignored in any calculations. However, for Clausewitz friction is everywhere in war and can accumulate with disastrous consequences. Therefore, friction cannot be dismissed as a minor and mostly insignificant deviation from the ideal mechanism; rather it is a fundamental and irreducible property of war. Clausewitz's use of the term "friction" is hence much closer to the understanding of thermodynamics than that of mechanism since unpredictability and chance are endogenous to the system.[69]

Clausewitz's greatest insights were slow to be recognised by the military establishment. Indeed Jomini was the more popular theorist for at least fifty years after the publication of On War. Even after he gained

---

67   Ibid., pp. 66-67.

68   Ibid., p. 67.

69   US Air Force Colonel John Boyd explicitly connected Clausewitzian friction with the second law of thermodynamics in his work on the warfighting decision cycle in the 1980s. The concepts of entropy and information are very closely linked, as we shall see in the next chapter. Barry D. Watts, "Clausewitzian Friction and Future War" (McNair Paper No. 52, Oct. 1996) http://www.ndu.edu/inss/McNair/mcnair52/m52c11.html.

pre-eminence, Clausewitz's indeterminacy has often been mistaken for a lack of clarity rather than an integral part of his philosophy. As Beyerchen points out, military students of his work have frequently made the "implicit and even explicit claim that, if Clausewitz were only less confused and understood his own concepts better, he would sound like Jomini."[70] Consequently emphasis has recurrently been put on those elements of his work which appeared to provide eternal rules for victory, such as the targeting of the enemy's "centre of gravity", and the maximum concentration of force and mass, those linear Newtonian concepts. Unsurprisingly, it is among the German military establishment that his ideas would be best appreciated and understood, notably by the general Helmut von Moltke the Elder:

No plan of action can look with any certainty beyond the first meeting with the major forces of the enemy [...] The commander is compelled during the whole campaign to reach decisions on the basis of situations than cannot be predicted. All consecutive acts of war are, therefore, not executions of a pre-meditated plan, but spontaneous action, directed by military tact.[71]

Auftragstaktik would be a logical response to a Clausewitzian understanding of war, distributing uncertainty, adjusting to contingency and navigating the inherent chaos of warfare.

Conclusion

If the harnessing of intimate sources of energy powered the rapid industrial development of Western societies and dreams of unlimited progress, it also brought with it instability and the recurring fear of their exhaustion. The linear certainties of mechanism appeared undermined by the discovery of an ineluctable and irreversible drive towards physical disorder. Thermodynamic warfare was marked by an increasing intensity and breadth of conflicts with the liberated energies and passions consuming continents until their eventual dissipation through the complete material and moral enervation of the societies engaged in them. An awareness of the irreducible uncertainty of warfare and

---

70   Alan D. Beyerchen, "Clausewitz, Nonlinearity and the Unpredictability of War", *International Security*, 17:3 Winter, 1992, p. 84.

71   Lynn, *Battle*, p. 212.

of the consequent futility of mechanistic warfare's previous attempts to impose order through a static, predetermined battle plan permeated the thought of the more astute of military observers. The quest for order was to continue however: the next milestone in technoscientific development would revolve around the concept of information and its potential for managing thermodynamic uncertainty. Communication and control now took centre stage through electromagnetic technologies, chief among which was the computer.

4

Cybernetics and the Genesis of the Computer

Information is information, not matter or energy. No materialism which does not admit this can survive at the present day.

Norbert Wiener[1]

I am thinking about something much more important than bombs. I am thinking about computers.

John von Neumann, 1946[2]

The two previous chapters have each covered a separate regime of the scientific way of warfare, combining a discussion of their respective key technologies and scientific principles along with an analysis of their relationship to the contemporaneous approaches to warfare. In the case of the next two regimes, each will be treated over the course of two chapters, with the first one establishing the crucial technological and scientific concepts and the second dedicated to their military embodiments. This is due partly to the need for a lengthier exposition of scientific ideas, which gain in complexity as we progress, but it is predominantly premised on the need for a more extensive analysis of military theory and

---

1   Norbert Wiener, *Cybernetics or Control and Communications in the Animal and the Machine* (New York: Wiley, 1949), p. 155.

2   Freeman Dyson, *Disturbing the Universe* (New York: Basic Books, 1981).

practice as we get closer to the present day. Indeed, from World War II onwards, the mantle of the scientific way of warfare was passed on to the United States, and its conduct of war remains the central focus of the rest of this book. With the particularly technologically-intensive American approach to warfare, reliance on science to think and practise warfare reached a new high point and hence requires particular consideration.

This chapter will provide an account of the genesis of the computer in the context of the lineage of electromagnetic technologies. We will look at the key role played by World War II in stimulating the development of the computer and its related sciences. This will be followed by a discussion of the scientific concept of information, the principles underpinning the cybernetic science of control and communications, and the latter's diffusion in fields as diverse as engineering, biology, human cognition, and the social sciences. The widespread military applications of cybernetics and computers will be left to the next chapter.

Electromagnetic Telecommunications and War

Whereas the clock harnessed the laws of motion (as subsequently theorised by classical mechanics) and the engine put to work the intimate sources of energy of inert matter by exploiting heat differentials (leading to the science of thermodynamics), the technologies of telecommunications and computing involved the mastering of the electromagnetic field. Electricity was a phenomenon that had been observed for millennia but a real understanding of its nature and its relation to magnetism had to wait for the nineteenth century and the work of such luminaries as Ampère, Faraday, and Maxwell. The application of electricity and radio waves to communications would enable the transmission of information at speeds attaining the very limits permitted by the known universe, that of light itself.

The electric telegraph heralded the start of a telecommunications revolution that would lead to present-day computer networks.[3] Previous to it, the speed of communication over large distances was broadly

---

3   Etymologically speaking, telegraphy refers to the long distance transmission of written messages without physical transport. By this definition this would include non-electromagnetic telecommunication technologies such as smoke signals or other visual signs, as well as modern technologies such as email or fax.

limited to that of the fastest existing means of transport. Beacons, smoke signals, or other visual signs could be relayed across vast expanses but weather and geography were major hindrances to the performance and reliability of these systems. Furthermore, the complexity of messages that could be transmitted was very limited; the semaphore network used by Napoleon could only transmit two words a minute and the cost of sending a message was roughly thirty times as high as for the electric telegraphs which would follow. Aside from being considerably more cost-effective, the latter could also transmit forty to fifty words a minute with the introduction of the Morse code in 1844.[4] The telecommunications device was an instant success, with telegraphs accompanying the construction of railroads, providing invaluable help in managing the expanding rail networks. By 1866, the first transatlantic telegraph cable had been completed, a formidable annihilation of distance. The telegraph also allowed for the precise synchronous setting of clocks and the establishment of standardised time, often called "railway-time" because of its initial purpose in coordinating railroad timetables. We have here an example of the complementarities of different technologies when they are combined in complex technosocial assemblages, the mutual dependencies of clock, telegraph and steam-powered transport promoting and reinforcing their individual potentials for organising social life.

Armies relied on telegraphy from the very beginning, both as early warning systems of the movements of any foreign army and to manage the huge logistical challenges of industrialised war. Because of their reliance on fixed stations and cables, both the telegraph and the telephone were best suited to defence than offence. The difficulty of extending a communications network in the field essentially limited their tactical application to siege warfare, an increasingly peripheral activity of war.[5] World War I saw the extensive use of the telephone for communication between military headquarters and the front, but the lines stopped at the latter. Beyond the trenches, command relied on traditional means, namely optical and acoustic signals that were increasingly drowned out by the noise and smoke of the industrial battlefield.

However, the term of telegraph will here describe only the electric telegraph that employed Morse code.

4   Pacey, *Technology in World Civilization*, p. 138.

5   Van Creveld, *Command in War*, p. 107.

Wireless telegraphy, the transmission of text through radio waves, was pioneered in the last decade of the nineteenth century. Its early uses were primarily naval, enabling ships to communicate with each other as well as with land using Morse code. Voice was added to radio communications at the turn of the century. It was not until the inter-war period however, that the technology was made reliable, mobile, and simple to use, accompanied by a broadening of the frequency spectrum, thereby reducing the problem of mutual interference that had plagued its tentative use in the trenches of the First World War. The Germany military was the first to apply wireless telecommunications in a systematic manner. During World War II, most of its tanks and planes were equipped with two-way radio communication for contact with other vehicles and headquarters. This enabled the high degree of coordination and tactical flexibility required for *Blitzkrieg*. As with virtually all major technological innovations, the successful use of radio by the German army had less to do with the quality and quantity of the device than with its integration within a new organisational and tactical scheme that could take full advantage of it.

Electromagnetic communications continued to grow in importance after World War II as miniaturisation proceeded, transmission of video was added to that of audio, and orbiting satellites layered a telecommunications network across the entire globe. This period was characterised also by the increasing convergence of those technologies with that of the computer, the genesis of which we now address.

The Computer: Genesis and Embodiment of an Abstract Machine

The computer's Anglo-Saxon name betrays the specificity of its original function, that of a complex calculator. Indeed the different names given to the computer in various languages are instructive in that they reveal specific understandings of the technology's purpose or nature. The French refer to it as an "ordinateur" – a machine that puts things in order. In Finnish, it is a "tietokone", which means "knowledge machine." In Chinese, the computer is called "dian nao" or "electric brain." Finally, the Icelandic language has a particularly poetic formulation with "tölva", the "number prophetess."

In fact the English term 'computer' initially referred to individuals, often women, employed to do arithmetic calculations whether assisted or not by mechanical aids. One of the first applications of this "primitive" computing power was the calculation of ballistics firing tables for artillery. Electronic computers were born as a technology designed for the automation of these calculations and in that sense they are part of the lineage of the slide rule and abacus. But the computer is first and foremost a *conceptual* machine that was imagined and theorised before its current embodiment was ever produced. This is in contrast to the clock and engine which only became abstract machines after the technologies reached a certain level of refinement through the trial-and-error work of countless artisans.

The principles of operation of the computer rest on logic. Computing is essentially the repeated application of a fixed and finite set of rules to incoming data. As a purely conceptual machine, a computer could therefore exist in any number of forms: from the simple use of pen and paper to a complex set of cogs and gears or its more familiar electronic embodiment. In the 1830s and following on from his work on gear-based calculators, mathematician Charles Babbage imagined the first programmable computer, the Analytical Engine. His design involved "programs" using loops of punched cards,[6] a "memory" which could store the results of intermediary calculations, a control unit and an output mechanism, all crucial features of modern electronic computers. However, unable to secure the necessary government funding, Babbage was never to build his Analytical Engine.[7]

The abstract computer would resurface in 1937 as part of Alan Turing's elaborate demonstration in the field of symbolic logic. For this purpose, Turing conceived of what became known as a "Turing Machine." The theoretical machine would be able to read, write and erase data, and employed a memory, a central processing unit, and a program controlling the machine's operations through a finite series of mathematical instructions known as algorithms. Although Turing had only conceptualised the machine to make a theoretical point, it would

---

6   The use of punched cards as an early form of software can be traced back to Jacquard's loom, which used cards to modify sewing designs at the turn of the nineteenth century.

7   In 1991, a team from the London Science Museum eventually built a working Analytical Engine, demonstrating the correctness of Babbage's design.

soon find a physical embodiment thanks to the progresses made in the harnessing of electromagnetic forces. The physical computer would have no doubt emerged sooner or later but it was the technological impulse of World War II that constituted the circumstances for its appearance. The brute calculating power of the computer became necessary for two vital technoscientific projects of the war: cryptanalysis and nuclear physics.

Cryptography, the secret coding of messages, had developed greatly in order to protect electromagnetic telecommunications from interception and impersonation. Throughout World War II, the Allies expended great effort in breaking the Enigma code used by the German military for its telecommunications. Doing so required a phenomenal computing power for its day, one that could only be achieved through an unprecedented efficiency in the automation of calculations. The technological break-through was so formidable that the German military, utterly convinced of the inviolability of the Enigma cipher, refused until the end to accept that it had been broken despite obvious indications that the Allies were receiving advance warning of their plans. Alan Turing was closely involved in the successful program in which Colossus, one of the first digital, programmable, and electronic computers, played a central role. Though not strictly speaking a Turing machine, it was nevertheless one of several significant milestones in the development of the modern computer.[8]

The development of the nuclear bomb was an unprecedented in-dustrial, technoscientific and military undertaking that mobilised up to one percent of the United States federal budget. Recent advances in theoretical physics had made a nuclear bomb a tangible possibility but there remained major obstacles to its realisation. Incredibly complex calculations were necessary to strengthen the basic understanding of nuclear fission and harness it into a practical device. The Manhattan Project began by relying on mechanical calculators operated by some of the wives of the scientists but it soon became apparent that greater computing power would be required. Under the impulsion of the math-

---

8   The title of first electronic computer is fiercely disputed with other candidates
     including the Z3 and ENIAC computers. The intricacies of the arguments are
     less important than the fact that they simply illustrate that the development of
     the general purpose computer (i.e. Turing-complete) was complex, piecemeal,
     and contingent on the applications to which the device was put to and on the
     availability and cost of other technologies, in contrast to its theoretical and
     abstract model.

ematician John von Neumann, modified IBM punched-card machines were introduced and allowed the completion of the project before the end of the war. One of the greatest scientific minds of his generation, von Neumann was a crucial figure in the development of both the computer and nuclear weaponry. Unlike other scientists, such as Robert Oppenheimer who became uncomfortable about the consequences of their work on the Manhattan project, he remained closely involved in the subsequent work on the nuclear arsenal until his death in 1957. A fervent proponent of nuclear build-up and even of a pre-emptive strike on the Soviet Union, he participated in the development of the hydrogen bomb and was appointed Commissioner of the Atomic Energy Commission in 1955.

With respect to the computer, von Neumann's greatest contribution was perhaps to provide the crucial bridge between the abstract mechanism imagined by Turing and the material work electrical engineers were pursuing. According to Herman Goldstine, a mathematician and army officer who brought him in as a consultant at the University of Pennsylvania in 1944 to work on the design of high-speed digital computers contracted by the Army, von Neumann was the first person "who understood explicitly that a computer essentially performed logical functions, and that the electrical aspects were ancillary."[9] By reducing all computing operation to logical functions, von Neumann was able to design a method whereby problems could be broken down into a sequence of discrete logical steps that could be programmed into a computer, establishing the approach of serial computing. He also gave his name to a computer architecture which distinguished itself from previous mechanical embodiments in that it used a single storage structure (memory) to contain both instructions and data. In this way, computers could be systematically reprogrammed for each new task rather than being purpose-built for a particular operation.

A diagram of the von Neumann architecture can be seen in Figure 3. The arithmetic logic unit (ALU) performs all the arithmetic computations according to instructions transmitted by the control unit (in practice, modern computers integrate these two elements in their central processing unit, the CPU). The memory unit serves as temporary storage for all the program instructions and data that are being executed

---

9   Heims, *John von Neumann and Norbert Wiener*, p. 182.

by the computer. Intermediate results can be stored in the memory and recalled when necessary during the computation of a problem with several discrete logical steps. Input and output connect the computer to its environment, allowing for both the introduction of new programs and data as well as the transmission of computation results to human users or other devices that will act upon them. The output can also serve as a new input for the computer, constituting a closed processing loop in which the computer responds to the stimulus of its own output. This point is particularly relevant to the discussion below of cybernetics.

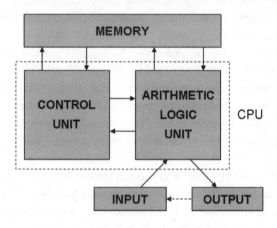

Figure 3: Diagram of the von Neumann computer architecture

Whereas clockwork transmits mechanical force and the engine converts an energetic release from inert matter into mechanical work, the electronic computer's "motion" is not to be found at the level of any of its components but rather occurs at that of the flow of electrons whose patterns express logical and mathematical relationships. The computer does not therefore perform any direct physical work but can be employed to control other machines via the transmission of information in the form of instructions. The computer's ability to apply conditional branching and run programs that can respond to their own results as much as to external inputs makes it an ideal control mechanism. It can thus regulate and modify its own behaviour as well as that of other machines connected to it on the basis of an incoming flow of information from its surroundings and its programmed responses to it. As we shall see in the next sections and Norbert Wiener's work on servomechanisms, this is not a feature unique to the computer but the latter has allowed a far greater complexity, precision and ubiquity of such control mechanisms.

But to focus exclusively on its ability to execute logical programs and its application as a control device would mean neglecting another essential feature of the computer, namely its capacity to manipulate any form of symbolic information and thus simulate any electronic symbol-producing machine. This includes all media technologies permitting the recording, processing or reproduction of audiovisual content. For a long time, these technologies remained quite distinct from the computer but their relatively recent digitalisation is erasing any fundamental distinction between the computer and the specific technologies of the television, camera or radio. We may distinguish devices by the type of media content they produce or transmit or by the interface with which we interact with them, but ultimately they are all increasingly being brought together under a common architecture of digital information-processing. This is seen in the current collapsing of devices: emails can be sent through a television, photographs taken with a mobile telephone, and films viewed on a handheld computer. The computer is therefore an abstract machine that encompasses all electromagnetic technology of symbolic representation.

Lastly, the conjunction of computing and telecommunication technologies has enabled computers to network together and share information and processing power, with the Internet as perhaps the most spectacular manifestation of this tele-interaction of computing devices. This has largely contributed to the convergence observed today in electronic devices while also greatly extending the distances across which a computer can act as a control mechanism, whether automated or under human operation.

The contemporary networked computer can thus be understood as a single device capable of four distinct yet interlocked functions:

- a logic machine applying finite rules to data;
- a control mechanism using information feedback (or what cyberneticists call a servomechanism);
- a semiotic machine handling any symbolic information including numbers, characters and images;
- an electromagnetic telecommunications device.

None of these functions is exclusive to the computer and conversely many modern computing devices only fulfil one or a few of these functions, depending on the purpose for which they were designed. Thus the computer finds itself at the point of convergence of several techno-scientific developments whose conjunction has amplified and transformed their respective capabilities and potentialities.[10] The computer's ability to imitate any symbol-producing machine has enabled it to "cannibalise" all such machines and integrate them under a single digital architecture. What ultimately brings together all these distinct technologies into a single device or abstract machine is the notion of *information*. Indeed, narrowed down to its barest definition, the computer is first and foremost an information-processing device. Already in the 1940s, the theories of Norbert Wiener and Claude Shannon were linking together the three functions of calculation, communication and control through the concept of information before they were ever combined in any single machine. If force was the core concept of Newtonian mechanics and energy that of thermodynamics, it is information which would fulfil a similar organising role for the science of cybernetics.

Bits and Negentropy: Information Becomes Physical

Before scientists began paying attention to it in the years preceding World War II, information was traditionally understood as the communication of human knowledge. However, the scientific concept of information which emerged in this period is quite distinct. The problem with the established definition of information as necessarily connected to meaning, and therefore context, was that it made scientific quantification and general theorisation extremely complicated. Engineers seeking to improve the efficiency of telecommunication technology therefore sought to detach the meaning of information from the process of transmission. Ralph Harltey, responsible for some of the foundations of information theory, wrote in 1928 of the need "to eliminate the psy-

---

10 A similar convergence was already observed when Alexander Graham Bell and others combined electric sound reproduction with telegraphy to give birth to the telephone in the last quarter of the nineteenth century.

chological factors involved and to establish a measure of information in terms of purely physical quantities."[11]

Such a measure emerged from Claude Shannon's war research on fire-control systems and cryptography at the AT&T Bell Labs. As an engineer, Shannon was concerned with the practical issue of the reliability of the transmission of a message, not its meaning. Communication and information were thus to be understood as a process between a sender and a receiver of communication that is distinct from the meaning being transmitted. Shannon's colleague Warren Weaver emphasised this distinction:

The word information, in this theory, is used in a special sense that must not be confused with its ordinary usage. In particular, information must not be confused with meaning [...] The word information in communication theory relates not so much to what you do say, as to what you could say. That is, information is a measure of one's freedom of choice when one selects a message [...] The concept of information applies not to the individual messages (as the concept of meaning would) but rather to the situation as a whole.[12]

For Katherine Hayles, this "meaninglessness" allowed information to become disembodied and "to be conceptualised as if it were an entity that can flow unchanged between different material substrates."[13] Information becomes "a pattern, not a presence."[14] Information could thus be theorised and mathematically expressed as an abstract quantity detached from its specific embodiments, in a similar way to matter and energy. Concomitantly, the process of communication was analogously abstracted from physical embodiment into a general diagram of operation. This understanding of information and communication would be central to the constitution of cybernetics as the science of control and communication of systems, be they organic, mechanical or social.

---

11   Hartley, R.V.L., "Transmission of Information", *Bell System Technical Journal*, Vol. 7, 1928, p. 536.

12   Tom Siegfried, *The Bit and the Pendulum: From Quantum Computing to M Theory – The New Physics of Information* (New York: John Wiley and Sons), p. 167.

13   N. Katherine Hayles, *How We Became Posthuman: Virtual Bodies in Cybernetics, Literature, and Informatics* (Chicago and London: University of Chicago Press, 1999), p. 54.

14   Ibid., p. 18.

Indeed for Shannon, the aim was to "consider certain general problems involving communication systems" which required the representation of "the various elements involved as mathematical entities, suitably idealised from their physical counterparts."[15] In other words, to conceptualise an abstract communication machine. The abstract machine presented by Shannon consists of five different components: an *information source* which produces the message to be communicated, a *transmitter* which operates on the message in order to produce a signal suitable for transmission, a *channel* which provides the medium for the signal be transmitted, a *receiver* which reconstructs the message from the signal, and a *destination* to which the message is intended (Figure 4). In addition, Shannon considered a noise source which would introduce a stochastic interference to the signal and impede communication; the question then becoming the level of redundancy necessary to avoid the pattern of the message being drowned out by the noise – how to preserve order from chaos.

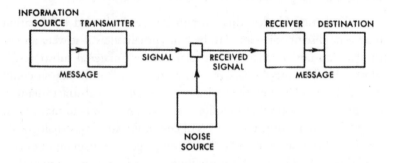

Figure 4: Shannon's schematic diagram of an abstract communication machine[16]

The basic unit of information would be the *bit* (binary digit), with one bit representing the choice between two mutually exclusive choices, e.g. the true or false of logic, the zero or one of the digital computer. Since Shannon had demonstrated that binary choices were the least expensive way to handle information, the transmission of any information could therefore be broken down into a sequence of optimal (i.e. more

---

15   Claude E. Shannon, "A Mathematical Theory of Communication", *Bell System Technical Journal*, Vol. 27, 1948, pp. 3-4.

16   Shannon, "A Mathematical Theory of Communication", p. 3.

or less equally probable) binary choices that would identify the correct message from the range of possible messages.[17] Shannon's probabilistic approach to information meant that the greater the uncertainty about a situation – in other words, the wider the range of equally probable alternative states that could be communicated – the larger the physical quantity of information necessary. Similarly, an improbable message would contain more information than a highly probable one. Shannon equated the mathematical measure of information with Boltzmann's formula for thermodynamic entropy (the measure of unusable energy or disorder within a closed system) because of the similarity in the probability distribution.

While Shannon's discovery was made outside of the realm of the physical sciences, the immediately apparent overlap between the measurement of information and that of entropy and the explanatory power it seemed to offer soon led scientists to make the connection into a meaningful physical one, thereby initiating a momentous transformation in the scientific worldview. According to Henri Atlan, "a real kinship between quantity of information and entropy means that not only does this notion of information has practical relevance for the statistical treatment of some communication problems but that it also expresses a universal physical reality in relation to other measurable physical magnitudes such as energy, temperature, etc… and that it thus fully enters the domain of the natural sciences."[18]

Crucially, the founder of cybernetics Norbert Wiener effected a change in sign to Shannon's equation, thus defining information as the opposite of entropy – negative entropy or *negentropy*:

The notion of the amount of information attaches itself very naturally to a classical notion in statistical mechanics: that of *entropy*. Just as the amount of information in a system is a measure of its degree of organisation, so the entropy of a system is a measure of its degree of disorganisation; and the one is simply the negative of the other.[19]

17   Von Baeyer, *Information*, pp. 30-31.

18   Henri Atlan, *L'Organisation Biologique et la Théorie de l'Information* (Paris: Editions du Seuil, 2006), p. 174.

19   Wiener, *Cybernetics*, p. 18. The term of negative entropy originated in Erwin Schrödinger's popular-science book *What is Life?* (1944), later shortened to negentropy by the physicist Léon Brillouin. Erwin Schrödinger, *What is Life? And Other Scientific Essays* (Garden City, NY: Doubleday Anchor, 1956). Léon

Information therefore became a measure of order and opposed to entropy as that of disorder and randomness. Anthropologist and cyberneticist Gregory Bateson further expanded on this new understanding of information:

> The technical term "information" may be succinctly defined as any difference which makes a difference in some later event. This definition is fundamental for all analysis of cybernetic systems and organisations. The definition links such analysis to the rest of science, where the causes of events are commonly not differences but forces, impacts, and the like. The link is classically exemplified by the heat engine, where available energy (i.e. negative entropy) is a function of a difference between two temperatures. In this classical instance, "information" and "negative entropy" overlap.[20]

Thus according to Wiener, the function of cybernetic systems driven by information feedback (i.e. systems endowed with the ability to adjust future conduct by past performance) is "to control the mechanical tendency towards disorganisation; in other words, to produce a temporary and local reversal of the normal direction of entropy."[21] The general tendency towards increasing entropy remains but, on the background of this rising chaos and indeterminacy – which Wiener designated as "evil", the diabolical arch-enemy of the scientist in search of the order governing the universe – information allows for the constitution of pockets of decreasing entropy and growing complexity which Wiener explicitly linked to progress.[22]

As Hayles points out, Shannon's original theory "defines information as a probability function with no dimensions, no materiality, and no necessary connection with meaning. It is a pattern, not a presence."[23] This shift was pursued further in cybernetics, reinforcing a conception of information which severed it from notions of meaning and the indi-

---

Brillouin, "The Negentropy Principle of Information", *Journal of Applied Physics*, vol. 24 (9) (1953), pp. 1152-1163.

20 Gregory Bateson, *Steps to an Ecology of Mind* (New York: Ballantine, 1972), p. 381.

21 Norbert Wiener, *The Human Use of Human Beings: Cybernetics and Society* (London: Eyre and Spottiswoode, 1954), pp. 24-25.

22 Wiener's view of evil here is that which St Augustine characterises as incompleteness (negative evil) rather than the malicious type of the Manicheans (positive evil). Wiener, *The Human Use of Human Beings*, p. 11 and pp. 34-35.

23 Hayles, *How We Became Posthuman*, p. 18.

vidual contexts in which it is found to become a universal pattern common to all forms of organisation. If this initially elevated information to a scientific concept as crucial as those of matter or energy, subsequent theories have posited that these are in fact merely expressions of information, thereby granting the latter the status of sole metaphysical building-block of the universe. Summing up this worldview, social theorist Kenneth Boulding described matter and energy as "mostly significant as encoders and transmitters of information."[24] The dominance of the scientific concept of information appears today complete, having gained pre-eminence over those entities previously taken to be the core constituents of our reality. But such a momentous ontological shift in the scientific view of nature began with considerably more limited pre-occupations centred around engineering problems and in the context of the rapid technological transformations wrought by World War II. The science of cybernetics that would emerge from this technoscientific endeavour would be the major contributor to the elaboration and the subsequent dissemination of the informational paradigm.

Cybernetics: the Science of Control and Communications

As with the computer, cybernetics drew on older ideas and research but was born from the imperatives of war. Indeed Norbert Wiener's wartime research played a major role in the elaboration of the central postulates of cybernetics. Wiener worked on one of the most urgent technological problems of the Second World War, namely the improvement of anti-aircraft defences. With the increases in the speed and altitude at which bomber aeroplanes could fly, it no longer became possible for anti-aircraft gunners simply to visually target a plane since it would have moved out of position in the short time necessary for the projectile to reach it. Anti-aircraft defences were thus notoriously inefficient and successful hits resulted more from chance than the gunner's accuracy. Whereas the traditional problem of ballistics required the production of lengthy tables detailing the appropriate artillery elevation according to type of gun, shell, and range to a fixed target, fire control against a

---

24   Arquilla and Ronfeldt, "Information, Power, and Grand Strategy" in Schwartzstein (ed.), *The Information Revolution and National Security*, p. 139.

rapidly mobile target was a real-time computational problem. Wiener therefore focused on first developing a mathematical theory for making a statistical prediction of the future course of a plane given available information on its position and motion. Real-time application of the theory required the processing of information provided by radar (yet another by-product of the discoveries of electromagnetism) into adjustments in the aiming of the gun. A missed shot would be followed by an adjustment of the aim, a new shot, and further adjustment if necessary. This led Wiener to think of this process as a *feedback loop* in which information gathering and processing precedes an action that results in a changed state and new flow of information.

The etymology of cybernetics refers to the Greek for steersman or governor and reflected Wiener's belief that a steersman and his rudder formed a feedback loop. The anti-aircraft unit, whether fully automated or incorporating a human controller, thus formed a self-steering device guided by an information feedback loop. Wiener designated all self-steering devices relying on information feedback as servomechanisms and insisted on their era-defining character:

The machines of which we are now speaking are not the dream of the sensationalist, nor the hope of some future time. They already exist as thermostats, automatic gyro-compass ship-steering systems, self-propelled missiles – especially such as seek their target – anti-aircraft fire-control systems, automatically controlled oil-cracking stills, ultra-rapid computing machines, and the like. They had begun to be used long before the war – indeed, the very old steam-engine governor belongs among them – but the great mechanisation of the Second World War brought them into their own, and the need of handling the extremely dangerous energy of the atom will probably bring them to a still higher point of development. [...] the present age is as truly the age of the servo-mechanisms as the nineteenth century was the age of the steam engine or the eighteenth century the age of the clock.[25]

A cybernetic system, or servomechanism, is characterised by three distinct components: (a) receptors or sensors that can absorb informational input from its environment, (b) a processing unit which can record and process this input, compare it with the desired state of the input, and issue the necessary instructions onwards to (c) an output mechanism which can impact the environment in the required way.

---

25   Wiener, *Cybernetics*, p. 55.

New outputs result in a new flow of input thereby closing the feedback loop. This continuous loop is enabled by the flow of information that links all the components together and allows the system to respond to changes in the perceived environment and adjust its behaviour accordingly (Figure 5). This contrasts markedly with clockwork mechanisms which can only follow the pre-programmed path built into them and have no ability for self-regulation.

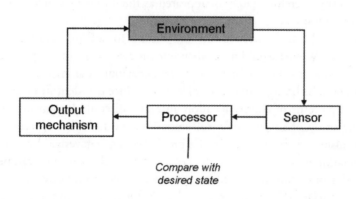

Figure 5: Information feedback loop in a cybernetic system

The servomechanism also distinguishes itself in that it replaces the simple chain of causality (A is the cause of effect B) suggested by clockwork and characteristic of traditional scientific theories with the notion of circular causality (A is the cause of effect B which is cause of A). Consequently, reductionist atomistic frameworks of interpretations give way to systemic holistic understandings of any object of study. Mechanism had sought to understand any whole by an analytical treatment of all of its individual components and of the sequential and linear causal relation of one component to the next. A clockwork mechanism could be perfectly theorised and subsequently perfected in this manner. In contrast, cybernetics and the affiliated methodologies focus on a holistic understanding of a system in which the components enter into relations of causal circularity. Thus in cybernetics the whole is superior to the sum of its parts.

In his engineering work during the war Wiener had dealt with the probabilistic problem of predicting the future path of an airplane. Also reflected in his earlier work on statistical mechanics and quantum physics, Wiener's view of the world was fundamentally probabilistic and his mathematical work revolved around the means to grasp stochastic processes and exert predictability and control over them. Wiener had a predilection for mathematical problems which "involved finding predictability through chaos or signal through noise"[26] and likened the discovery of laws of nature to the identification of repetitive patterns involved in breaking a secret communications cipher.[27] Cybernetic mechanisms therefore naturally appeared as the means by which order could be imposed over chaos.

Nor would such mechanisms be limited to solving engineering problems – Wiener would find cybernetic processes at work everywhere among living organisms. In this way the behaviour of animal and machine could be brought under a single theory since the identification of abstract patterns of communication and control could be substituted for the study of specific physical embodiments. Indeed a cybernetic mechanism is defined in terms of a process which is governed by rules of operation and a continuous flow of data to which these rules can be applied. Its function and operation can therefore be formulated in terms of logical relationships and modelled accordingly by a computing device, the specific structure of the mechanism being deemed irrelevant.

Homeostasis was a term coined in the 1930s to describe the process by which living organisms adjust their internal environment to maintain a stable state. Examples would include the regulation of body temperature and cardiac rhythm or the concentration of nutrients and waste products within the tolerable limits of the organism. Wiener adopted the term and applied it more generally to all systems whose behaviour relies on feedback to stave off entropy: "it is my thesis that the physical functioning of the living individual and the operation of some of the new communications machines are precisely parallel in their analogous attempts to control entropy through feedback."[28] Homeostasis was thus the means by which a system could maintain its goal – survival in the case of a biological life form ("the process by which we living

---

26   Heims, *John Von Neumann and Norbert Wiener*, pp. 146-147.

27   Wiener, *The Human Use of Human Beings*, p. 124.

28   Theodore Roszak, *The Cult of Information* (Berkeley, CA: University of California Press, 1994), pp. 9-10.

beings resist the general stream of corruption and decay"[29]), the continued regulation of a mechanical process within defined boundaries for a servomechanism – in the midst of a changing environment which could never be predicted with complete certainty. The pursuit of such a goal via feedback loops is what Wiener understood as the teleology of a system since its behaviour is goal-directed, here towards a desired stable state.

It should be noted that if another cybernetic system was put in the place of the environment in Figure 5, we would have two cybernetic systems interacting with one another as each tries to impose its own desired state on the other. If the respective goals are incompatible, the systems will be in a state of conflict or competition; if the goals can be conciliated, a mutually satisfactory equilibrium may be reached. A control relationship is established when one system can dominate another system and impose its preferences over it. In cybernetics, control and communication are inextricably linked since control "is nothing but the sending of messages which effectively change the behaviour of the recipient."[30] Complex control systems are thus composed of a hierarchy of nested cybernetic systems, each with its own goal but subservient to the goal of the system above it. For example, a machine or organism whose overall goal is survival might have a set of subsidiary goals that serve this purpose: a regular supply of energy, the evasion of a threat, or any other behaviour that addresses a disturbance that takes the system away from its overarching desired state. The more complex the environment and the greater the variety of possible perturbations, the more control loops will be required to attain and sustain the system's goal. These nested hierarchies constitute a top-down architecture of control which cyberneticists see as explanatory of the "increasing complexity which characterises such fundamental developments as the origin of life, multicellular organisms, the nervous system, learning, and human culture."[31] Bureaucratic organisations and their top-down command

---

29   Wiener, *The Human Use of Human Beings*, p. 95.

30   Ibid., p. 8.

31   Francis Heylighen and Cliff Joslyn, "Cybernetics and Second-Order Cybernetics" in R.A. Meyers (ed.), *Encyclopedia of Physical Science and Technology* - 3rd edn (New York: Academic Press, 2001).

layers linked by two-way communication channels offer another obvious example in human societies.

Cybernetic Organisms: From Computerised Brains to Biological Computers

While the clock and engine allowed frequent comparisons between machines and humans, the computer blurred even more drastically their boundaries since it theorised and enabled their combination under a single system linked by information feedback, as with the integration of the human operator in an anti-aircraft unit. Human and machine would thus come to be described and analysed in the same terms. For Kenneth Craik, a British psychologist working on the problem of radar tracking during the war, "the human behaves basically as an intermittent correction servo" and could be described by the same equations.[32] Similarly, Norbert Wiener and his colleague Arturo Rosenbluth were convinced that "as objects of scientific enquiry, humans do not differ from machines."[33]

Cybernetics was concerned from the very beginning with describing the universal patterns of organisation behind biological and mechanical systems and thereby enhancing the possible interfaces between them.[34] This produced a discourse that combined the mechanisation of biology and the anthropomorphising of machines which quickly moved from the explicitly metaphorical to the literal. Neurophysiologist Ralph Gerard made this last observation at the seventh session of the Macy conferences, the inter-disciplinary events during which cybernetics was developed in the post-war period:

We started our discussion in the "as if" spirit. Everyone was delighted to express any idea that came to his mind, whether it seemed silly or certain or merely a stimulating guess that would affect someone else. We explored possibilities for

---

32   Kenneth J.W. Craik, "Theory of the Human Operator in Control Systems", *British Journal of Psychology* 38 (1947), pp. 56-61.

33   Norbert Wiener and Arturo Rosenbluth, "Purposeful and Non-Purposeful Behaviour", *Philosophy of Science* 17, Oct 1950, p. 326.

34   Michael Heim defines an interface as "where two or more information sources come face-to-face." Michael Heim, *The Metaphysics of Virtual Reality* (New York: Oxford University Press, 1993), p. 77.

all sorts of "ifs." Then, rather sharply it seemed to me, we began to talk in an "is" idiom. We were saying much the same things, but now saying them as if they were so.[35]

Concerned about the military applications of his ideas after the war, Wiener turned to seemingly more benign uses and showed great interest in prosthetics, viewing improvements in the condition of the invalid as one the most immediate promises of cybernetics. But there is only one step from rehabilitation to enhancement and the term of cyborg (cybernetic organism) was later coined during research into cybernetic technologies that would enable humans to operate in hostile extraterrestrial environments, the battlefield being of course one of the most hostile *terrestrial* environments.

Research into the brain and nervous system was greatly influenced by the development of computers and played a central role in cybernetic discourse. Wiener insisted that:

The ultra-rapid computing machine, depending as it does on consecutive switching devices, must represent an almost ideal model for the problems arising in the nervous system. The all-or-none character of the discharge of the neurones is precisely analogous to the single choice made in determining a digit on the binary scale, which more than one of us had already contemplated as the most satisfactory basis of computing machine design.[36]

It was known that neurons are connected to each other via synapses through which electrical and chemical signals are transmitted. The input from other neurons determine whether an individual neuron will "fire", that is send out a signal to those neurons connected to its output. A neuron can therefore be thought of as in being in one of two states: "firing" or "not firing." This binary choice naturally appeared analogous to the 0 or 1 states of computing logic gates.

Von Neumann's conceptual formulation of the computer was developed in parallel with an analogous theory of the human mind such that both coevolved together and it is virtually impossible to establish a clear precedence of either over the other. Arthur Burks, a collaborator of von Neumann notes that the mathematician thought of computers in two ways: one as a "general-purpose computational device" and the

---

35   Slava Gerovitch, *From Newspeak to Cyberspeak: A History of Soviet Cybernetics* (Cambridge, MA and London: MIT Press, 2002), p. 90.

36   Wiener, *Cybernetics*, p. 22.

other as a "general theory of automata, natural and artificial."[37] The discipline of artificial intelligence therefore emerged at the same time as modern computing and the general assumption was that computer science was uncovering the mechanisms of human thought. Cognition became therefore predominantly conceived in terms of information processing, the treatment of incoming data on the basis of a limited set of rules. In the field of linguistics, Noam Chomsky's influential theory posited a universal grammar, a logical set of rules that governs all human languages and determines the correct construction of sentences without consideration for semantic meaning (variability across languages being accounted for by different second-order rules).[38]

Lily Kay has provided a detailed account of the manner in which cybernetics and information theory impacted research into biochemistry and genetics after the war, shifting the scientific discourse from one based on notions of chemical and biological specificity to one articulated around informational conceptions.[39] Nucleic acids became eventually designated as the carriers of informational content, bearers of a genetic "code" to be broken by molecular biologists. The 1950s saw the discovery of the structure of DNA, the nucleic acid believed to carry the genetic instructions for the development of all cellular life forms. Composed of only four different types of chemical bases (abbreviated as A, T, G, and C) that connect the two strands of the famous double helix, DNA was seen as being able to account for the enormous differentiation and specialisation of life-forms. Sequences of those elementary building blocks have been compared to the computer code which provides instructions to a computer. Small sequences of three bases (e.g. ACT, CAG, TTT) translate into "instructions" for specific amino acids which then form proteins (amino acid sequences) according to a set of "rules." Kay has persuasively related this informational discourse to the rise of cybernetics and information theory and the military contexts in which they emerged so that within molecular biology "the genetic

---

37   M. Mitchell Waldrop, *Complexity: The Emerging Science at the Edge of Order and Chaos* (London: Viking, 1992), pp. 161-2.

38   Noam Chomsky, *Syntactic Structures* (The Hague: Mouton, 1957). Perhaps unsurprisingly, Chomsky's hierarchical classification of grammars was subsequently applied to the analysis of formal programming languages in computer science.

39   Kay, *Who Wrote the Book of Life?*.

code became the site of life's command and control."[40] Indeed for the geneticist and Nobel Prize winner Jacques Monod, the organism was nothing but "a cybernetic system governing and controlling the chemical activity at numerous points" and gene-enzyme regulations constituted a system "comparable to those employed in electronic automation circuitry, where the very slight energy consumed by a relay can trigger a large-scale operation, such as, for example, the firing of a ballistic missile."[41]

Even as the structure of DNA was being discovered, Wiener was putting forward a view of life as a pattern of organisation determined by its informational content and whose physical embodiment was both sustained and renewed by homeostasis:

Our tissues change as we live: the food we eat and the air we breathe become flesh and bone of our body, and the momentary elements of our flesh and bone pass out of our body every day with our excreta. We are but whirlpools in a river of ever-flowing water. We are not stuff that abides, but patterns that perpetuate themselves.[42]

For Wiener therefore, the organism is the message. In the final instance, life remains however nothing but a local and temporary reversal of entropy in a universe in which overall randomness and chaos is necessarily increasing – "life is an island here and now in a dying world."[43]

Sociocybernetics

In the 1950s, cybernetics appeared to offer a whole new interdisciplinary theory and methodology with anthropologists, linguists, physiologists, sociologists, philosophers, engineers and computer scientists all applying cybernetic principles to their field. Cybernetics was not so much a traditional scientific discipline than a convergence of engineering techniques, scientific theories and philosophical concepts under a common discourse that allowed the discussion and analysis of artificial machines, biological organisms, and social organisation as equivalent systems of control and

---

40   Ibid., p. 5,

41   Quoted in ibid., p. 17,

42   Wiener, *The Human Use of Human Beings*, p. 96,

43   Ibid., p. 95.

communication operating under a single set of principles. Upon opening the Third Congress of the International Association of Cybernetics in 1961, its president Georges Boulanger announced that cybernetics:

intends to investigate freely in the domain of the mind. It wants to define intelligence and to measure it. It will attempt to explain the functioning of the brain and to build thinking machines. It will assist the biologist and the doctor, and also the engineer. Educational practice, sociology, economics, law, and philosophy will become tributary to it. And it can be said that there is not a sector of human activity that can remain foreign to it.[44]

Initially, Wiener's already ambitious goal for cybernetics was a theory of "control and communications in the animal and the machine"[45] but the definition was soon expanded to the understanding of the behaviour of all complex systems, including social.[46] After the first Macy conference in 1946, Wiener had proposed that fields as diverse as statistical mechanics, communication engineering, the theory of control mechanisms in machines, biology, psychology and social science could all be understood through an emphasis on the role of communication:

The neuromuscular mechanism of an animal or of man is certainly a communication instrument, as are the sense organs which receive external impulses. Fundamentally the social sciences are the study of the means of communication between man and man, or, more generally, in a community of any sort of being. The unifying idea of these disciplines is the MESSAGE, and not any special apparatus acting on messages.[47]

He further claimed in 1948 that "it is certainly true that the social system is an organisation like the individual, that is bound together by a system of communication, and that it has a dynamics in which circular processes of a feedback nature play an important role."[48] Several social scientists would later develop these ideas and apply many of the

---

44   Céline Lafontaine, *L'Empire Cybernétique – Des Machines à Penser à la Pensée Machine* (Paris: Editions du Seuil, 2004), p. 25.

45   Heims, *John Von Neumann and Norbert Wiener*, p. 184.

46   Charles R. Dechert, "The Development of Cybernetics" in Charles R. Dechert (ed.), *The Social Impact of Cybernetics* (Notre Dame, IN: University of Notre Dame Press, 1966), p. 20.

47   Steve J. Heims, *The Cybernetics Group* (Cambridge, MA: MIT Press, 1991), p. 22.

48   Quoted in Capra, *The Web of Life*, p. 62.

principles of cybernetics and systems analysis to their fields of study. Karl Deutsch explicitly drew from cybernetics to introduce notions of information feedback to the understanding of social systems and the "steering" of government in his seminal *Nerves of Government*. David Easton formulated a theory of the political system defined as "a means whereby certain inputs are converted into outputs" and where the properties of feedback allow it "to regulate stress by modifying or redirecting its own behaviour."[49] For Talcott Parsons, cybernetic notions of hierarchies of control provided "the fundamental basis for classifying the components of social systems" and reducing the functional imperatives of such systems to "pattern maintenance, integration, goal-attainment, and adaptation."[50]

But while Norbert Wiener did see the potential applications of his theory to social organisation, he was reluctant to grant this interpretation the same scientific credibility as to the study of machines and organisms. A liberal humanist at heart, Wiener was particularly concerned about the implications for the liberal subject of a cybernetic management of society:

I have spoken of machines, but not only of machines having brains of brass and thews of iron. When human atoms are knit into an organisation in which they are used, not in their full right as responsible human beings, but as cogs and levers and rods, it matters little that their raw material is flesh and blood. *What is used as an element in a machine, is in fact an element in the machine.* Whether we entrust our decisions to machines of metal, or to those machines of flesh and blood which are bureaus, and vast laboratories and armies and corporations, we shall never receive the right answers to our questions unless we ask the right questions.[51]

---

49   David Easton, *A Framework for Political Analysis* (Chicago, IL: University of Chicago Press, 1979), pp. 112 and 128; David Easton, *A Systems Analysis of Political Life* (New York: John Wiley and Sons, 1965); Karl Deutsch, *The Nerves of Government* (New York: The Free Press, 1963).

50   Talcott Parsons and Leon H. Mayhew, *Talcott Parsons on Institutions and Social Evolution: Selected Writings* (Chicago, IL: University of Chicago, 1982), pp. 158-159.

51   Wiener, *The Human Use of Human Beings*, pp. 185-186. On the subject of Wiener's anxiety over the potential threat posed to liberal subjectivity by cybernetics, see Hayles, *How We Became Posthuman*, chapter 4.

If Wiener was uneasy about "social machines", his own language contributed to this logical extension of the cybernetic conceptual apparatus. It is also quite obvious that no social machine tends to treat individuals as "cogs and levers and rods" so completely than the military. Wiener tended to see a democratic potential in cybernetics with its promise of feedback and reciprocal influence. However cybernetics could just as well serve a hierarchical organisation in which subservient systems fulfilled individual homeostatic roles set by the overarching system.

Conclusion

The scope of the ambition of cybernetics entailed the development of a new language that would be common to all the scientists and social scientists studying systems of control and communications across all disciplines. However, the promise of a new unified natural philosophy was never realised as cybernetics became a victim of both its own success and the overambitious goals it had set itself. Wildly popular in the fifties and sixties, it attracted a lot of research funding for many projects that yielded disappointing results and led to an inevitable fall from grace. Furthermore, the constitution of something as broad as a science of systems could only be sustained across such a broad range of disciplines and subject areas by diluting the conceptual and explanatory apparatus to the point at which its usefulness and incisiveness were severely impaired. The term itself fell out of favour in the 1970s and 1980s and few scientists or academics would refer to themselves as cyberneticists today.

However, rather than disappearing altogether, cybernetics dispersed itself into all the fields it had touched and thus much of its ontology and core concepts – namely those of information, circularity, and feedback – continue to play a major role in many disciplines. In a 1994 interview, Heinz von Foerster, one of the founding fathers of the cybernetics movement, stated that "cybernetics melted, as a field, into many notions of people who are thinking and working in a variety of other fields."[52] In some ways, the influence of cybernetic ideas is now more pervasive than

---

52   Stefano Franchi, Güven Güzeldere, and Eric Minch, "Interview with Heinz von Foerster", *Stanford Humanities Review*, Volume 4, Issue 2, 1995 http://www.stanford.edu/group/SHR/4-2/text/interviewvonf.html.

when it was identified as a single discipline. The servomechanism became indeed the defining technology of its age, rarely referred to as such but subsumed as one of the functions of the ubiquitous information-processing computer. The work of the early cyberneticists would later feed into the development of the theories of chaos and complexity in the 1970s and 1980s, marking a crucial transformation in the informational paradigm. A full discussion of this will however have to wait until chapter 6. It is necessary to first turn to the profound effects of cybernetics and the computer on American military theory and practice during the Cold War.

5
Cybernetic Warfare:
Computers at War

Modern war has become too complex to be entrusted to the intuition of even the most experienced military commander. Only our giant brains can calculate all the possibilities.

John Kemeny, RAND Consultant and co-creator of
the BASIC computer language, 1961[1]

Where is your data? Give me something I can put in the computer. Don't give me your poetry.

Robert McNamara on being told by a White House aide that
the Vietnam War was doomed to failure [2]

The smouldering embers of World War II had barely been extinguished than the world lurched into a new conflict which for the best part of four decades would threaten the complete mutual annihilation of its belligerents. The Cold War certainly inaugurated a fundamental redistribution of power in world politics with the United States and Soviet Union standing as the two sole superpowers in the wake of Europe's

---

1 Sharon Ghamari-Tabrizi, *The Worlds of Herman Kahn: The Intuitive Science of Thermonuclear War* (Cambridge, MA: Harvard University Press, 2005), p. 149.

2 Edwards, *The Closed World*, pp. 127-128.

final exhaustion in two successive global conflagrations. But perhaps no less era-defining were the radical transformations in the theories and practices of warfare. If the role of nuclear weapons has been the subject of much commentary, the influence of other technologies and in particular the scientific ideas which accompanied them has been afforded less attention. This chapter concerns itself with the computerisation and cyberneticisation of the American military in the aftermath of World War II and throughout the Cold War.[3] Grappling with the fearsome power unleashed by nuclear weapons and the challenges of coordinating vast war machines to spring into action within the shortest of delays, state and military adopted new conceptual frameworks, techniques, and organisational dispositions which promised to restore control and predictability. Cybernetic concepts and technologies were vital in erecting an understanding of war in which the use of force was thought of as an activity totally amenable to scientific analysis, to the detriment of other forms of thinking on military affairs.

The computer is naturally a central figure in this chapter. Following its initial genesis for the purposes of code-breaking and the Manhattan project, the computer subsequently continued to play a key role in the post-war military, involved not only in the design of thermonuclear devices based on nuclear fusion but on numerous other military programs. The electromagnetic computer was thus not only born but also evolved as a military technology since in the first two decades of its existence its development was driven above all by the needs and funding of the United States armed forces. For Gene Rochlin, computers fulfilled five main roles in the military after World War II as either: embedded means of fire control for artillery and anti-aircraft guns; solvers of long, complex technical and engineering problems; elements of advanced command and control; basic tools for strategic analysis and war gaming; or

---

3   The focus on the United States is a choice determined by two factors. Firstly, the US was the most enthusiastic adopter of the computer and its related sciences, making it the truest heir of the scientific way of warfare. Secondly, although interesting parallels can no doubt be found in the Soviet Union, limits on the available literature and the greater secrecy of that society constitute an important obstacle to an in-depth discussion of the role of the computer in its military. Nonetheless, it is hoped that further research in this area will be conducted and made available in the English-speaking world.

embedded and programmed controllers for self-guided weapons.[4] All these aspects will be considered here but, as with the clock and the engine in previous chapters, the treatment of the computer as a tool is doubled by an analysis of its metaphorical function within the nexus of ideas and practices that make up the third regime of the scientific way of warfare: *cybernetic warfare.*

Cybernetic warfare will first be discussed in terms of the "closed world" constituted by it. In this world, cybernetic technologies proliferate alongside a conceptual and methodological apparatus which emphasises the controllable and predictable nature of war. Subsequent sections turn to the regime's more specific features: the shift from traditional notions of command to that of "command and control", the reduction of war to a set of mathematical functions and cost-benefit calculations susceptible to optimisation through the techniques of operations research and systems analysis, and the increasing modelling and simulation of conflict. The chapter concludes with an examination of the Vietnam War, a conflict in which those principles were truly put to the test and incurred spectacular reversals thereby exposing the severe limitations of the cybernetic warfare approach.

The "Closed World" of Cybernetic Warfare

In *The Closed World*, Paul Edwards relates the rapid computerisation of the military to the constitution of a "closed world" discourse conveying "a radically bounded scene of conflict, an inescapably self-referential space where every thought, word, and action is ultimately directed towards a central struggle."[5] Framed by the permanent threat of nuclear devastation, the Cold War opposing the West and the East became the exclusive geopolitical framework through which all policies, events and rhetoric were interpreted and formulated, with in mind the goal of, if not victory, at least the preservation of the status quo and survival. Within this discourse, computers acted as powerful tools and metaphors

---

4   Gene I. Rochlin, *Trapped in the Net: The Unanticipated Consequences of Computerization* (Princeton, NJ: Princeton University Press, 1997), p. 138.

5   Edwards, *The Closed World*, p. 12.

promising "total oversight, exacting standards of control, and technical-rational solutions to a myriad of complex problems."[6]

Edwards identifies several key features and articulations in this "closed world" discourse. Engineering and mathematical techniques which allow for the creation of models of aspects of the world as closed systems combine with technologies such as the computer which enable large scale simulation, systems analysis and central control. A language of systems, gaming, communication and information is erected, privileging abstract formalisms over "experiential and situated knowledge." Visions of omnipotence through air power and nuclear weapons assisted by "centralised, instantaneous, automated command and control" are summoned in response to fears of an expansionist Soviet Empire.[7]

Within this conceptual framework, uncertainty and unpredictability – chaos in other words – are understood as information deficiencies and thus susceptible to be overcome by the appropriate deployment of negentropic information technologies and computerised simulations of conflict. Edwards does indeed explicitly connect the "closed world" discourse to the development of cybernetics and computerisation. Computers are seen as participating in the creation and perpetuation of this worldview in two ways. "First, they allowed the practical construction of central real-time military control systems on a gigantic scale. Second, they facilitated the metaphorical understanding of world politics as a sort of system subject to technological management."[8] Hence the closed world is not simply the proliferation and imposition of the discursive framework of super-power confrontation on all international and domestic politics but also an understanding of the world that defines the latter as finite, manageable and computable. Edwards convincingly relates cybernetics and the computer sciences to an overarching set of "tools, techniques, practices and languages which embody an approach to the world as composed of interlocking systems amenable to formal mathematical analysis."[9]

6   Ibid., p. 15.

7   Ibid.

8   Ibid.

9   Paul N. Edwards, "The Closed World: Systems Discourse, Military Policy and Post-World War II US Historical Consciousness" in Les Levidow and Kevin Robins (eds), *Cyborg Worlds: The Military Information Society* (London: Free Association Books, 1989), pp. 138-139.

As direct experience of total war receded and new inconceivably destructive weapons were developed, mathematical and logical models and simulations of warfare became increasingly fetishised for their promises of predictability and control. Defence intellectuals were their keenest practitioners and most outspoken proponents, wielding these instruments to the very highest spheres of executive power. Convinced of the superiority of their method, they were determined to apply scientific rationalism to the entire spectrum of war. Sharon Ghamari-Tabrizi has noted that the quantitative studies they conducted and promulgated "often aimed toward an ideal of omniscient information management."[10]

Founded on a *Weltanschauung* that drew its conviction from the practical engineering successes of the informational sciences, cybernetic warfare strove to shape military affairs into a perfectly modelled and controlled closed world. By importing this methodological and conceptual baggage, military thinkers internalised many of their assumptions. If, as "engineering approaches designed to solve real-world problems, systems theories tend in practice to assume the closure of the system they analyse," military problems framed within the same conceptual and methodological framework naturally tended to be also perceived in terms of closed systems.[11] Such closed systems lend themselves perfectly to modelling and simulation, the ability to run and re-run scenarios in the belief that all factors have been incorporated and appropriately weighted. These models have come to exert a powerful influence on military leaders and policymakers, all looking for certainty and mastery over events, however illusory. Bill Nichols points to the role of cybernetic systems in:

creating a world of simulacra amenable to total control [...] cybernetic simulation renders experience, and the real itself, "problematic". It draws us into a realm, a design for living, that fosters a fetishised relationship with the simulation as a new reality all its own, based on the capacity to control, within the domain of the simulation, what had once eluded control beyond it.[12]

10   Ghamari-Tabrizi, *The Worlds of Herman Kahn*, p. 128.

11   Paul N. Edwards, "The Closed World: Systems Discourse, Military Policy and Post-World War II US Historical Consciousness" in Les Levidow and Kevin Robins (eds), *Cyborg Worlds: The Military Information Society* (London: Free Association Books, 1989), pp. 138-139.

12   Les Levidow and Kevin Robins, "Towards a Military Information Society?" in Levidow and Robins (eds), *Cyborg Worlds*, p. 173.

The promises of cybernetic warfare fuelled the dream of a complete automated dominance of the battlefield which was embraced by some of the most prominent military commanders and policy-makers. In 1969, General William Westmoreland, Commander-in-Chief of US forces in Vietnam, prophesised the imminent arrival of the fully cyberneticised and frictionless battlefield:

On the battlefield of the future, enemy forces will be located, tracked, and targeted almost instantaneously through the use of data links, computer as- sisted intelligence evaluation, and automated fire control. With first round kill probabilities approaching certainty, and with surveillance devices that can con- tinually track the enemy, the need for large forces to fix the opponent becomes less important. I see battlefields that are under 24-hour real or near-real time surveillance of all types. I see battlefields on which we can destroy anything we can locate through instant communications and almost instantaneous applica- tion of highly lethal firepower. [...] In summary, I see an Army built into and around an integrated area control system that exploits the advanced technology of communications, sensors, fire direction, and the required automatic data processing [...]With cooperative effort, no more than 10 years should separate us from the automated battlefield.[13]

As we shall see, such a drive for certainty and predictability was common among those who put faith in computerised systems and the analytical techniques of operations research and systems analysis in the 1950s and 1960s. For Edwards, Westmoreland's speech epitomises the "vision of a closed world, a chaotic and dangerous space rendered or- derly and controllable by the powers of rationality and technology."[14]

The appeal of such certainty to an institution in which the train- ing of troops is, according to Keegan, designed "to reduce the conduct of war to a set of rules and a system of procedures – and thereby to make orderly and rational what is essentially chaotic and instinctive" is obvious.[15] It is therefore not surprising that the military embraced computers as the panacea to the eternal problem of uncertainty and

---

13   William Westmoreland, Address to the Association of the US Army, Oct. 14, 1969.

14   Edwards, "Why Build Computers?" in Merritt Roe Smith and Gregory K. Clancey (eds), *Major Problems in the History of American Technology: Documents and Essays*, Boston: Houghton Mifflin, 1998), pp. 454-462.

15   Keegan, *The Face of Battle*, pp. 18-19.

unpredictability in war. Van Creveld facetiously sums up the attraction of computers to the military machine:

Computers with their binary on-off logic seem to appeal to the military mind. This is because the military, in order to counter the inherent confusion and danger of war, is forever seeking ways to make communications as terse and unambiguous as humanly possible. Computers by their very nature do just that. Had they only been able to stand at attention and salute, in many ways they would have made ideal soldiers.[16]

There are, however, specific cultural factors which made the United States military a particularly fertile ground for computerisation and a technoscientific approach to warfare even before World War II. Indeed the American experience and culture of war is one in which engineering, logistics, and technology have historically played a central role. As the first modern industrial war, the American Civil War had required the extensive uses of railways and the North eventually prevailed due in large part to its industrial and economic superiority. Later, the entry of the US into World War I in April 1917 had also necessitated a rapid mobilisation and the solving of numerous logistical problems in transporting troops and material across the Atlantic. Nor can the weight of the West Point military academy in the training of the country's military elite be discounted. Following its founding in 1802 on the model of the French Ecole Polytechnique, West Point emphasised civil engineering as the foundation of its curriculum and many of its graduates were responsible for the construction of the American transport infrastructure in the nineteenth century. If the curriculum has since been broadened, engineering and military science remain an important part of it and contribute to fostering a conception of warfare as a problem to be solved through scientific rationality.

We may also relate the drive for informational omniscience and almost godlike certainty in military affairs to the increasingly instrumentalist understanding of war that has developed in the West, and particularly the United States. For Christopher Coker, the twentieth century has seen the existential and metaphysical dimensions of war progressively recede in the West's understanding of war to the benefit of its view as "a rational instrument employed by states in a controlled manner for purposes that are

---

16   Van Creveld, *Technology and War*, p. 239.

either economic or political." [17] Such an instrumental approach naturally finds in technoscience the tools best suited to its realisation. Cybernetic thought provides a comforting lens through which to view the use of force as it reduces military strategy to what Gibson calls "a one-factor question about technical forces; success or failure is measured quantitatively [...] machine-system meets machine-system and the largest, fastest, most technologically advanced system will win. Any other outcome becomes *unthinkable.*"[18] This tendency to think of armies as "machine-systems" is a product of the scientific and technological way of warfare and the increasing reliance on an industrial base to sustain war efforts.

Military commanders have always sought to maintain order in the face of the chaos of the battlefield and the constant threat of a breakdown in the cohesion of their armies. Different epochs have responded in different manners to this challenge. Mechanistic warfare was an attempt to impose order over chaos by reducing the behaviour of soldiers to that of pre-programmed clockwork automatons. With thermodynamic warfare, the increasingly powerful releases of energy made communication of orders on the battlefield extremely difficult but the industrialisation of warfare implied a development of processes of production and logistics over which a great degree of centralising control could be achieved. The ability to marshal resources appropriately and manage vast integrated assemblages of bodies and material became the paramount factor determining military and strategic victory in those wars of attrition, over and above tactical and operational brilliance. The integration and operation of these systems of ever-greater complexity would only be made possible by the development and extension of information and telecommunication technologies, leading to the establishment of centralised command and control structures.

From Command to Command and Control

Command and control has become the common term employed by the military brass to describe its main function. The addition of the term "control" to what previously had simply been referred to as "command"

---

17   Coker, *The Future of War*, p. 6. "War has become almost entirely an instrument for solving problems and managing crises or risks." Christopher Coker, *Waging War Without Warrior?* (London: Lynne Rienner, 2002), p. 62.

18   Gibson, *The Perfect War*, p. 23.

is revealing in itself. Command suggests the mere transmission of orders while control suggests a process that involves a feedback mechanism allowing the controller to obtain new information from the system, adjust orders accordingly and thus exert continuous direction on subordinates. As Rochlin puts it:

Command was historically an open cycle process: the commander set up the battle, gave instructions, provided for whatever contingencies could be planned for, and then issued the command to execute. After that, the ability to intervene was minimal. In contrast, control is a closed cycle process with feedback, analysis, and iteration; it was not possible even to consider the transition from command to command and control until modern technical means for intelligence and communications became available. [19]

Military strategist John Boyd contrasted command as directing, ordering, or compelling and control as regulating, restraining, or holding to a certain standard.[20] Command and control infrastructures thus brought with them the hope that the disorder of the battlefield could be overcome through information flows in the same way cybernetic systems stave off entropy. In 1995, Lt. Gen. Carl O'Berry spoke of Horizon, an effort to ensure compatibility among all information systems in the US military, in the following terms: "[Horizon] brings order out of something that until now has been an atmosphere of entropy. For the first time we have taken interoperability to the domain of science instead of emotion. I'm taking the guesswork out of C⁴I systems architecture."[21] The shift from command to command and control is indicative of new expectations about the role and capabilities of the hierarchy in directing the operations of the military machine. That this evolution is directly related to information is clearly illustrated by the litany of acronyms that have since followed: C³I (Command, Control, Communications, and Information – or Intelligence), C⁴I² (C³I plus Computers and Inter-operability), C³ISR (C³I plus Surveillance and Reconnaissance), C³ISRT (C³ISR plus Targeting), etc.

---

19   Rochlin, Trapped in the Net, p. 204.

20   Gregory A. Roman, "The Command or Control Dilemma: When Technology and Organizational Orientation Collide" (Maxwell AFB, Alabama: Air University Press, Feb. 1997), p. 4.

21   Arquilla and Ronfeldt, "Information, Power, and Grand Strategy" in Stuart J.D. Schwartzstein (ed.), The Information Revolution and National Security, p. 146.

Integration of armed forces into a coherent system maintained by information and communication technologies (ICTs) amenable to centralised control has been an observable trend in all modern industrial armies. As the range and specialisation of military personnel and equipment increase along with the concomitant logistical challenges characteristic of industrial warfare, reliable channels of communication become essential. Furthermore, as van Creveld notes, information demands tend to increase exponentially with the growth in the number of specialities since "the amount of information needed to coordinate their performance grows not arithmetically but geometrically, everybody (or groups of every kind) having to be coordinated with everybody else."[22] The limitations of early ICTs in terms of their availability and the volume of information that could be processed and transmitted made centralisation all the more appealing since it reduced the number of potential channels of communication. For the major part of their existence, computers were too bulky and unwieldy to be brought onto the battlefield and computer engineers privileged centralised processing of information to maximise the limited processing power available.

However, there were also specific geopolitical conditions that combined with the new technology of nuclear weapons to particularly drive centralisation of the military in the post-war era. Indeed concerns over the eventuality of nuclear war, be it intentional or accidental, were omnipresent in the 1950s and continued, somewhat abated, throughout the Cold War. Due to the incredible destructive power of nuclear weapons and the speed of the delivery systems (first bombers then intercontinental ballistic missiles), it became crucial to ensure a very tight control over their use, as well as develop effective early warning mechanisms for a credible nuclear deterrent.

The emergence of jet engine aircraft and the further concomitant increases in speed and altitude at which these planes operated had now rendered gun-based systems largely obsolete. Anti-aircraft missile systems were therefore developed, building upon the research initiated into fire control by Wiener and others during the Second World War. Under its Ajax and Hercules iterations, Project Nike saw the deployment of missile systems in the proximity of major industrial and urban centres throughout the 1950s. Aside from an improvement in speed

---

22   Van Creveld, *Command in War*, p. 235.

and range over gun defences, Nike missiles could be guided from the ground so as to home in on their target. Radar stations would track the radar signature of the missile and target aircraft, feeding this data to a computer which would calculate the missile's optimal course for achieving interception, adjusting its flight as new information came in. At the point of closest approach, the computer would send a "burst command" that would cause the missile to detonate. A clear cybernetic loop is here in evidence: the radar acting as a sensor, the computer as the processor, and the missile's behaviour as the output.

Simultaneously, it was necessary to integrate these new anti-aircraft weapons into an overarching air-defence system that would be able to detect a full-out air assault and coordinate an appropriate response. With the development of jet-powered aircraft, the time available in the window of opportunity for detection and interception of bombers potentially carrying nuclear weapons shrunk and existing command structures were no longer adequate. This problem was further compounded by the fact that in a nuclear war every aircraft that was not intercepted would have potentially catastrophic consequences. Computers presented a clear technological solution to the problem of effective and rapid processing and transmission of both incoming information (provided by radar and observation posts) and outgoing information (sent to anti-aircraft defences such as interceptor fighter planes or land-based weapons). As an article in the *Air University Quarterly Review* of Winter 1956-57 put it, "the speed with which these weapons could react, each to the other, seems to indicate that only a machine with vast memory and instant response could be expected to indicate a successful counter strategy in sufficient time to be useful."[23]

Within a year of this article, the Air Force announced SAGE (Semi-Automated Ground Environment), the first computer-based command, control and communications system designed to provide a centralised air defence network. Based on information from radar echoes, the calculation of precise positions and speeds of multiple planes required massive computing power while the efficient and prompt transmission of this data to anti-aircraft weapon systems necessitated a reliable communications

---

23   Sharon Ghamari-Tabrizi, "US Wargaming Grows Up: A Short History of the Diffusion of Wargaming in the Armed Forces and Industry in the Postwar Period up to 1964", StrategyPage.Com http://www.strategypage.com/articles/default.asp?target=Wgappen.htm.

network. Target information collected and processed by SAGE would be transmitted to air defences, namely interceptor aircraft or missile systems.

SAGE broke significantly with existing computer technology because of its requirement for real-time processing and responses to user inputs. Until then, the norm was batch-processing, the execution of series of non-interactive jobs all at one time. Users programmed the computer, entered the data to be processed, and waited for its output to be generated and displayed via print-outs. Expanding on MIT's Whirlwind research project into a military flight simulator, SAGE resulted in several crucial developments in computer technology. Real-time processing required a revolutionary user interface, so SAGE was able to present data to a hundred operator stations via a cathode ray tube and responded to requests for additional information from operators handling light guns directed at the screen. The resulting decrease in the delay between inputs and outputs created a close cybernetic loop between computer and user which has only gained in complexity and intimacy since (Figure 6). The use of telephone lines to transfer computer data was also pioneered by SAGE, an early premise of the technology that would eventually lead to the development of the Internet.

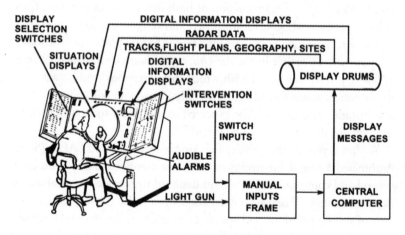

Figure 6: SAGE man-machine cybernetic loop[24]

---

24   As presented in SAGE technical documents. Courtesy of The MITRE Corporation.

Although obsolete by the time of its completion in 1963, the deployment of ICBMs by the Soviet Union having rendered anti-aircraft defences largely irrelevant, the system drove the development of crucial information technologies as well as the adoption of certain organisational principles. As such, Edwards is correct to underline that "SAGE was less important as an actual defence system than as a symbol of things to come [...] it is the idea of automated control and information processes – the concept itself – that has shaped, more than any technology, the contemporary US armed forces."[25] In total, between US$8 and 12 billion were spent on developing and implementing SAGE, a higher level of expenditure than had been dedicated to the Manhattan Project.

SAGE was followed by numerous related projects, most notably the World Wide Military Command and Control System (WWMCCS) in 1962. Progressively extended from Strategic Air Command to the rest of the military, WWMCSS strove for centralised global command and control of American troops through the integration of all independent systems via a broad spectrum of telecommunication systems including military satellites. In 1996, WWMCCS was deactivated and replaced by the Global Command and Control System (GCCS). Both projects have in common the extension and operation of command and control structures across the globe, establishing cybernetic system closure over the entire planet. [26]

Such global reach requires the availability of reliable telecommunications anywhere in the world. No technology has been more crucial in this respect than the artificial satellites now orbiting the earth in their thousands, our communication relays and eyes in the sky. The enclosure of the world within global command and control architectures required the militarisation of space and its occupation by human artefacts.[27] The space race between the US and USSR triggered

---

25   Edwards, "The Closed World" in Levidow and Robins (eds), *Cyborg Worlds*, p. 143. Also see chapter 3 of Edwards, *The Closed World* for a detailed account of the development of SAGE.

26   There were also civilian applications of the technology such as air-traffic control systems and SABRE, the airline reservation system in operation since 1964.

27   While satellite technology was initially exclusively reserved for scientific and military purposes, a majority of operational satellites are today in the civilian field, providing commercial services from meterology to telecommunications.

by the launch of Sputnik was therefore not merely a matter of prestige and propaganda for both nations. The balance of power in space had immediate practical implications for security and warfare back down on Earth. As early as 1946, the RAND Corporation published its first study entitled *Preliminary Design of an Experimental World-Circling Spaceship* in which it was claimed that "a satellite vehicle with appropriate instrumentation can be expected to be one of the most potent scientific tools of the twentieth century" and that its achievement "would produce repercussions comparable to the explosion of the atomic bomb."[28]

Encircling the globe in a mesh of geocentric orbits would allow not only for the final abolishing of distance by enabling instantaneous communications from any location on the planet, but it would also permit the precise coordinates of individuals or objects to be known and transmitted. The first satellite navigation system, NAVSAT, was made operational in 1964, initially for ballistic missile submarines. With an accuracy of about two hundred metres provided by ten orbiting satellites, it was sufficient for the guidance of nuclear missiles. 1967 saw the Russians launch their own satellite navigation system called Tsyklon. Research on a system providing greater precision and coverage was initiated by the United States in 1973 and eventually led to the NAVSTAR Global Position System (commonly known as GPS) through a network of 24 satellites made fully operational in 1995. While 40,000 US troops were using GPS devices by 2002, the service has also been made commercially available resulting in sales of several million receivers and will soon become a standard feature of all mobile consumer electronic devices.[29] Concerned with its potential use by the military of enemy states, the US has retained the right and means to degrade its reliability through a feature named "Selective Availability" that reduces accuracy from 15 to 100 metres. This dependency on America, along with the appeal of significant commercial benefits, has prompted the European Union to launch its own satellite navigation system, Galileo, which will function with an accuracy of five metres

---

28   Project RAND, "Preliminary Design of an Experimental World-Circling Spaceship" (1946), pp. 13-14 http://www.rand.org/pubs/special_memoranda/2006/SM11827part1.pdf.

29   David Hambling, *Weapons Grade* (London: Constable and Robinson, 2005), p. 43.

when it is operational around 2013. The expressed hostility of the US to this project underlines the importance attached to positioning systems and the military and strategic value of the information provided by them.[30]

The Strategic Defense Initiative, or "Star Wars", project is a clear descendent of SAGE as a computer-controlled and centrally-commanded scheme, and epitomises the militarisation of space and its potential impact on earth-bound warfare. An air defence system designed to intercept ballistic missiles fired at the United States through a complex network of sensors and precision-guided missiles (some located on earth, others space-based), it was only possible to construe SDI as a workable system with a profound faith in the potential for information technology to grant omniscience and omnipotence and provide an infallible shield against attack. The technological feats required for the effective operation of such a system are enormous, then and now, with many experts casting doubts over their feasibility and reliability as well as pointing to their vulnerability to relatively inexpensive counter-measures.[31] In a somewhat analogue way to SAGE, SDI is thus perhaps best understood not so much as an effective defence system than as an ideological weapon, an early testing ground for future technological applications, and an idealised totalising model of the cybernetic regime of warfare in which the entire planet is secured and brought under computerised control.

As Edwards point out, what was erected during the Cold War was a "nested hierarchy of cybernetic devices", each composed of an assemblage of bodies and machines fulfilling its own individual regulative

---

30   In Sept. 2007, the US Department of Defense announced it would no longer procure GPS satellites with the selective availability capability, probably to fend off the future commercial competition of Galileo or even to dissuade the Europeans from pursuing the much troubled venture. In any case a number of global and regional satellite navigation systems being developed by Russia, China, India, and Japan look set to further challenge the present American monopoly.

31   Even the present National Missile Defense project and its considerably more modest goal of shielding the United States from only a small number of ICBMs launched by a "rogue state" are subject to similar criticisms. L. Garwin, "Holes in the Missile Shield", *Scientific American*, Nov. 2004 http://www.sciam.com/article.cfm?chanID=sa006andcolID=1andarticleID=000A45A2-E044-115D-A04483414B7F0000.

functions according to formalised rules while communicating with the lower and upper echelons of the hierarchy:

Airplanes, communications systems, computers, and anti-aircraft guns occupied the micro levels of this hierarchy. Higher-level "devices", each of which could be considered a cyborg or cybernetic system, included aircraft carriers, the WWMCCS, and NORAD early warning systems. At a still higher level stood military units such as battalions and the Army, Navy, and Air Force themselves. Each was conceptualised as an integrated combination of human and electronic components, operating according to formalised rules of action. Each level followed directives taken from the next highest unit and returned information on its performance to that unit. Each carried out its own functions with relative autonomy, issuing its own commands to systems under its control and evaluating the results using feedback from them.[32]

James Constant's discussion of command and control encapsulates this cybernetic thinking on military organisation. In his *Fundamentals of Strategic Weapons*, he proposes a diagram conceptualising the relationship of the different military systems in the face of an adversary (Figure 7). The behaviour of a threat (T) is registered by early warning system (EW) which passes on the information to command and control (C^2) which can then indicate the appropriate actions, if any, to be initiated by the weapon systems (W). This will likely result in a changed state or behaviour in the threat triggering a new cycle of the loop. The different early warning, command and control, and weapon systems are all connected together by a flow of information transmitted via communication links (C). Constant observes that "the command and control loop is basically a servomechanism" and that "as such, it is possible to apply the standard theory of servomechanisms in order to optimise the system operation, performance and response." The diagram captures the behaviour of entities at both the tactical and strategic levels, granted that at the latter we find "a plurality of interrelating loops, each with a portion of the threat" and serving the overall objectives of military system as a whole.[33]

---

32   Edwards, *The Closed World*, p. 206.

33   James Constant, *Fundamentals of Strategic Weapons: Offense and Defense Systems* (The Hague: Martinus Nijhoff, 1981), p. 390.

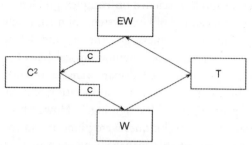

Figure 7: Command and control loop [34]

This understanding of military operations as interlocked systems obeying formalised rules invited, and indeed required, their analytical treatment through the lenses of mathematics and logic. In order to determine the formalised rules of action according to which each level of the hierarchy of cybernetic devices should operate on the basis of incoming information, it was necessary to specify the parameters and signals upon which to act and identify the range of states available to the system. Exhaustive models of the behaviour of both the US military and that of its potential enemies were thus developed, thereby reducing war to a complex equation to be resolved by a technoscientific priesthood.

Operations Research and Systems Analysis: Solving the War Equation

"The representation and analysis of real world processes using logic, mathematics and computer science," operations research (OR) and its offspring systems analysis (SA) transformed the manner in which war was prepared for, planned and imagined.[35] Despite initial resistance by military officers, statistical control, OR and SA gained a rapidly growing influence over planning and operations in the post-war era. By 1962, this approach had become so popular and ubiquitous since its early applications in World War II that OR could proclaim itself to

---

34   Reproduced from ibid., p. 390.

35   Department of the Army Pamphlet 600–3–49, "Operations Research/Systems Analysis" (Washington, DC: Department of the Army, 1987) http://www.army. mil/usapa/epubs/pdf/p600_3_49.pdf.

be "the attack of modern science on complex problems arising in the direction and management of large systems of men, machines, material and money in industry, business, government and defence."[36] Systems analysis likewise "served as the methodological basis for social policy planning and analysis across such disparate areas as urban decay, poverty, health care, education, and the efficient operation of municipal services such as police protection and fire fighting."[37] However, as DeLanda has observed, most of these techniques were pioneered in the military and the broad application of this management science effectively marked the transfer of "command and control structures of military logistics to the rest of society and the economy."[38]

Operations research seeks to improve operations by studying an entire system rather than exclusively concentrating on specific elements. In the context of the transfer of operations research to business in 1950s-60s but equally applicable to military affairs, Gene Rochlin tells us that "the new agenda differed from the old in a major expansion of the scope of analysis; instead of treating the firm as a series of isolated, interacting operations to be integrated from the top, it was now visualised as single, complex, interrelated pattern of activities, to be analysed, coordinated and optimised as a whole."[39] In this sense OR and SA are very much in the cybernetic mould in their belief in a whole that is superior to the sum of its parts and their assumptions about the closure of the systems being modeled. Operations researcher Stafford Beer explicitly connected cybernetics to OR, publishing the influential *Cybernetics and Management* in 1959.[40] He was later entrusted with a project to develop a national

---

36   Nigel Cummings, "How the World of OR Societies Began" (The OR Society) http://www.orsoc.org.uk/orshop/(awaqdrfkrmznlwneegwigdqi)/orcontent. aspx?inc=article_news_orclub.htm.

37   The RAND Corporation, "A Brief History of RAND" http://www.rand.org/ about/history/. For a detailed account of the applications of cybernetics, systems analysis, and computer simulations to urban planning and management in the US, notably by former defence intellectuals, see Jennifer S. Light, *From Warfare to Welfare: Defense Intellectuals and Urban Problems in Cold War America* (Baltimore, MD and London: John Hopkins University Press, 2003).

38   DeLanda, *War in the Age of Intelligent Machines*, p. 5.

39   Rochlin, *Trapped in the Net*, p. 59.

40   Stafford Beer, *Cybernetics and Management* - 2nd edn (London: English Universities Press, 1967).

real-time computerised system to run the entire Chilean economy according to cybernetic principles under the Allende government from 1970 to 1973. For Beer, cybernetics was nothing less than "the science of which operational research is the method":

Operational research comprises a body of methods which cohere to provide a powerful tool of investigation. Cybernetics is a corpus of knowledge which might reasonably claim the status of a science. My contention is that the two are methodologically complementary; that the first is the natural technique in research of the second, and the second the natural embodiment in science of the first. By definition, each is concerned to treat a complex and interconnected system or process as an organic whole. By methodology, each is concerned with models and analogies from every source. By science, neither is departmental. By philosophy, each attests to the indivisible unity of knowledge.[41]

The computer is here again central since the optimisation of the mathematical models constructed by operations researchers and systems analysts is achieved through the use of computer-based algorithms that calculate changes in the system's behaviour resulting from any changes in the multiple variables that constitute the models. Without the computer, the widespread application of OR and SA and the increasing complexity of the models developed would have been impossible. In this sense, these analytical techniques are inseparable from the technologies that support them. The viability of the models is dependent on their ability to be translated into computer code, that is into a program that can convert quantifiable inputs into quantifiable outputs. As system analysts James Martin and Adrian Norman put it, "a model without numbers cannot be manipulated so *measurement* and *quantification* is a fundamental part of the description resulting from analysis, and the basis of the evaluation of systems design."[42] Consequently, that which cannot be assigned a number or expressed in terms of logical relationships is necessarily excluded.[43]

---

41   Stafford Beer, "What Has Cybernetics to do with Operational Research?", *Operational Research Quarterly*, Vol. 10, No. 1, 1959).

42   James Martin and Adrian R.D. Norman, *The Computerised Society* (Harmondsworth: Penguin Books, 1973), p. 569.

43   Operations researchers do occasionally pursue qualitative research such as conducting interviews and open-ended surveys. These exercises are clearly secondary to the manipulation of quantitative data and not the basis on which OR and its extended family of management sciences have asserted their institutional

The present section will offer a brief history of OR and SA, focusing on their rapid, although not uncontroversial, rise within the American defense establishment, culminating in the nomination of Robert McNamara to the position of Secretary of Defense. Information on the use of operations research and systems analysis in the Soviet Union is harder to come by given the society's highly secretive character and the unavailability of sources in the English language.[44] It is however clear that they also found widespread applications in the other main protagonist of the Cold War where they were simply known as cybernetics, a discipline which, after at first being denounced as bourgeois "philosphical obscurantism", was hailed at the 1961 Party Congress as a vital factor in the Soviet "revolution of the military system."[45]

Operations research was originally pioneered by the British in the late 1930s and enthusiastically embraced by the US military during the Second World War. OR Air Force studies multiplied exponentially in this period: "offensive ones dealing with bombing accuracy, weapons effectiveness, and target damage [...] defensive ones dealing with defensive formations of bombers, battle damage and losses of our aircraft, and air defence of our bases [...] studies of cruise control procedures, maintenance facilities and procedures, accidents, in-flight feeding and comfort of crews, possibility of growing vegetables on South Pacific islands, and a host of others."[46]

Van Creveld accounts for the initial success of this mathematical approach with the particular nature of strategic bombing and the defensive measures deployed against it. The development of air defences necessitated the establishment of socio-technical systems of a greater complexity than had ever been previously constructed. The integration of radar required the creation of an extended coverage of the airspace

---

authority to analyse and determine organisational and operational structures. Therefore these analytical techniques will here be understood as being defined by their use of logic, mathematics and computer science.

44   One notable exception is Slava Gerovitch's fascinating work, *From Newspeak to Cyberspeak: A History of Soviet Cybernetics.*

45   Andrew Wilson, *The Bomb and the Computer* (London: Barrie and Rockliff, 1968), p. 49.

46   Clayton J. Thomas and Robert S. Sheldon, "Air Force Operations Analysis" in Carl Harris and Saul Gass (eds), *Encyclopaedia of Operations Research and Management Science* (Norwell, MA: Kluwer Academic Publishers, 2000), p. 8.

through individual radar stations (with particular attention paid to reducing overlap and mutual interference) along with a communications network that could transmit the relevant information to a centralised headquarters for processing and then onwards to air defence units such as anti-aircraft guns or fighter planes. Faced with such heavy defensive systems, bombers had to fly at altitudes that were frequently too high for the crews to observe directly their targets. Consequently, operations had to be planned days ahead, as well as coordinated and integrated with ground facilities, air support and a host of anti-radar measures. "Thus strategic bombing not only found itself opposed by a technological system but itself assumed all the characteristics of such a system."[47] War in this arena thefore took on the characteristics of a battle of attrition between two competing technological systems. This configuration naturally lent itself to being run by centralised, statistically-based forms of management.

Naval warfare, particularly anti-submarine activities, was the other field in which operations research obtained impressive results during World War II. When British anti-submarine aircrafts reduced the depth at which depth charges were to detonate on the recommendation of operations researchers, the increase in successful attacks was so great that the German military became convinced the British were using a new type of explosive. OR was also able to reduce the loss rate of naval convoys when analysts realised that larger convoys suffered lower percentage losses than smaller ones.

The greater simplicity and homogeneity of the aerial and marine environments certainly played a crucial factor in the success of OR since warfare in those milieus was easier to model mathematically than land operations. More generally, modern war involved "more repetitive operations susceptible to analysis" in that "a men-plus-machines operation can be studied statistically, experimented with, analysed, and predicted by the use of known scientific techniques just as a machine operation can be."[48] Scientists, Wilson tells us, felt that they were ideally trained to grapple with the problems of modern war with their ability "to get

47   Van Creveld, *Technology and War*, p. 194.

48   Clayton J. Thomas and Robert S. Sheldon, "Military Operations Research" in Harris and Gass (eds), *Encyclopaedia of Operations Research and Management Science*, p. 514.

down to the fundamentals of a question – to seek out broad underlying principles through a mass of sometimes conflicting and irrelevant data [...] with the result that they were often able to discredit what the military regarded as 'commonsense' solutions."[49]

After the war, operations research – the optimising of existing systems – soon morphed into systems analysis – the design of the most effective system for the accomplishment of a defined objective – granting analysts planning powers. After 1945 the length of procurement cycles increased with the time necessary for the research and development, production, and deployment of any new technology. Furthermore, closer cybernetic integration of vehicles, projectiles, communications, radar, and electronic counter-measures created weapon systems whose components could not be designed separately if integration into a functioning whole were to be successful. This naturally empowered those analysts who proposed a scientific methodology according to which technological and budgetary decisions could be determined. Systems analysis was perfectly suited to this task since its cost-benefit analysis and optimisation routines enabled planners to determine the best allocation of resources given a limited supply of resources. Reviewed through a range of possible future security and military environments, alternative systems could be compared and judged in terms of efficiency and cost.

This approach promoted a view of warfare which reduced it to a mathematical problem with a number of variables that could be manipulated and a production model that could be scientifically managed along Taylorist lines.[50] The RAND Corporation, the think-tank created

---

49   Wilson, *The Bomb and the Computer*, p. 43.

50   Fortun and Schweber have drawn out the similarities between Taylorism's "scientific management" and operations research in their efforts to improve system efficiency, but also underlining that the central difference between them is that whereas the former used exclusively deterministic models in which "the effect of a given action was assumed to result in a well-defined and well-determined effect" (in other words, along the lines of the clockwork model of science), OR dealt principally with "stochastic processes and with probabilistic models that explicitly recognised uncertainty as an intrinsic feature of the processes being modelled." Here, OR rejoins cybernetics again in that the latter also sought to grapple with problems of a stochastic nature, such as the future positions of an enemy airplane that an anti-aircraft system was trying to track. M. Fortun and SS. Schweber, "Scientists and the Legacy of World War II: The Case of Operations Research (OR)", *Social Studies of Science*, Vol. 23, 1993, p. 624.

by the US Air Force, became the home of systems analysis, often to the detriment of any other forms of thinking about national security. As Kaplan puts it, "for an organisation dominated by mathematicians, systems analysis appeared to be *the* way to get the scientific – the right – answer. Projects that involved no systems analysis, such as most of the work produced by the social science division, were looked down upon, considered interesting in a speculative way at best."[51]

Models grew to astonishing levels of complexity, fuelled by the desire to create an accurate simulation of conflict, a scientific understanding of a quite literal war machine. The father of systems analysis, RAND researcher Ed Paxson, was symptomatic of this trend. Witness the minutiae of his obsession in planning for World War III:

His dream was to quantify every single factor of a strategic bombing campaign – the cost, weight, and payload of each bomber, its distance from the target, how it should fly in formation with other bombers and their fighting escorts, their exact routing patterns, the refueling procedures, the rate of attrition, the probability that something might go wrong in each step along the way, the weight and inaccuracy of the bomb, the vulnerability of the target, the bomb's "kill probability," the routing of the planes back to their bases, the fuel consumed, and all extraneous phenomena such as the weather – and *put them all into a single mathematic equation.*[52]

Planning for the use of nuclear weapons in a bombing campaign was a particularly urgent task during the Cold War and required continuous reviewing since the technology and availability of bombs and missiles were subject to rapid change. The explosive power of individual devices – first triggered by nuclear fission in atomic bombs, then nuclear fusion for hydrogen bombs – escalated vertigineously with 1952 witnessing the American test of a 10.4 megaton bomb, nearly 700 times more powerful than that dropped on Hiroshima and superior to the combined total explosive ordnance employed in the two world wars.[53] Launch-

---

51   Fred Kaplan, *The Wizards of Armageddon* (New York: Simon and Schuster, 1984), p. 87.

52   Kaplan, *The Wizards of Armageddon*, p. 87.

53   In a game of one-upmanship typical of the Cold War, the Soviet Union detonated a completely impractical bomb of 50 megatons baptised Tsar Bomba (the "Emperor Bomb") in 1961. This remains the most powerful nuclear device ever detonated, even though the same bomb design could have been used for a 100 megaton explosion.

ing systems gained in range and accuracy; with the evolution from the medium-range bomber B-29 in 1945 to the intercontinental ballistic missile (ICBM) in 1957, full-blown nuclear war could be initiatied within a few hours of the executive decision. Further shortened by the unavoidable delay in the detection of such an attack from either of the Cold War protagonists, this window might be the only one available to policy-makers in which to retaliate in kind before being struck.

There was to be no rehearsal or practice run for nuclear war, and perhaps no second chance. Consequently, a "hot" World War III had to be planned for by being analysed, quantified, systematised, and simulated. Systems analysis, game theory[54] and the whole range of available mathematical and statistical instruments were the only means to rationalise armageddon and "think the unthinkable."[55] The expected levels of casualties and destruction of a full-blown nuclear war were such that they threatened to render meaningless any notion of strategy as the rational use of force for political aims, in accordance with Clauswitz's dictum. Perhaps even more terrifyingly, analysts believed that it might become rational for any one of the adversaries to initiate nuclear war if it either believed that an attack against it was imminent or that it might be possible to survive retaliation after a first strike.

Faced with such a chilling prospect, defense intellectuals saw it as their duty to salvage strategic thinking and bring the nuclear face-off under rational and scientific management, viewing it as the only means by which to prevent or limit nuclear war. The priority of analysts

---

54   Founded by John von Neumann and Oskar Morgenstern with the 1944 pub-
      lication of their *Theory of Games and Economic Behavior*, game theory seeks to
      capture mathematically the strategic interaction of actors in situations where
      the actions of each actor impact the outcome of the "game" for the other par-
      ticipants. Applied to a broad range of areas of enquiry in the social sciences, in
      particular economics, game theory was employed in the Cold War to model
      the nuclear face-off and determine the likely outcome of specific policies of
      deterrence on the behaviour of the participants. As the economist and nuclear
      strategist Thomas Schelling made clear, the theory "is based on the assumption
      that the participants coolly and 'rationally' calculate their advantages according
      to a consistent value system" which allows for the modelling of games according
      to the rules of logic. Thomas C. Schelling, *The Strategy of Conflict* (Cambridge,
      MA: Harvard University Press, 1960), p. 16.

55   *Thinking about the Unthinkable* was the title of a 1962 book by the notorious
      nuclear strategist Herman Kahn.

therefore became to preserve the "delicate balance of terror"[56] over and above any notion of winning the face-off, to ensure that the "Cold War system" could return to homeostatic equilibrium and ward off the possibility of it exceeding the bounds beyond which it would self-destruct in an apocalyptic spasm dubbed "wargasm" by the nuclear strategist Herman Kahn. Initially, the focus of systems analysts was to ensure that the United States could incur a Soviet first strike and still retain enough nuclear weapons to ravage the Soviet Union under a policy of "mutual assured destruction" (MAD). It would thus never be rational to initiate a first strike, argued the proponents of deterrence.[57] On the recommendation of senior analysts, reinforced missile silos and airbases were constructed and a system whereby fleets of bombers carrying nuclear payloads were permanently in flight and others were ready to launch at short notice was established. Subsequently, some defence intellectuals such as Kahn sought to chart a path between the either/or of complete restraint and full-blown Armageddon by conceiving of a rationalised limited use of nuclear weapons. Under such a scheme, a graduated use of nuclear weapons was imagined according to which a form of tit-for-tat bargaining with the enemy could proceed and avert automatic

---

56   Albert Wohlstetter, "The Delicate Balance of Terror" (1958) http://www.rand. org/publications/classics/wohlstetter/P1472/P1472.html.

57   Stanley Kubrick's film *Dr Strangelove* satirised deterrence theory by pushing the logic of mutual assured destruction to its absurd conclusion with the Doomsday Machine. Actually first imagined by Hermann Kahn, the device is constituted of a computer hooked up to a huge stock of thermonuclear bombs that will be automatically detonated and shroud the earth in radiation upon detection of a nuclear attack by the adversary. In taking the human out of the loop, deterrence could be made more effective since the adversary could not be tempted to gamble on a failure of nerve. As the eponymous Dr Strangelove puts it: "deterrence is the art of producing in the mind of the enemy the fear to attack. And so, because of the automated and irrevocable decision-making process which rules out human meddling, the Doomsday Machine is terrifying. It's simple to understand. And completely credible, and convincing." It has more recently been claimed that a program very much akin to the Doomsday Machine was in fact secretly made operational in the Soviet Union in 1984 under the name of Perimetr and may even still be active. Stanley Kubrick (director), *Dr Strangelove or How I Learned to Stop Worrying and Love the Bomb* (Columbia Pictures, 1964); P. D. Smith, *Doomsday Men: The Real Dr Strangelove and the Dream of the Superweapon* (London: Allen Lane, 2007); Rosenbaum, Ron, 'The Return of the Doomsday Machine?' (2007) http://www.slate.com/id/2173108/pagenum/all/.

escalation to complete annihilation. Although detailed plans for this form of nuclear bargaining were formulated, they were never adopted as a formal policy because of widespread concern that full esclation might be impossible to prevent once the nuclear threshold had been crossed.

In the absence of any experience of actual thermonuclear war, systematic mathematical calculation of the theoretical damage it would inflict on urban areas and troops was the only means by which to assess offensive and defensive requirements. Consequently, nuclear payloads, delivery systems, military and civilian defensive measures along with the tactics and strategies within which these would be inserted were also given the system analysis treatment. Nor was systems analysis limited to nuclear aspects of warfare since the entire spectrum of conventional military operations was to become subject to its scrutiny. As RAND's first vice-president Alan Henderson declared in 1949, "systems analysis seeks to cover the full range of possible future weapons characteristics and simultaneously analyse each set of possible characteristics in all possible tactics and strategies of employment."[58] Such an all-encompassing remit necessarily posed significant computational challenges. Indeed while the consideration of systems with just ten binary variables yields already over a thousand different combinations for assessment, simply doubling the number of variables being considered results in a system with over a million possible states for evaluation. Only the computer and its formidable processing power would be able to manage this exponential increase in possible permutations, allowing for the creation of complex models with multiple variables and providing a rapid calculation of the effects on any changes in their values.

The same modelling techniques were also employed for a vast range of wargames which simulated an array of operations from the tactical to the operational to the strategic, from individual battalions to anti-aircraft defences to global geopolitical exercises. While wargaming had long been practised – the Germans had been keen enthusiasts of *Kriegsspiel* from the nineteenth century onwards – the new generation of wargames and simulations were an extension of OR and SA since they relied on the same methodology for their models. Ghamari-Tabrizi points to the manner in which these wargames constituted their own closed worlds:

---

58   Ghamari-Tabrizi, *The Worlds of Herman Kahn*, p. 138.

Following the thread of systems thinking, the gamers tried to shoehorn everything of importance into game design and play. Since a major war would batter every department of life, they were tempted to expand their model into infinitely complex details in the simulation of reality. But at the same time, they were determined to set upper and lower boundaries, limits and constraints of every kind onto that surging impulse towards the *Weltbild*. In other words, in war game design, one makes out a wish to catch a richly furnished world, but one sealed off like a terrarium or a tableau in a paperweight. This snug little world, in which the totality could be grasped all at once, encompasses the universe of miniature life.[59]

Computers became increasingly employed in wargames, first to calculate the outcome of any decision by the players by processing it through complex models of warfare and international relations (thereby avoiding lengthy calculations on paper and references to rulebooks), and later as an interface for the players. With the aim of providing greater realism, the environments of decision-makers were often reproduced painstakedly. Mediated through computerised displays and interfaces, real wartime situations and simulations would be largely indistinguishable. Wargamers at RAND would eventually grant computers an even greater role by making them fully-fledged players. Faced with human players that would persistently refuse to cross the nuclear threshold in simulated excercies, the simulationists developed artificial intelligences that could play the role of the Soviet Union or United States, creating a variety of iterations characterised by different personalities and willingnesses to resort to force.[60] Computers were effectively the ideal wargamers: cold, logical, purely instrumental and devoid of the messy cultural, social and historical attributes that plagued human players and could not be mathematically modelled. Fully computerised wargames allowed for the rapid testing of an entire range of weapon system characteristics, logistics, tactics, and strategies for the purpose of identifying the optimal combination.[61] But the use of wargames was not restricted

---

59   Ibid., p. 166.

60   DeLanda, *War in the Age of Intelligent Machines*, p. 103.

61   In the 1983 film *Wargames*, the US military entrusts the launching of nuclear weapons to a computer called WOPR (War Operations Plan and Response) in a bid to eliminate the potential for human error and failure of nerve. A teenage hacker, convinced he is playing the latest computer game, inadvertently triggers a countdown to thermonuclear war. At the climax of the film, the hero succeeds

to testing models; they could also provide their own facts and statistics for interpretation and inclusion in the models. As one wargamer observed: "as we recede from such sources of empirical data as World War II and Korea, an ability to generate synthetic battlefield facts becomes increasingly important."[62] These synthetic facts drawn from the experiences of simulated conflict could then be fed back into further models of war – simulation begetting simulation in a hyperreal feedback loop increasingly removed from situated experience of real life combat.

If institutional resistance from the Air Force, RAND's main sponsor, to studies that attempted to model warfare in its entirety forced the organisation into publicly downgrading the ambition in the scope of their research projects, in practice, the systemic interelationship of areas of study and the commonly-held belief of analysts in the superiority of their methodology made such restrictions difficult to maintain. Alain Enthoven, Deputy Assistant Secretary for Systems Analysis under McNamara, once pointed out to a general that "I have fought as many nuclear wars as you have." In fact, given his time at RAND modelling them and playing war games, Enthoven may well have believed that he had actually fought *more* nuclear wars, albeit simulated. Enthoven's quip was symptomatic of the attitude of RAND analysts towards the military brass, and to whom Ghamari-Tabrizi attributes the belief than "in order to approach nuclear war properly, one had to become a perfect amnesiac, stripped of the intuitions, judgements, and habits cultivated over a lifetime of active duty."[63] Combat experience and traditional common wisdom of the military were thus devalued in favour of the cool rational calculations of the defence intellectual. In 1961, this latter vision appeared to have triumphed over the generals as Robert McNamara was made Secretary of Defense and proceeded to apply the tools of systems analysis across the military more systematically than ever before.

---

in convincing the computer to play out all the simulated scenarios and strategies for a full-blown nuclear exchange with the Soviet Union, resulting in the artificial intelligence's realisation that these all lead to mutual annihilation and that therefore the only manner to win this particular "game"is not to play. John Badham (director), *Wargames* (MGM, 1983).

62   Ghamari-Tabrizi, *The Worlds of Herman Kahn*, p. 169.

63   Ibid., p. 48. Kahn echoed Enthoven's sentiment when he asked officers who were critical of his approach, "how many thermonuclear wars have *you* fought recently?".

Robert Strange McNamara had first risen to prominence during the Second World War, distinguishing himself as one of the most brilliant analysts in the Statistical Control Office, where he conducted operations research on the Air Force operations using human computers and IBM counting machines. He was notably involved in the strategic bombing campaign of Japan, recommending the switch to firebombing and lower altitude bombing which the notorious Air Force General Curtis LeMay (later head of Strategic Air Command during the Cold War) adopted with devastating results for Japanese cities. After the war, he left the armed forces to join the Ford Corporation in 1946 and applied the same principles of scientific management with great success before being offered the role of Secretary of Defense by President Kennedy. Surrounding himself with a team of ex-RAND analysts that shared his outlook, McNamara set out to extend these principles to all branches of the military. A controversial figure, particularly unpopular with certain sections of the military over which he asserted previously unseen levels of civilian control, McNamara was once referred to as a "'human IBM machine' who cares more for computerised statistical logic than for human judgments."[64]

McNamara instigated the Planning, Programming and Budgeting System (PPBS) in 1962, perhaps his most lasting legacy, by institutionalising systems analysis in the decision-making process of military planning and procurement. With PPBS, cost-benefit and cost-effectiveness analysis were applied across all branches of the military so that various military programs from different services could be evaluated, compared, and granted funding accordingly.[65] Department of Defense Comptroller Charles Hitch (ex-RAND) was responsible for the implementation of PPBS, defining the system analysis approach that was being applied as:

economic analysis applied to the public sector. Economic analysis is concerned with the allocation of resources. Its maxim is: maximise the value of objectives achieved minus the value of resources used. In business this reduces itself to maximising profits. In Defence [...] we lack a common valuation for objectives and

---

64   US Department of Defense, "Biography of Robert S. McNamara" http://www.defenselink.mil/specials/secdef_histories/bios/mcnamara.htm.

65   Kaplan, *The Wizards of Armageddon*, p. 254.

resources and therefore have to use one of two weaker maxims – maximise our objectives for given resources, or minimise our resources for given objectives.[66]

PPBS was subsequently extended across the federal bureaucratic structure, in particular the social welfare agencies of the Departments of Health, Education and Welfare and Office of Economic Opportunity. Hitch insisted that systems analysis acted merely as an instrument assisting decision-makers rather than being the decisive factor in determining spending plans. Gregory Palmer agrees that PPBS was often more of a heuristic or ideal, but that "in its pristine form, PPBS was a closed system, rationally ordered to produce carefully defined outputs."[67] But if the ascendancy of operations research and systems analysis now seemed complete, they were not without their critics who claimed these instruments were prone to mislead dangerously if applied uncritically and to the detriment of other forms of reasoning about military affairs.

In his Farewell Address to the people on January 17, 1961, President Eisenhower famously warned against "the acquisition of unwarranted influence, whether sought or unsought, by the military-industrial complex." Less frequently quoted are his words about the "danger that public policy could itself become the captive of a scientific-technological elite."[68] A military man, Eisenhower may well have been thinking of the operations researchers and system analysts which rose to prominence during his presidency and were about to take control of the Pentagon yielding instruments they believed could be used to tackle all problems. "The military effect of cybernetics and computers did more than bring about changes in administration, logistics, communications, intelligence and even operations," van Creveld tells us, "they also helped a new set of people to take charge, people who thought about war – and hence planned, prepared, waged, and evaluated it – with the aid of fresh criteria and from a fresh point of view."[69]

Indeed the rapid diffusion of information and communication technologies empowered those individuals which had mastered the language and methodology of the sciences that accompanied them. This was to

---

66   Wilson, *The Bomb and the Computer*, p. 49.

67   Gregory Palmer, *The McNamara Strategy and the Vietnam War: Program Budgeting in the Pentagon, 1960-68* (Westport, CT: Greenwood Press, 1978), p. 5.

68   President Dwight Eisenhower, Farewell Address to the People, Jan. 17, 1961.

69   Van Creveld, *Technology and War*, p. 246.

the detriment of established traditions of military thought and practice of warfare. Via an "'organised scientific discourse' through multiple, but centralising relationships among high-bureaucratic positions, technobureaucratic or production logic in the structure of its propositions, and the conventional educated prose style," cybernetic warfare excluded accounts of the war which did not conform to the exigencies of technoscientific discourse. For Gibson, this amounted to a neglect of "warrior knowledge" which he describes in terms of Foucault's notion of "subjected knowledge,"[70] understood as forms of knowledge that are "disqualified as inadequate to their task or insufficiently elaborated: naïve knowledges, located low down on the hierarchy, beneath the required level of cognition or scientificity."[71]

Because of the scientific and mathematical methodology upon which this worldview relied, analysts systematically privileged the quantifiable aspects of warfare which were susceptible to being integrated into mathematical models and input-output calculations. Anything which could not be quantified was therefore excluded. Intuition, courage, and willpower, those attributes which been considered central to war for centuries, were thereby devalued. John Lewis Gaddis explicitly criticised a tendency in American strategic thought in postwar era "to equate the importance of information with the ease of measuring it – an approach better suited to physics than to international relations."[72]

But even that which could be quantified could not necessarily be precisely measured or estimated and would be frequently only the result of more or less inspired guesswork. Solly Zuckerman, an early operations research pioneer, warned of the dangers of applying this type of scientific methodology to problems which were ill-suited to it and for which empirical data and a reliable understanding of all the variables was lacking:

Operational analysis implies a kind of scientific natural history. It is a search for exact information as a foundation for extrapolation and prediction. It is not so much a science in the sense of a corpus of exact knowledge, as it is the

---

70   Gibson, *The Perfect War*, p. 467.

71 · Foucault, *Power/Knowledge*, p. 82.

72   John Lewis Gaddis, *Strategies of Containment: A Critical Appraisal of Postwar American National Security Policy* (Oxford: Oxford University Press, 1982), p. 84.

attempted application of rigorous methods of scientific method and action to new and apparently unique situations. The less exact the information available for analysis, the less it is founded on experience, the more imprecise are its conclusions, however sophisticated and glamorous the mathematics with which the analysis is done.[73]

Thus, for all their scientific rigour, systems analysis and wargames relied heavily on intuitive and speculative estimations about numerous factors for which there was limited reliable information available. As such, the outcome of systems analysis studies or war games was heavily dependent on the assumptions underpinning their models, some acknowledged by the analysts, others largely concealed or unquestioned.[74] Driven by their desire for predictability, analysts constrained uncertainty by either setting the possible variations of factors within clearly delineated numerical ranges and probability sets or by simply discounting all those elements that could not be treated in this bounded way. Princeton academic Klaus Knorr noted some of the uncertainties frequently neglected by systems analysis:

Costs may be uncertain, technology may be uncertain, the properties of military conflict situations may be uncertain, and the reactions and capabilites of the potential enemy nations are apt to be uncertain. The last uncertainty is of particular import; it is imperative that military choices be examined within a framework of interaction. An opponent's responses to our choices may, after all, curtail ot altogether nullify the advantage we seek. Nor is it enough to

---

73   Perry, "Commentary" in Wright and Paszek (eds), *Science, Technology and Warfare*, p. 117. See also Solly Zuckerman, "Judgment and Control in Modern Warfare", OR, Vol. 13, No. 3. (Sep. 1962), pp. 245-266. "If we are to avoid the imposition of arbitrary limits to the exercise of judgment and control, let us be careful not to create in a mathematical vacuum situations which are based neither on past experience of affairs, nor on any conception of the innumerable variables and factors that determine social decision either today or tomorrow." (p. 266)

74   Perhaps more so than any of his colleagues, Herman Kahn was particularly forthright about the speculative nature of much of his work and how much of it relied on crucial assumptions that had little if any empirical foundation. This frankness did not make Kahn's work any less controversial, both pilloried and applauded for provocatively broaching the taboo subject of the conduct of a "winnable" nuclear war and envisaging a post-war world in *On Thermonuclear War* (1961).

recognise the conflict aspects of the problem. The possibilities of tacit or formal co-operation may be equally significant.[75]

In fairness, senior system analysts recognised some of the limitations of their studies and it would be erroneous to claim that policy was solely dictated by them. As Alain Enthoven himself put it, operations research and systems analysis "cannot be 'objective' in the sense of being independent of values [...] value judgments are an integral part of the analysis: and it is the role of the analyst to bring to light for the policymaker exactly how and where value judgments enter so that the latter can make his own value judgments in the light of as much relevant information as possible."[76] Nevertheless, government policies increasingly required some form of scientific costing and analysis for their justification, even if other motives drove their promotion and adoption. The leeway for intuition and guesstimates opened up the systems analysis models to manipulation for political and institutional motives. McNamara frequently used systems analysis to placate the insatiable demands of the air force for more nuclear warheads, insisting on "scientific" justification for such expenditure. The services soon caught on to this new way of determining procurement needs and created their own systems analysis departments that would produce reports that endorsed their own preferences. Systems analysis could thus be made to serve as a mere front for procurement and budgetary demands which satisfied commercial and political interests or inter-service rivalries that had nothing to with military effectiveness or strategic needs but could not be so easily dismissed once they had mastered the requirement of "scientificity." As senior RAND analyst Albert Wohlstetter bemoaned it, "the problem with the use of numbers was that you've bequeathed them to people of bad faith and to people of good faith as well."[77]

McNamara himself came to be disillusioned with the approach he had championed, recognising the impossibility of making war into a fully rational and predictable instrument of policy: "war is so complex, it's beyond the ability of the human mind to comprehend all the vari-

---

75   Wilson, *The Bomb and the Computer*, p. 114.

76   Perry, "Commentary" in Wright and Paszek (eds), *Science, Technology and Warfare*, p. 117.

77   Gregg Herken, *Counsels of War* (New York: Alfred A. Knopf, 1985), p. 230.

ables. Our judgement, our understanding, are not adequate."[78] McNamara was to learn this lesson during his tenure as Secretary of Defense between 1961 and 1967, when the United States became mired in a Vietnam War it could not win despite its army of system analysts in the Pentagon. Hindsight is a precious commodity but Vice Admiral Rickover summed up what had long been military wisdom during a 1966 subcommittee hearing of the House Committee on Appropriations in which he attacked the cost-effectiveness studies of the Department of Defense:

All wars and military development should have taught us that [...] a war, small or large, does not follow a prescribed "scenario" laid out in advance. If we could predict the sequence of events more accurately, we could probably avoid war in the first place.[79]

Vietnam and the Failure of Cybernetic Warfare

The limits of the centralising cybernetic model became clear with the Vietnam War in which the world's most powerful and technologically advanced military was unable to overcome a Third World guerrilla army. James Gibson has perhaps done the most to document the dramatic failure of "technowar", an approach to military conflict which views war as "a production system that can be rationally managed and warfare as a kind of activity that can be scientifically determined by constructing computer models."[80] Indeed the principles of operations research and systems analysis were systematically applied to provide analysis of the war and guidance to the policymakers while cybernetic command and control technologies were widely deployed. With the development of computers allowing for the gathering and processing of vast amounts of data, it was inferred that it would be possible to gain a far superior understanding and control of military operations than ever before. Furthermore, the repetitiveness of military operations in Vietnam, whether in terms of aerial bombardment or infantry missions, appeared ideally suited to centralised statistical management. In practice however, this

---

78   Errol Morris (director), *Fog of War* (Sony Pictures, 2004).

79   Wilson, *The Bomb and the Computer*, p. 110.

80   Gibson, *The Perfect War*, p. 156.

approach produced a distorted picture of the conflict which prevented a realistic assessment of the war, encouraged a counter-productive remote micro-management of the war, and impeded an understanding of the adversary's strategic behaviour and reasoning by erecting a mirror image of the American mindset.

It is true that because of the ebb and flow of the conflict, the absence of a clear front, and the guerilla tactics of the Vietcong, it was extremely difficult to gain any insight into the conflict without statistical means. Nevertheless, what manifested itself in Vietnam was an obsession with statistical evaluations and directing the war from the top, perceived as the point of omniscience. Endless statistics of enemy bodycounts, bomber sorties, and "pacified" hamlets were circulated among policy-makers and Pentagon officials and presented to the media and public as proof of progress in the war. The production of these statistics required that a regular flow of information be collected and recorded by troops before being centrally processed and aggregated for the consumption of the war managers. The pressure on troops to produce detailed reports of their operations and particularly to match their "production" targets in terms of enemy casualties led to wildly inaccurate and overblown estimates that masked the extent to which the US strategy was failing. A further problem was that the measure of information gathering was frequently one of quantity over quality, such that operations in the intelligence field were gauged primarily on data volumes:

Collection departments received most agency budgets and collection departments represented their progress in terms of how many "bits" of information they collected, or how many hours of radio messages were recorded. Since their work was so tangible and measurable, collection departments got the most. As one senior staff member of the National Security Council said, "95 percent of the US intelligence effort has been on collection, and only 5 percent on analysis and production [intepretation]."[81]

The paradox of this informational approach to warfare is noted by van Creveld: "designed to produce accuracy and certainty, the pressure exercised at the top for more and more quantitative information ended up by producing inaccuracy and uncertainty."[82] Instead of providing a picture of military operations of unparalled precision and exactness, the

---

81   Gibson, *The Perfect War*, p. 367.

82   Van Creveld, *Command in War*, p. 259.

collection and production of information for its own sake generated a fictional account of the conflict based on a misplaced sense of omniscience and on the basis of which incorrect decisions were taken. As the Pentagon systems analyst Alain Enthoven was to eventually recognise, "you assume that there is an information system that will tell you what you want to know. But that just isn't so. There are huge amounts of misinformation and wrong information."[83] Thus, far from eliminating the Clausewitzian "fog of war", information-processing techno-social assemblages generated their own "kind of twilight, which, like fog or moonlight, often tends to makes things seem grotesque and larger than they really are."[84]

Beside masking the reality of the conflict, the informational demands of this approach eventually overwhelmed the military infrastructure despite the deployment of an unprecedented telecommunications network in a field of operations. Electronic communications gear accounted for a third of all major items of equipment brought into the country and the first use of satellite communications for military purposes was inaugurated in 1965.[85] Nevertheless the volumes of data transferred and requiring processing within a highly centralised command and control structure were such that that saturation and bottlenecks frequently resulted. Intelligence on Vietcong positions and movements often arrived too late to be actionable, delayed in an information-processing infrastructure unable to treat all the data it was fed. As Arquilla and Ronfeldt point out, "informational overload and bottlenecking has long been a vulnerability of centralised, hierarchical structures for command and control."[86]

Vietnam was also the site for the deployment of wide-scale cybernetic systems operating on similar principles to the domestic air-defense systems discussed above. Between 1967 and 1972, the Air Force ran Operation Igloo White at the cost of nearly $1 billion a year. Through an

---

83   Herken, *Counsels of War*, p. 220.

84   Clausewitz, *On War*, p. 90.

85   Van Creveld, *Command in War*, p. 239. Van Creveld also tells us that there was one radio set for every 4.5 soldiers in the Vietnam War compared to one for every 38.6 soldiers during the Second World War.

86   John Arquilla and David Ronfeldt, "Cyberwar is Coming!" in John Arquilla and David Ronfeldt (eds), *In Athena's Camp: Preparing for Conflict in the Information Age* (RAND, 1997), p. 45.

array of sensors designed to record sound, heat, vibrations, and even the smell of urine, feeding information to a control center in Thailand which sent on the resulting targeting information to patrolling jet aircraft (even the release of bombs could be controlled remotely), this vast cybernetic assemblage was designed to disrupt the Ho Chi Minh Trail, a network of roads and trails providing logistical support to the North Vietnamese. Extravagant claims about the performance of the system were made at the time with the reported number of destroyed trucks in 1970 exceeding the total number of truck believed to be in all of North Vietnam.[87] In reality, far fewer truck remains were ever identified, there were probably many false positives in target identification, and the North Vietnamese and their Laotian allies became adept at fooling the sensors. In spite of all this, the official statistics still trumpeted a 90% success rate in destroying equipment travelling down the Ho Chi Minh Trail, an assertion difficult to sustain given that the North Vietnamese conducted major tank and artillery operations in South Vietnam in 1972.

Not only were the statistical indicators pointing to US success in the Vietnam frequently erroneous and misleading, the models on which war managers relied were equally faulty. Trapped in a mindset which treated the war as a purely technical problem to be solved through overwhelming application of *matériel* according to a scientific methodology, these officials failed to grasp the sheer determination of their opponents and the extent of the success of their political strategy. Equally misguided was the attempt to frame the behaviour of the Vietcong within abstract models of rationality such as game theory had constructed and which then underpinned much of nuclear strategy. Indeed the American bombing campaign in Vietnam from 1965 onwards applied a gradation in the use of force through which signals were to be sent to the North Vietnamese. This amounted to a communicative theory of war according to which the level of violence is alternatively ratcheted up or alleviated depending on the message to be sent. In this manner, the government wished to convince the North Vietnamese that they could not win and that the costs of their ongoing support of guerrillas in the South outweighed any benefits, thereby forcing them to negotiate. In effect, the North Vietnamese were being treated as a cybernetic system

---

87   Paul N. Edwards, "Cyberpunks in Cyberspace: The Politics of Subjectivity in the Computer Age" in Susan Leigh Star (ed.), *Cultures of Computing* (Keele, UK: Sociological Review and Monograph Series, 1995), pp. 69-84.

which could be steered towards the desired behaviour by a selective input of information in the form of targeted aerial bombardment. This thinking emerged from attempts by defence intellectuals, frustrated by the paradoxical powerlessness of nuclear weapons so destructive they could not be used, to theorise and rationalise their limited use against the Soviet Union as bargaining chips in an eventual showdown. This strategy which had been ultimately abandoned because of the impossibility of guaranteeing that nuclear war would not rapidly escalate into an apocalyptic war of extermination now resurfaced in the context of the Vietnam War. As a result of treating the bombing campaign in this manner, relevant decisions were highly centralised with President Johnson and the White House exerting direct oversight and veto over target selections. However, instead of resulting in the predicted outcome, the bombings only strengthened the resolve of the North Vietnamese who refused any negotiations before a complete cessation of the air campaign. Furthermore, the naked determination to prevail in what was seen as a national war of liberation which had begun with the struggle against the French guided North Vietnamese strategy far more than any calculation of immediate interests.

By applying bargaining models based on game theory which assumed a common utility-maximising rationality and cost-benefit framework of analysis on all sides, American strategists erected an understanding of the enemy that was a mere reflection of the their own worldview and was presumed to obey to the same strategic rationales. American policymakers likewise also assumed that the tight top-down control exerted over its own military operations were echoed in the organisation of their adversaries. The famous attack on an American warship in the Gulf of Tonkin in August 1964 was immediately interpreted as a deliberate escalation of the conflict by the North Vietnamese. In fact, command in the North Vietnamese army was far more decentralised and the decision to attack the warship had been taken at a low level in the chain of command.[88] The US thus assumed a greater coherence and clarity of intent of individual actions by the North Vietnamese than reality warranted, premised on a view of warfare as a frictionless activity

---

88   James G. Blight and Janet M. Lang, *The Fog of War – Lessons from the Life of Robert S. McNamara* (Lanham, MD: Rowman and Littlefield Publishers, 2005), pp. 107-108.

in which all acts are unambiguous and calculated in perfect conformity to an overall strategic plan.

Gibson further submits that technowar not only altered the conduct of war but even the likelihood of the use of force: "by adopting micro-economics, game theory, systems analysis, and other managerial techniques, the Kennedy administration advanced "limited" war to greater specificity, making it seem much more controllable, manageable, and therefore *desirable* as foreign policy."[89] Henry Kissinger illustrated this very point and the dangerous hubris which resulted from it when he claimed in 1968 that "a scientific revolution has, for all practical purposes, removed technical limits from the exercise of power in foreign policy."[90] This perception was further bolstered by the military and civilian leadership's conception of war as determined principally by the management of complex industrial systems:

Limited war fought as a war of attrition means that only information about technological-production systems will count as valid knowledge about the enemy. For the military as well as civilian, the enemy becomes a mirror image of ourselves, only "less" so.[91]

Since military effectiveness could only be measured by the yardstick of "technological-production systems," the North Vietnamese were necessarily inferior and victory was the only conceivable outcome for the American war machine. The closed self-referentiality of cybernetic warfare effectively blinded its practitioners to the effectiveness of the asymmetric strategy deployed by their adversaries. Colonel Harry Summers relates a story circulating towards the end of the conflict which, although probably apocryphal, nonetheless captures the spirit of the thinking that dominated the conduct of the war:

When the Nixon Administration took over in 1969 all the data on North Vietnam and the United States was fed into a Pentagon computer – populations, gross national product, manufacturing capability, number of tanks, ships, and aircraft, size of the armed forces, and the like. The computer was then asked,

---

89   Gibson, *The Perfect War*, p. 80.

90   Henry Kissinger, "Central Issues of American Foreign Policy" in Henry Kissinger, *Agenda for a Nation* (Washington, DC: The Brookings Institution, 1968).

91   Gibson, *The Perfect War*, p. 23.

"When will we win?" It took only moments to give the answer: "You won in 1964!"[92]

The military systems assembled under cybernetic warfare had been designed to combat other similar systems in what was to be a high-intensity mechanised war of attrition, perhaps all the way to (mutual) annihilation. If they thankfully remained untested throughout the Cold War, they may well have performed as expected in such a conflict. Indeed in the Gulf War of 1991 Saddam Hussein opposed the hierarchical system of the US army with his own inferior rigid and centralised system and was comprehensively defeated. Centralised command and control is best suited to high-intensity wars in homogeneous environments such as was presented by Saddam's attempt to fight a modern industrial war in the Iraqi deserts. However, when faced with low-intensity conflicts of the counter-insurgency type in which a dispersed enemy merges into a complex environment (such as the Vietcong in the jungles of Vietnam), the productivist logic and centralised command of cybernetic warfare was susceptible to spectacular inefficiency and failure. Attempts to simplify the battlespace through the practice of deforestation and the use of Agent Orange made little difference against an opponent that played to its strengths and understood its enemy far better than the Americans did. Witness North Vietnamese General Vo Nguyen Giap's piercing observation:

The United States has a strategy based on arithmetic. They question the computers, add and subtract, extract square roots, and then go into action. But arithmetical strategy doesn't work here. If it did, they would already have exterminated us with their airplanes.[93]

The reasons for American defeat in Vietnam are multi-faceted and certainly cannot be reduced to the influence of systems analysis and the failings of an information-driven conduct of warfare. Furthermore, the military was not in any conventional sense of the word defeated by the North Vietnamese but the latter succeeded in convincing the American public and political class that the war could not be won either. While the war was therefore ultimately lost on the political battlefield, it was none-

---

92   Beatrice Heuser, *Reading Clausewitz* (London: Pimlico, 2002), p. 170.

93   Jeff Mustin, "Flesh and Blood: The Call for the Pilot in the Cockpit", *Air and Space Power Journal - Chronicles Online Journal*, July 2001 http://www.airpower.maxwell.af.mil/airchronicles/cc/mustin.html

theless a misplaced faith in the technoscientific approach to war which gave the war planners an illusory sense of what could be achieved through only military means and caused them to pay insufficient attention to both their own political strategy and that of the North Vietnamese.

Conclusion

Defeat in Vietnam exposed the shortcomings of cybernetic warfare and revealed the inherent limitations of its attempt to make war into an entirely controllable and predictable activity. The cybernetic model of warfare erected by the system analysts was one that was frictionless, a perfectly oiled machine resting on elegant mathematical constructs. Rather than eternal attributes of the battlefield, uncertainty and unpredictability became understood merely as a lack of information which could be overcome through the deployment of the proper information and communication technologies and elaboration of appropriate models of conflict.

If the debacle of Vietnam provoked some serious soul-searching among American strategists and military men, it did not result in an immediate or widespread abandonment of the central principles of cybernetic warfare or in a significant revaluation of other forms of thought on war. Throughout the rest of the Cold War and beyond, information technology continued to be embraced as the panacea to the chaos and indeterminacy of war. The Strategic Defense Initiative promised an invulnerable shield against nuclear attack through a combination of computers and space weapons while revolutions in military affairs in the mould of Westmoreland's vision have been repeatedly heralded. However, the miniaturisation and diffusion of computers and telecommunication devices, accompanied by developments in the informational paradigm with the scientific theories of chaos and complexity, has led to the emergence of a new understanding of warfare revolving around the notion of the network and decentralised command. It is to this latest regime of the scientific way of warfare that we can now turn.

6

A New Informational Regime: From Chaos Theory to Complexity Science

Chaos often breeds life, when order breeds habit.

Henry Brooks Adam

Networks in the regime near the edge of chaos – this compromise between order and surprise – appear best able to coordinate complex activities and best able to evolve as well.

Stuart Kauffman[1]

The focus of the original cyberneticists on control mechanisms as a means of overcoming disorder (or entropy) has in recent decades progressively given way to a consideration of the distributed emergence of "complexity." While information remains the key organising concept at the core of this new approach, the sciences of chaos and complexity have reconceptualised disorder as a necessary condition of order as opposed to an unruliness to be warded off. Where the clock, engine, and computer served as central technological metaphors within previous scientific frameworks, it is the more abstract yet no less ubiquitous figure of the

---

1   Stuart A. Kauffman, *At Home in the Universe: The Search for Laws of Self-organization and Complexity* (Oxford University Press, 1995), p. 26.

network that fulfils this role here. As was the case with cybernetics, chaos theory and complexity science have constituted broad fields of interdisciplinary enquiry that have left practically no area untouched and can be located with a broader cultural moment.[2] These scientific developments are reflected in military thought with a move away from computerised hierarchical centralisation towards decentralised self-synchronising networks, as we shall see in the next chapter.

For now, the focus will be on presenting the conceptual framework erected by the new scientific theories of chaos and complexity, dubbed "chaoplexity" by some commentators in light of their theoretical prox-imity and overlap.[3] Particular attention will be paid to the challenge they pose to previous assumptions about the possibility of exerting complete predictability and control over systems as well as to the novel account they propose of the key processes underlying both change and life it-self. Central to this are the non-linear dynamics and positive feedback loops underpinning "chaotic" phenomena and the distributed networks through which the emergence and self-organisation of complex systems is made possible.

The Rediscovery of Non-Linearity: Chaos Theory and Positive Feedback

Early cybernetic thought focused mainly on how systems use informa-tion and control mechanisms to steer towards and maintain the goals that are assigned to them and counteract the various disturbances which might cause them to deviate from these same goals. Originating in the study of engineering problems before being subsequently extended to the enquiry of organic or social entities, cybernetics examined systems that were viewed as organisationally closed (in the sense of having a pre-established finite number of possible states) and pursuing overarching goals determined exogenously. Control hierarchies adjusted to changes

---

2   Mark Taylor has notably shown how the ideas of complexity are echoed in a number of developments in architecture, art, and social theory. Mark C. Taylor, *The Moment of Complexity: Emerging Network Culture* (Chicago, IL: University of Chicago Press, 2001).

3   John Horgan, *The End of Science: Facing the Limits of Knowledge in the Twilight of the Scientific Age* (London: Abacus, 2002), pp. 191-192.

in the environment and the system parameters via information feedback loops with the ultimate objective being the homeostasis of the system. As Stafford Beer put it:

A self-regulating servomechanism needs to operate as a closed system […] The whole point of homeostatic self-regulation in cybernetic machines is that the system should deal with disturbances; moreover with disturbances that have not been foreseen in principle by the designer. This requirement can be met only by a closed system in the servomechanism model.[4]

If information feedback is the main mechanism through which cybernetic systems self-regulate, it is necessary to introduce here a distinction between negative and positive feedback. Negative feedback occurs in a system that responds to disturbances with a stabilising adjustment in order to guide or return the system to the desired state. Positive feedback is present when disturbances are amplified and thus move the system further away from its point of origin. Cybernetics was essentially preoccupied with the first form of feedback since positive feedback's amplification of disturbances was seen primarily as a disruptive process to be avoided, countered, or appropriately tamed to serve the overall homeostatic objectives.[5] Furthermore, the focus of early cybernetics was predominantly on linear processes since engineers traditionally strove to keep their systems linear as it made them simpler to build and to predict.[6] The assumptions of closed systems, negative information feedback, and linearity dominated the cybernetic outlook of the immediate post-war era, with Cold War planners tasked with the integration of large technological systems adopting much of this conceptual and

---

4   Beer, *Cybernetics and Management*, p. 166.

5   In 1963, Magoroh Maruyama called for a "second cybernetics" which would pay greater attention to "deviation-amplifying mutual causal systems" and connected such systems to evolutionary, economic, cultural, and psychological processes. Magoroh Maruyama, "The Second Cybernetics: Deviation-Amplifying Mutual Causal Processes", *American Scientist*, 5:2 (1963), pp. 164-179.

6   "In the early system sciences of cybernetics, information theory, and general systems theory emergent phenomena per se were not explicitly the focus of research, since the systems investigated by these earlier approaches were simple, linear and equilibrium seeking, in contrast to the complex, nonlinear, and non-equilibrium systems in which complexity theory is interested." Jeffrey Goldstein, "Emergence as a Construct: History and Issues", *Emergence: Complexity and Organization* 1:1 (1999), pp. 54-55.

methodological baggage. Yet it is these very assumptions that came to be all progressively challenged by the new scientific discoveries.

A number of cyberneticists and system theorists began to broaden their field of enquiry beyond questions of self-regulation and homeostasis to probe how systems reproduced themselves and even emerged in the first place. While the earlier approach had been suited to dealing with engineering problems and the practical issues of machine design, it soon appeared limited for the consideration of certain physical and biological phenomena. It was through their study of biological systems that Humberto Maturana and Francisco Varela formulated the concept of autopoeisis ("self-creation" in Greek) in the early 1970s. For the two scientists, an autopoietic system such as those encountered in the biological world was:

a dynamic system that is defined as a composite unity as a network of productions of components that (1) through their interactions recursively regenerate the network of productions that produced them and (2) realise this network as a unity in space in which they exist by constituting and specifying its boundaries as surfaces of cleavages from the background through their preferential interactions within the network.[7]

As with the systems of first wave cybernetics, these were defined by sets of relations between parts but here these relations not only accounted for their operation but also for their continual reproduction. "The living organisation is a circular organisation which secures the production or maintenance of the components that specify it in such a manner that the product of their functioning is the very same organisation that produces them."[8] The living organism was thus conceived of as a self-perpetuating process through which its constitutive components and its pattern of organisation mutually sustain and reproduce one other in a closed causal loop.[9]

7   Humberto Mathurana, "Man and Society" in Frank Benseler, Peter Heil and Wolfgang Koch (eds), *Autopoiesis, Communication, and Society: The Theory of Autopoietic Systems in the Social Sciences* (Frankfurt: Campus Verlag, 1980), p. 29.

8   Humberto Mathurana, quoted in Hayles, *How We Became Posthuman*, p. 138.

9   Niklas Luhmann subsequently developed Maturana and Varela's notion of autopoeisis within the social sciences under his sociological systems theory. Niklas Luhmann, *Social Systems* (Stanford, CA: Stanford University Press, 1995).

Along with self-production, interest in the notion of self-organisation grew in the 1970s in order to explain the dynamic emergence of systems and here the departure from early cybernetics is particularly significant. Certainly the notion of self-organisation was not absent from early cybernetics since scientists like Ross Ashby and Heinz von Foerster had developed the concept in their respective studies of the nervous system and biological systems. However, as Fritjof Capra points out, the crucial novelty of the new understandings of self-organisation lay in allowing for the creation of new structures and new modes of behaviour, in contrast with the models of the early cyberneticists. "For Ashby all possible structural changes take place within a given "variety pool" of structures, and the survival chances of the system depend on the richness, or "requisite variety" of that pool. There is no creativity, no development, no evolution."[10]

The new inquiry into processes of self-organisation led to an exploration of the phenomenon of positive information feedback, which had until then been primarily seen in terms of a harmful process since it took systems away from their desired equilibrium. In theories of self-organisation, positive feedback accounts for the emergence of complexity in systems in which outputs feed back into them as inputs, allowing for runaway processes of change. The study of non-linear relationships in which outputs are not proportional to inputs allowed for the formulation of exponential processes of change central to the scientific theories of chaos and complexity. "While negative feedback is the essential condition for stability, positive feedbacks are responsible for growth, self-organisation, and the amplification of weak signals."[11] Ilya Prigogine related positive feedback to self-organisation in his Nobel Prize-winning work on dissipative structures, as summed up by Jenner:

The initial step in the development of self-organising systems, in Prigogine's analysis, occurs when energy flowing into a system increases and generates chaotic, or random, behaviour. Such behaviour arises through "positive feedback", in which an initial change in the value of any parameter or value of the system results in an amplification of change elsewhere in the system. As a result, the system's components grow increasingly random and chaotic, and threaten to destroy the system altogether. If certain conditions are present, however, the

10   Capra, *The Web of Life*, p. 85. W. Ross Ashby, *An Introduction to Cybernetics* (London: Chapman and Hall, 1956).

11   Heylighen and Joslyn, "Cybernetics and Second-Order Cybernetics", p. 12.

system undergoes a radical transformation; at some point, the energy is chan-nelled into new forms of behaviour, and the elements of the system interact in a uniform way, and what had been, or might have become, uncontrolled random behaviour is now channelled into highly structured interactions.[12]

Or to put it in Capra's words: "self-organisation is the spontaneous emergence of new structures and new forms of behaviour in open sys-tems far from equilibrium, characterised by internal feedback loops and described mathematically by non-linear equations."[13]

Independent studies of systems characterised by positive feedback and non-linear processes in a variety of fields including meteorology, fluid dynamics, chemistry, and population biology eventually led to the constitution of a new interdisciplinary scientific corpus which came to be known as chaos theory. The common thread to all the studies gathered under this banner was the use of non-linear mathematics to model physical systems and explore the complex patterns of behaviour displayed by such models. Mechanistic science had focused its atten-tion on linear phenomena since the mathematical functions by which they could be expressed were easy to understand and solve. In contrast, non-linear equations have very complex behaviours, can have multiple solutions for any given value, and are largely impervious to analytical techniques.[14] While the privileging of linear equations by scientists was essentially due to their greater ease of manipulation and study, this methodological constraint eventually came to be interpreted as reflect-ing the fundamental nature of reality. As mathematician Ian Stewart has observed, "classical mathematics concentrated on linear equations for a sound pragmatic reason: it could not solve anything else [...] so docile are linear equations that the classical mathematicians were willing to compromise their physics to get them."[15] In other words, scientists came to view phenomena as essentially linear with non-linearity construed

---

12   R A. Jenner, "Dissipative Enterprises, Chaos, and the Principles of Lean Or-ganizations", *Omega: The International Journal of Management Science*, Vol. 26, No. 4, Dec., 1998.

13   Capra, *The Web of Life*, p. 85.

14   Their property of non-additivity means non-linear equations cannot be broken up into smaller parts that are individually solved before being recombined, as is possible with their linear counterparts. In other words, they do not fit the clockwork model of science erected by mechanism.

15   Beyerchen, "Clausewitz, Nonlinearity and the Unpredictability of War", p. 63.

as a negligible aberration or deviation from the linear norm, a mere mathematical curiosity.

Most scientists now hold precisely the reverse to be true – both mathematically and physically, linear processes are the exception and not the rule. Nature is fundamentally non-linear. While the behaviour of all linear systems is consistent in the sense that they tend towards a fixed equilibrium, non-linear systems display a broad range of behaviours dependent on their mathematical properties. Some tend towards fixed equilibrium in the same way as linear systems, others may enter a periodic pattern of regular oscillation between different points. Yet others revealed an unexpected behaviour that became the foundation of chaos theory. Indeed certain non-linear functions produce incredibly intricate patterns and non-periodic behaviour which seem completely random and disorderly. The great discovery of chaos theory was that "simple deterministic models could produce what looked like random behaviour. The behaviour had an exquisite fine structure, yet any piece seemed indistinguishable from noise."[16] Thus, it became possible to identify a structure and order to phenomena which previously appeared to have none. In this sense, chaos theory is a misnomer; the phenomena it models are not random, probabilistic, or truly chaotic since they obey deterministic laws. Disorder finds with chaos theory its own hidden order.

It was the computer that provided the tool for the exploration of non-linear functions, its processing power allowing for the iteration of calculations that uncovered the hidden patterns produced by these mathematical systems.[17] Striking images can be produced when such patterns are represented graphically, perhaps best exemplified by Benoit Mandelbrot's work on fractals (Figure 8). Fractals are infinitely detailed geometric objects generated by the repeated application of simple mathematical rules. The property of self-similarity across scales characteristic of fractals entails a geometrical resemblance or physical correspondence between the parts of a system and the system as a whole. Indeed similar or identical patterns can be observed at different levels of magnification

---

16   Gleick, *Chaos*, p. 79.

17   David Campbell, Jim Crutchfield, Doyne Farmer, and Erica Jen, "Experimental Mathematics: The Role of Computation in Nonlinear Studies", *Communications of ACM* 28(4), 1985, pp. 374-384.

Figure 8: Mandelbrot set fractal

of a given structure, with increased detail never resulting in a decrease in the complexity of the patterns (Figure 9). This phenomenon is a result of the iteration of simple rules governing the constitution of complex forms. Far from being limited to mathematical oddities, Mandelbrot's work uncovered fractal structures in fern leaves, clouds, bronchia, rock formations, and even stock market prices.[18] In his book *The Fractal Geometry of Nature*, Mandelbrot insisted on both the novelty of his work relative to traditional geometry and its replication in the observable world: "many patterns in Nature are so irregular and fragmented, that, compared with *Euclid* [...] Nature exhibits not only a higher degree but an altogether different level of complexity."[19]

Such discoveries constituted unexpected scientific developments that emerged from the use of computers. It had originally been thought that computers might finally provide the necessary computational power to perfectly map the past and future states of physical systems, given a full understanding of the natural laws governing them. Recall Laplace's

---

18   For the latter, see Benoit B. Mandelbrot and Richard L Hudson, *The (Mis) Behaviour of Markets: A Fractal View of Risk, Ruin and Reward* (London: Profile Books, 2004).

19   Quoted in Hayles, *Chaos Bound*, p. 164.

Figure 9: Self-similarity in a Mandelbrot set fractal

invocation of a theoretical intelligence which could "comprehend all the forces by which nature is animated" and for which consequently "nothing would be uncertain and the future as the past, would be present to its eyes."[20] But such an ambition relied on a Newtonian conception of the world which was to be terminally undermined by chaos theory. Indeed the presumption of classical physics on which the Laplacian dream rested was that "arbitrarily small influences don't blow up to have arbitrarily large effects."[21] In accordance with linear mathematics, small influences could thereby be safely ignored and the value of the variables of any system could be approximated within a reasonable margin of error without jeopardising a model's predictions.

What computer simulations of non-linear systems revealed was their *sensitive dependence on initial conditions*, that is the non-proportionality of cause to effect or input to output. In other words, minute variations in the initial conditions of a dynamical system can produce large variations in its long term behaviour. The popular metaphor employed to illustrate this phenomenon is the "butterfly effect", the notion that a butterfly flapping its wings in Tokyo can cause a tornado in California. The

20   Laplace, "Théorie Analytique des Probabilités".
21   Gleick, *Chaos*, p. 15.

implications of sensitivity to initial conditions is that any finite model of such a dynamic system is necessarily limited in its predictive capacity as there will always be unavoidable imprecisions in our measurement of initial conditions. These imprecision are due not only to limitations in the accuracy of measurement instruments but more fundamentally to the practical need of rounding off figures at some decimal point. Hence, beyond a certain number of iterations precise predictions become virtually useless. This characteristic of non-linear systems is notably evoked to explain the persistent inability of meteorology to make any reliable forecasts beyond about a week.

It should be noted that the late-nineteenth century mathematician Henri Poincaré had anticipated much of chaos theory by distinguishing chance as statistical randomness from chance as a deterministic process that could not be predicted due to sensitivity to initial conditions:

A very slight cause, which escapes us, determines a considerable effect which we cannot help seeing, and then we say this effect is due to chance. If we could know exactly the laws of nature and the situation of the universe at the initial instant, we should be able to predict exactly the situation of this same universe at a subsequent instant. But even when the natural laws should have no further secret for us, we could know the initial situation only *approximately*. If that permits us to foresee the subsequent situation *with the same degree of approximation*, this is all we require, we say the phenomenon has been predicted, that it is ruled by laws. But this is not always the case; it may happen that slight differences in the initial conditions produce very great differences in the final phenomenon; a slight error in the former would make an enormous error in the latter. Prediction becomes impossible and we have the phenomenon of chance.[22]

Unfortunately Poincaré did not have at hand the computational instruments to demonstrate his powerful intuition and this remarkable insight could not seriously challenge the dominant linear paradigm of the physical sciences until the last decades of the twentieth century.

Although chaos theory has imposed a limitation on the *long-term* predictability of non-linear systems, it has simultaneously revealed an inherent order in phenomena that had previously appeared completely disordered, thereby allowing for a *short-term* predictability where there was none before. Furthermore, if precise long-term pre-

---

22   Ian Stewart, Does God Play Dice?: The New Mathematics of Chaos, MA: Blackwell Publishing, 2002, p.364.

dictability as classically understood is now found to be impossible, a qualitative understanding of the behaviour of a system may in certain circumstances replace a now foreclosed quantitative one. The exact future state of a non-linear system may be impossible to predict but it is often possible to identify and model its overall behaviour through the identification of certain patterns and regularities in its dynamics. Prediction thus shifts from quantitative analysis (calculating precisely in what state a system will be in at a particular moment) to qualitative analysis (understanding the general behaviour of the system). Not only is prediction of chaotic systems therefore not completely impossible, but even a certain degree of control appears within reach. Indeed experiments in "chaos control" have shown that with a sufficient grasp of their dynamics some systems can be nudged into particular patterns of behaviour.[23] While chaos control is still largely at an experimental stage, it demonstrates that chaos theory does not stand against or outside the technoscientific project of control but rather recasts it so that order is not so much imposed against chaos as made to emerge from disorder by utilising the latter's properties. Further ways to mould reality would be suggested with the emergence of complexity science since this next stage in the development in the study of nonlinear dynamical systems would seek to uncover the processes underpinning the very spontaneity and malleability of life.

Complexity, Networks, and Emergence: Life at the Edge of Chaos

Despite the significant contributions of chaos theory, there was a sense among certain scientists that the theory didn't go far enough. It certainly explained how the iteration of certain simple rules could give rise to astonishingly complicated dynamics but it did not sufficiently address the apparently inexorable growth of order and structure in the universe, such as witnessed in the evolution of biological life forms and human societies. Further research into these areas, conducted in particular at the Santa

---

23   One of the earliest papers on chaos control was Edward Ott, Celso Grebogi, and James A. Yorke, "Controlling Chaos", *Physical Review Letters*, 64, 1990, pp. 1196–1199. Research is ongoing into chaos control in optical and electronic systems as well as cardiac dynamics.

Fe Institute in New Mexico, eventually led to the formation of another interdisciplinary field known as complexity science.[24] Its focus would be on the behaviour of complex systems, understood as systems composed of many independent parts which are coupled in a non-linear fashion.

Complexity turns out to an exceedingly difficult term to define in a precise and definite manner and disagreements abound on the criteria which should determine whether an object of study should be considered complex or not. The nebulous characteristic of the term reflects in part the fact that it covers a broad field of enquiry into non-linear dynamic systems rather than denoting a clearly defined scientific theory. For the physicist Murray Gell-Mann, the appropriateness of the word refers back to its etymology – *plexus* means braided or entwined, from which is derived *complexus,* meaning braided together.[25] Hence complexity suggests the "intricate intertwining or interconnectivity of elements within a system, and between a system and its environment."[26]

The notion of network is therefore critical to describing the patterns of interaction which are constituted by the interplay of multiples entities in a complex system. Capra makes the connection between the network and the notions of non-linearity and positive feedback which chaos theory had previously developed:

The first and most obvious property of any network is its non-linearity – it goes in all directions. Thus the relationships in a network pattern are non-linear relationships. In particular, an influence, or message, may travel along a cyclical path, which may become a feedback loop. The concept of feedback is intimately connected with the network pattern.[27]

Another central concept is that of emergence, defined by Goldstein as "the arising of novel and coherent structures, patterns and proper-

---

24   The Santa Fe institute is located in the close vicinity to the Los Alamos National Laboratory where the Manhattan Project was conducted during the Second World War. While still one of the key research centres for the development of new nuclear weaponry, Los Alamos also collaborates with the Santa Fe Institute on a number of complexity science projects.

25   Murray Gell-Mann, "Let's Call It Plectics", *Complexity Journal*, Vol. 1/ No. 5 (1995/96).

26   James Moffat, *Complexity and Network-Centric Warfare* (CCRP Publications, 2003), p. 68.

27   Capra, *The Web of Life*, p. 82.

ties during the process of self-organisation in complex systems."[28] Self-organisation occurs through the autonomous interaction of individual entities, sometimes on the basis of relatively simple rules governing behaviour. As scientist Stephen Wolfram put it:

> Whenever you look at very complicated systems in physics or in biology, you generally find that the basic components and the basic laws are quite simple; the complexity arises because you have a great many of these simple components interacting simultaneously. The complexity is actually in the organisation – the myriad possible ways that the components can interact.[29]

This view is in direct opposition to reductionist approaches such as mechanism which view properties of the system as the mere aggregation of those of their constituent parts. Emergent properties, however, are properties of the whole that cannot be deduced from the properties of the individual parts making it up and only manifest themselves through the organisation of the parts.

Complex adaptive systems constitute a special case of complex systems that are capable of changing and learning from experience. Complexity theorist John Holland defines a complex adaptive system as a dynamic network of many agents acting in parallel, constantly acting and reacting to what the other agents are doing. Since the control of a complex adaptive system tends to be highly dispersed and decentralised, any coherent behaviour in the system arises from competition and cooperation among the agents themselves. It is the accumulation of all the individual decisions taken by the multitude of agents which produces the overall behaviour of the system, which can thus be said to be emergent.[30]

Complex adaptive systems include living organisms, insect colonies, bird flocks, ecosystems, businesses, stock markets, and other forms of social organisation with the constituent agents being cells, species, individuals, firms, or nations. According to John Holland, there are common characteristics to all these systems which complexity science is best equipped to understand and manipulate to solve many of the world's most intractable troubles:

---

28   Goldstein, "Emergence as a Construct", p. 49.

29   Waldrop, *Complexity*, p. 86.

30   Waldrop, *Complexity*, pp. 145-146.

Many of our most troubling long-range problems – trade imbalances, sustainability, AIDS, genetic defects, mental health, computer viruses – centre on certain systems of extraordinary complexity. The systems that host these problems – economies, ecologies, immune systems, embryos, nervous systems, computer networks – appear to be as diverse as the problems. Despite appearances, however, the systems do share significant characteristics, so much so that we group them under a single classification at the Santa Fe Institute, calling them *complex adaptive systems* (CAS). This is more than terminology. It signals our intuition that there are general principles that govern all CAS behaviour, principles that point to the way of solving the attendant problems. Much of our work is aimed at turning this intuition into fact.[31]

We see here that the explanatory scope attributed to complexity theory by its proponents is no less ambitious than that of the original cyberneticists.

The exploration of non-linear functions with computers also revealed the phenomenon of bifurcation in the study of dynamical systems. The discovery was made that a small change made to the parameter or control values of a system could cause a sudden qualitative change in the system's long-run dynamical behaviour. The notion of bifurcation was to become key in explaining the transformation and evolution of systems. As Urry puts it, "systems reach points of bifurcation when their behaviour and future pathways become unpredictable and new higher order, more differentiated, structures may emerge."[32] For certain control values, the system will respond to all perturbations by settling back down to an established stable state. When the control values are such that the system reaches its first point of bifurcation, the system will develop two alternative stable states either of which it will settle in, depending on the perturbations applied to it. As the parameters' values continue to change, each stable state will further bifurcate, multiplying the number of possible states. Beyond certain parameter values, the system will shift to chaotic behaviour. It is just before the onset of this behaviour, where bifurcations are greatest but stable states still exist, that system flexibility and adaptability is maximised, at the "edge of chaos" (Figure 10).

---

31   Horgan, *The End of Science*, pp. 195-196.

32   John Urry, *Global Complexity* (Cambridge: Polity, 2003), p. 28.

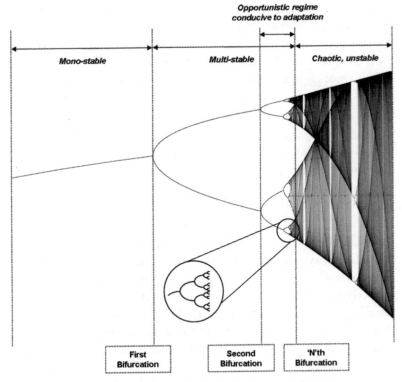

Figure 10: Bifurcation diagram of a non-linear system[33]

Complexity science thus redefines "life" as a balance between forces of order and forces of disorder, between fixed rigid structures and chaotic motion. As Waldrop sums it up:

Right in between the two extremes [of order and chaos], at a kind of abstract phase transition called "the edge of chaos", you also find *complexity*: a class of behaviours in which the components of the system never quite lock into place, yet never quite dissolve into turbulence, either. These are the systems that are both stable enough to store information, and yet evanescent enough to transmit it. These are the systems that can be organised to perform complex computations, to react to the world, to be spontaneous, adaptive, and alive.[34]

---

33   Based on Linda P. Beckerman, "The Non-Linear Dynamics of War", Science Applications International Corporation, 1999.

34   Waldrop, *Complexity*, p. 293.

Building on the discoveries of chaos theory, complexity theorists claim that it is at frontier of the phenomena of chaos, the "narrow domain between frozen constancy and chaotic turbulence," that the most complex and adaptive structures can be found. [35]

It is through mechanisms of information processing, distribution and exchange that complex adaptive systems are seen to emerge and evolve. According to Gell-Mann:

A complex adaptive system acquires information about its environment and its own interaction with that environment, identifying regularities in that information, condensing those regularities into a kind of "schema" or model, and acting in the real world on the basis of that schema. In each case, there are various competing schemata, and the results of the action in the real world feed back to influence competition among these schemata. [36]

By identifying patterns and correlations, schemata allow the complex adaptive system to extract regularities from the raw data flow that traverses it. On this basis, the complex adaptive system can constitute a description of an observed system, predict events, or create prescriptions for its own behaviour. Through a process of continuous learning, these schemata are always being adjusted and rebuilt as the complex adaptive system interacts with its environment and other systems, and new information is absorbed.

Gell-Mann proposed that the length of description of schemata be used as a measure of complexity. Descriptions of systems showing completely regular, highly ordered, patterns of behaviour would be low in informational content (since the pattern could be expressed in very few terms) while descriptions of completely random behaviour would have no informational content at all (since no pattern at all can be discerned). Hence informational content and complexity are maximised in between these two extremities, at "the edge of chaos" (Figure 11).

---

35   Francis Heylighen, "Complex Adaptive Systems" (Principia Cybernetica Web, 1996) http://pespmc1.vub.ac.be/CAS.html.

36   Murray Gell-Mann, *The Quark and the Jaguar: Adventures in the Simple and the Complex* (London: Little, Brown, 1994), p. 17.

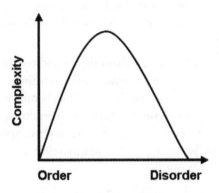

Figure 11: Complexity is highest in between the poles of order and disorder

Crucially, the sense in which complex systems are adaptive is quite distinct from traditional scientific understandings of the adaptation and optimisation of systems in that it allows for radical transformation by virtue of which new types of behaviours and goals can emerge. Whereas servomechanisms seek to regulate behaviour within the confines of an existing structure and pre-determined goals via negative feedback, complex systems can modify their internal structure and redefine their objectives through positive feedback. As John Holland puts it, "adaptation, whatever its context, involves a progressive modification to some structure or structures."[37] Prigogine and Stengers make a similar distinction here:

It is obvious that the management of human society as well as the action of selective pressures tend to optimise some aspects of the behaviour or modes of connection, but to consider optimisation as the key to understanding how populations and individuals survive is to risk confusing causes with effects. Optimisation models thus ignore both the possibility of radical transformations – that is, transformations that change the definition of a problem and thus the kind of solution sought – and the inertial constraints that may eventually force a system into a disastrous way of functioning. Like doctrines such as Adam Smith's invisible hand or other definitions of progress in terms of maximisation and minimisation criteria, this gives a reassuring representation of nature as an all-powerful and rational calculator, and of a coherent history characterised by

---

37   John H. Holland, *Adaptation in Natural and Artificial Systems* (Cambridge, MA: MIT Press, 1995), p. 3.

global progress. To restore both the inertia and the possibility of unanticipated events – that is, restore the open character of history – we must accept its fundamental uncertainty.[38]

If the major contributions of chaos theory and complexity have been to uncover the vital role of decentralised co-ordination and positive feedback mechanisms, it would be nevertheless misleading to assume from this that hierarchical control and negative feedback are now viewed as irrelevant. Rather, the new scientific corpus views opposing processes as complementary, balancing change and stability. Complexity theorist Doyne Farmer points out that:

Evolution thrives in systems with a bottom-up organisation, which gives rises to flexibility. But at the same time, evolution has to channel the bottom-up approach in a way that doesn't destroy the organisation. There has to be a hierarchy of control – with information flowing from the bottom up as well as from the top down.[39]

Likewise, both forms of feedback can generally be observed in complex systems as negative feedback serves to constrain the growth of positive feedback. Without the former, the latter would likely eventually either extinguish itself when it runs out of resources to fuel its process of expansion (as in the case of a virus epidemic or the chemical process of combustion) or risk the system's dissolution when run-away processes become too strong to preserve the fine balance between frozen constancy and chaotic turbulence. Nonetheless, chaoplexic science affirms the primacy of positive feedback and decentralised emergence since they are the prerequisites for creation and change through which mechanisms for negative feedback and hierarchical control can subsequently appear. In other words, an emergent structure may subsequently exert some downward causation on the parts whose interaction produced it in the first place but this is a secondary effect of bottom-up self-organisation.

---

38 Prigogine and Stengers, *Order out of Chaos*, p. 207. In the 19th century, Nietzsche had already criticised contemporary physiological and biological thought for only understanding organisms in terms of adaptation (in the sense of optimisation): "it fails to appreciate the paramount superiority enjoyed by those plastic forces of spontaneity, aggression, and encroachment with their new interpretations and tendencies, to the operation of which adaptation is only a natural corollary." Friedrich Nietzsche, *The Genealogy of Morals*, II 12 (Dover Publications, 2003), p. 52.

39 Waldrop, *Complexity*, p. 294.

The worldview constituted by chaoplexity marks a seismic shift away from the dominant conceptions of the natural world. No longer is order to be seen as the product of a natural tendency towards equilibrium. On the contrary, it is with non-equilibrium that order emerges from chaos, at the point where instability and creative mutation allow for the genesis of new forms and actions.[40] Consequently, the systems produced through these processes of self-organisation have distinct emergent features which cannot be understood solely through an analysis of their atomistic components since it is their patterns of interaction which constitute their complexity. In the field of genetics, this has lead to a break from an understanding of strands of genes in DNA as a biochemical computer executing a genetic program in favour of the view that the genome, the complete set of genes in an organism, "forms a vast interconnected network, rich in feedback loops, in which genes directly indirectly regulate each other's activities."[41] Hence, according to Francesco Varela, "the genome is not a linear array of independent genes (manifesting as traits) but a highly interwoven network of multiple reciprocal effects mediated through repressors and depressors, exons and introns, jumping genes, and even structural proteins."[42] Nevertheless, complexity remains within the informational paradigm since these non-linear interactions "do not have to be physical, they can also be thought of as the transference of *information*."[43]

Complex systems also tend to be open systems in their interactions with their environment, as such their borders may not always be easy to ascertain. Consequently, these characteristics pose many analytical challenges and have major implications for the approach of any model or simulation of a complex system, as King points out:

Rather than trying to figure out all the chains of causality, the [non-linear] modeller looks for nodes where feedback loops join and tries to capture as many of the important loops as possible in the system's "picture." Rather than shaping the model to make a forecast about future events or to exercise some central control, the non-linear modeller is content to perturb the model, trying out different variables in order to learn about the system's critical points and its

---

40   Prigogine and Stengers, *Order out of Chaos*, p. 287.

41   Capra, *The Web of Life*, p. 199.

42   Ibid.

43   King, *Social Science and Complexity*, pp. 76-77.

homeostasis (resistance to change). The modeller is not seeking to control the complex system by quantifying it and mastering its causality; (s)he wants to increase his/her "intuitions" about how the system works so s(he) can interact with it more harmoniously.[44]

As with chaos theory, the traditional goal of attaining complete and precise quantitative knowledge of a system – and with that the possibility of gaining full control of it – gives way to a more limited and qualitative understanding which relies more on a certain "intuition", perhaps the same continuous learning process described by the theory of complex adaptive systems. Indeed Gell-Mann sees schemata and adaptive learning at the heart of all cognitive processes.

Decentralised self-organising systems are also better equipped than centralised systems to deal with limited predictability and contingency. According to the biologist Christopher Langton, "since it's effectively impossible to cover every conceivable situation, top-down systems are forever running into combinations of events they don't know how to handle. They tend to be touchy and fragile, and they all too often grind to a halt in a dither of indecision."[45] In contrast, decentralised systems of quasi-autonomous units can operate more effectively and with a greater degree of adaptability on the basis of the local calculations of the networked agents constituting them.

Conclusion

Whereas early cybernetics had focused primarily on self-regulating and stabilising systems, the sciences of complexity and chaos which followed have studied self-organising systems which develop emergent properties through non-linear relationships and positive feedback mechanisms. While the former were interested in stable systems maintaining themselves and converging towards a determined goal (homeostasis), the latter have turned to the decentralised networked processes by which complex adaptive systems emerge, change, and reproduce themselves (autopoiesis and self-organisation).

---

44   King, *Social Science and Complexity*, p. 54.

45   Waldrop, *Complexity*, p. 279.

These two approaches are not contradictory *per se*; rather the sciences of self-organisation see the self-regulating systems studied by early cyberneticists as only special cases within a broader study of systems. There is continuity in that systems remain the focus of analysis with the whole privileged over the parts and information the key operational concept. Circularity is also central to both approaches but these differ with regard to the circular processes which are emphasised. Early cybernetics saw positive feedback as essentially undesirable since it took systems away from their equilibrium and could even threaten their dissolution with order giving way to disorder (entropy). Chaoplexic theorists have on the other hand turned to positive feedback in order to explain systemic change and seemingly unpredictable yet deterministic forms of behaviour – here apparent disorder finds its own order.

In summary, the discoveries of chaoplexity can be condensed into three main points to carry through to the rest of this study:

- non-linearity and sensitivity to initial conditions as observed in chaotic systems impose severe limits on attempts to predict the behaviour of such systems. Precise quantitative analysis must yield to a more qualitative understanding via the identification of more or less hidden patterns in the system's behaviour;
- decentralised and distributed network relations and positive feedback allow for the bottom-up emergence and evolution of complex systems;
- complexity and adaptability are greatest at the "edge-of-chaos" where systemic structure can be retained but is also at its most flexible and creative. Such systems are best suited to responding to contingency and unpredictability.

Having established the fundamental claims of the new non-linear sciences, we can now turn to their growing influence within military thought and examine the emerging theories and practices of the latest regime in the scientific way of warfare: *chaoplexic warfare*.

Towards Chaoplexic Warfare? Network-Centric Warfare and the Non-Linear Sciences

The fundamentally complex and interactive nature of war generates uncertainty. Uncertainty is not merely an existing environmental condition; it is a natural byproduct of war.

US Marine Corps Command and Control Doctrine, 1996[1]

Possibly the single most transforming thing in our force will not be a weapons system, but a set of interconnections.

Donald Rumsfeld[2]

If the pairings of mechanism and clockwork, thermodynamics and the engine, and cybernetics and the computer can all be related to specific contemporary approaches to the conduct of war, does the emergence of sciences of chaos and complexity alongside the figure of the network herald the appearance of a new chaoplexic way of warfare? On one level, there is ample evidence of the impact the non-linear sciences are having on the development of technologies with potential military applica-

---

1   *MCDP 6: Command and Control*, United States Marine Corps, 1996, p. 55.

2   Tim Weiner, "A 'God's-Eye View' of the Battlefield", *The New York Times*, Nov. 20, 2004.

tions. Indeed these have ramifications for the development of virtually all technologies deemed high priority by the military, including but not limited to semiconductor materials, microelectronics circuits, software engineering, high-performance computing, machine intelligence and robotics, simulation and modeling, radar, sensors, signal and image processing, and biotechnology.[3] However, this chapter will not be concerning itself with these direct applications of chaos and complexity theories to technological development but rather with the manner in which their concepts and principles can be seen working through present theories and practices of warfare. The non-linear sciences have clearly permeated a sizeable portion of military literature in the United States, particularly the highly-influential one on network-centric warfare, now the official doctrine of the US Department of Defense. However, since we still stand at the threshold between cybernetic and chaoplexic eras, serious questions remain as to whether network-centric warfare really represents a full engagement with the principles and implications of the non-linear sciences or simply a re-branding of established cybernetic approaches.

The first section of the chapter will turn to the influential ideas of John Boyd, in particular his famous OODA loop, as they represent a first strain of military theory to draw from scientific conceptions to move beyond the limitations of the cybernetic understanding of warfare. Restoring contingency and unpredictability to military affairs with an understanding of the decision cycle analogous to that of complex adaptive systems, Boyd made creative change central to success in war. The second section turns more specifically to the role of uncertainty in war with a rereading of Clausewitz through the lens of the non-linear sciences and further considers the implications for the organisation and tactics of armed forces, a discussion that is carried on through to the following sections on networks and swarming. Finally, the chapter concludes with an analysis of the doctrine of network-centric warfare in the light of earlier sections, arguing that although ideas and practices derived from the new sciences

---

3   Glenn E. James, "Chaos Theory: The Essentials for Military Applications" (Naval War College, Newport, Rhode Island, Center for Naval Warfare Studies, Newport Paper No. 10, Oct. 1996), p. 4. Panel on Mathematics (Nonlinear Science and the Navy), Naval Studies Board, Commission on Physical Sciences, Mathematics, and Applications, National Research Council, "Nonlinear Science" (Washington DC: National Academy Press, 1997).

are emerging within it, they are yet to fully emancipate themselves from many of the central assumptions underpinning cybernetic warfare.

John Boyd and the OODA "loop"

John Boyd is a crucial pivotal figure in the emergence of scientifically in-spired military thought which, in the aftermath of the Vietnam War, began to challenge many of the entrenched principles of cybernetic warfare. One of the most successful fighter pilots in the history of the US Air Force (he was known as "Forty-Second Boyd" for his ability to defeat any opponent in aerial combat in less than forty seconds), Boyd developed a theory of aerial combat and was closely involved with the development of the F-15 and F-16 fighter planes. If Boyd is increasingly considered to be one of the most important military thinkers of recent times, he never wrote a key text, preferring instead a few short articles and numerous briefings to both military and civilian audiences. While Boyd was something of an iconoclast whose uncompromising stance and unconventional ideas generated hostil-ity from the Air Force hierarchy, his ideas have gained widespread exposure within the US military. The first organisation to adopt his ideas, and which remains probably the one that has stayed closest to their original spirit, is the Marine Corps. Boyd was closely involved in the elaboration of the Corps's 1989 military manual, *Warfighting* (subsequently updated in 1997), which will be discussed in the next section.

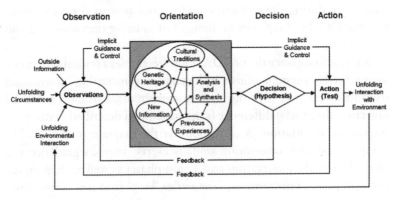

Figure 12: John Boyd's OODA "loop"[4]

---

4   Based on Boyd's sketch in John Boyd, "The Essence of Winning and Losing" (Briefing, Jan. 1996)

His most enduring contribution was the elaboration of the OODA "loop" (Figure 12), a theory of the decision-making process of the fighter pilot which subsequently became extended to all aspects of warfare, including the strategic dimension.

OODA stands for Observe-Orient-Decide-Act and seeks to model the decision-making process a combatant goes through when engaged in the warfighting environment. It is effectively a cognitive theory that can be applied to any situation, which accounts for its current enthusiastic adoption in business management literature. In the *observation* phase, the actor (or system) absorbs information from his environment, his situation within it, and the actions of his adversary. In the *orientation* phase, the actor interprets this information through an existing framework of analysis which creates meaning, discerns existing opportunities and threats, and provides a range of responses to initiate. The *decision* phase sees the actor commit to a course of *action* which is subsequently carried out in the following phase. Not only does the actor then return to the observation phase on the basis of the new information following from the action phase and consequent unfolding interaction with the environment, but feedback loops are operating between all stages in the cycle and the observation phase as the actor continually absorbs new information in order to adjust his frameworks and behaviour accordingly. For Boyd, the OODA "loop" was applicable across all levels of warfighting from the individual combatant to command and control structures: "the process of observation-orientation-decision-action represents what takes place during the command and control process – which means that the OODA "loop" can be thought of as being the command and control loop."[5]

While at first glance the OODA "loop" resembles a typical cybernetic loop whereby a system adjusts its behaviour to incoming information from its interaction with the environment in order to meet a desired objective, the crucial difference is the stage Boyd described as the most important: orientation. A closer look at the diagram of the OODA "loop" reveals that orientation actually exerts "implicit guidance and control" over the observation and action phases as well as shaping the decision phase. Furthermore, "the entire 'loop' (not just orientation)

5   John R. Boyd, "Organic Design for Command and Control" (Briefing - May 1987).

is an ongoing many-sided implicit cross-referencing process of projection, empathy, correlation, and rejection" in which all elements of the "loop" are simultaneous active.[6] In this sense, the OODA "loop" is not truly a cycle and is presented sequentially only for convenience of exposition (hence the scare quotes around "loop").

With the orientation phase, Boyd allows for the analytical framework itself to be modified through the comparison of observations of the external world with the system's internal framework, and thus for the system to act in new, unforeseen, ways. He distinguishes between two different processes that occur during orientation: "analysis (understanding the observations in the context of pre-existing patterns of knowledge) and synthesis (creating new patterns of knowledge when existing patterns do not permit the understanding needed to cope with novel circumstances)."[7] Boyd lists several elements which come into play in determining new frameworks (cultural traditions, genetic heritage, previous experiences, new information) but these are less important than the very principle that such frameworks can and must change.

Cybernetic warfare conceptualised as a negative feedback system necessitates a complete modelling of war in which all factors and parameters have to be accounted for. Indeed for a negative feedback system to adjust to changes in the environment, it must be designed so that all eventualities have been foreseen and/or all parameters to be monitored have been designated; otherwise, it will be enable to initiate the required self-correcting behaviour. This fuels attempts to effect a systemic closure of our understanding of the phenomenon of war that characterise the drive of operations research and systems analysis to model and simulate war. However, Boyd explicitly rejects the possibility of such a final and total understanding of war and points to the irreducibly incomplete and evanescent character of any theoretical framework seeking to encapsulate reality.

Indeed Boyd repeatedly insists that regular overhauls of such frameworks are both necessary and unavoidable. Invoking the second law of thermodynamics, Boyd postulates that, as closed systems, internal

---

6   Boyd, "The Essence of Winning and Losing".

7   Chuck C. Spinney, "Genghis John", *Proceedings*, US Naval Institute, July 1997, pp. 42-47.

frameworks are unavoidably subject to rising entropy as the mismatch between a changing environment and model increases.[8] For Boyd, entropy here designates "the potential for doing work, the capacity for taking action, or the degree of confusion and disorder associated with any physical or information activity."[9] Tinkering with the inner structure of the framework in order to preserve it is a self-defeating effort: "any inward-oriented and continued effort to improve the match-up of concept with observed reality will only increase the degree of mismatch."[10] Rigidly adhering to the same closed model of reality leads to chaos (entropy) and eventually death. In order to counter this, Boyd advocates taking apart existing frameworks and reconstructing new ones through a perpetually ongoing process of "destruction and creation":

People using theories or systems evolved from a variety of information will find it increasingly difficult and ultimately impossible to interact with and comprehend phenomena or systems that move increasingly beyond and away from that variety – that is, they will become more and more isolated from that which they are trying to observe or deal with, unless they exploit the new variety to modify their theories/systems or create new theories/systems.[11]

Akin to chaos and complexity theorists, Boyd reinvents entropy as the condition through which creation and novelty can emerge: "an entropy increase permits both the destruction or unstructuring of a closed system and the creation of a new system to nullify the march toward randomness and death."[12] The essence of Boyd's theory can be summed up by the following formula: "a changing and expanding

---

8   Boyd also draws on Heisenberg's quantum uncertainty principle (it is impos-
     sible to simultaneously fix or determine precisely the velocity and position of
     a particle or body at the quantum level) and Gödel's incompleteness theorem
     (no logical or mathematical system can be complete in the sense that there
     are necessarily propositions that cannot be either proven or disproven from
     the axioms or postulates of the system) to argue for the impossibility of ever
     achieving a perfectly consistent and stable system.

9   John R. Boyd, "Destruction and Creation" (1976).

10   Ibid.

11   John R. Boyd, "The Conceptual Spiral" (unpublished briefing).

12   Boyd, "Destruction and Creation".

universe of mental concepts matched to a changing and expanding universe of observed reality."[13]

The similarities between the OODA "loop" and Murray Gell-Mann's theory of schemata in complex adaptive systems are striking: "a complex adaptive system acquires information about its environment and its own interaction with that environment, identifying regularities in that information, condensing those regularities into a kind of 'schema' or model, and acting in the real world on the basis of that schema."[14] Gell-Mann's own diagram of the operational process of complex adaptive systems mirrors that of the OODA "loop" (Figure 13).[15] While Gell-Mann's cycle differs from Boyd's OODA "loop" in that in that it is truly sequential and lacks the latter's complex feedback loops and "implicit guidance and control" which prevent it from being a straightforward cycle,[16] the essential remains that both theories postulate the need for ever-changing conceptual frameworks to cope with novelty. Indeed Gell-Mann insists on the perpetually evolving nature of schemata when faced with new information. In Mark Taylor's words:

When there are too many discrepancies between the theory and the data of experience, new ideas must be explored and concepts formulated. If the input of the so-called real world cannot be effectively processed, the schema either adapts or becomes obsolete.[17]

---

13   Ibid.

14   Gell-Mann, *The Quark and the Jaguar*, p. 17. One could also note similarities between Boyd's process of synthesis of new frameworks and the ideas of Thomas Kuhn concerning the emergence and collapse of scientific paradigms.

15   The similarity between Gell-Mann's diagram and Boyd's OODA "loop" has been independently observed by Frans Osinga in his in-depth examination of Boyd's ideas and of his personal library. Osinga's study provides the most thorough discussion of Boyd's thought to date and is particularly valuable in detailing the extent to which the military thinker was influenced by scientific developments. Frans Osinga, *Science, Strategy and War: The Strategic Theory of John Boyd* (Abingdon, UK: Routledge, 2007).

16   This particular insight is owed to a personal communication with Chet Richards, one of Boyd's former close associates.

17   Mark C. Taylor, *The Moment of Complexity*, p. 206.

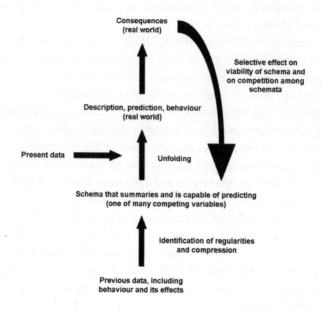

Figure 13: Diagram of the functional organisation of a complex adaptive system[18]

Certainly, Boyd's theory became no less ambitious in the scope of phenomena it eventually strove to explain. According to Grant Hammond, the OODA "loop" is nothing less than a theory of life since the "process of seeking harmony with one's environment, growing, interacting with others, adapting, isolating oneself when necessary, winning, siring offspring, losing, contributing what one can, learning, and ultimately dying – is for Boyd reducible to a series of OODA 'loops.'"[19]

For Chuck Spinney, a close collaborator of Boyd, the connections between the OODA "loop" and developments in the field of complexity and evolutionary biology are clear:

Each of us bases decisions and actions on observations of the outside world that are filtered through mental models that orient us to the opportunities and threats posed by these observations [...] these mental models, sometimes called paradigms, *shape* and are *shaped by* the evolving relationship between

---

18   Reproduced from Gell-Mann, *The Quark and the Jaguar*, p. 25.

19   Grant T. Hammond, "The Essential Boyd". http://www.belisarius.com/mod-ern_business_strategy/hammond/essential_boyd.htm.

the individual organism and its external environment [...] Evolutionary biologists, ethologists, and cyberneticists will immediately recognise that the
words "shape" and "shaped by" tell us the OODA loop is the product of a co-
evolutionary interaction. Since all co-evolutionary processes embody positive
as well as negative feedback loops, the OODA loop is necessarily a non-linear
system and will exhibit unpredictable emergent behaviour.[20]

This notion of unpredictability is crucial since Boyd believes in a perpetually renewed world that is "uncertain, everchanging, unpredictable"[21]
and thus requires continually revising, adapting, destroying and recre-
ating our theories and systems to deal with it. Understandings of the
world are always playing catch-up with reality and our systems must
consequently remain open to structural and behavioural change. Such a
stance is in perfect accordance with the systems described by complexity
theorists: "since the system has to cope with unpredictable change in the
environment, the development of the structure cannot be contained in
a rigid [deterministic] programme that controls the behaviour of the
system."[22] Therefore conceptual frameworks must stay open to change
on the basis of new information from the external world and avoid at
all cost closing on themselves, interpreting all new information through
the prism of rigid and untouchable schemata.[23]

Boyd thus moves from the dominant view of uncertainty as a threat
that must be overcome to one in which it is an irreducible characteristic of being and nothing less than the very condition of possibility of
change and creativity:

Ambiguity is central to Boyd's vision. It is not something to be feared but
something that is a given. Being creative organisms, we should welcome it and

---

20   Chuck Spinney, "Asleep at the Switch in Versailles... or ... Why Nonlinear Re-
      alities Overwhelm Linear Visions ... or ... Why did Slobo Cave?" (Defense and
      the National Interest, Sept. 6, 1999) http://www.d-n-i.net/fcs/comments/c317.
      htm.

21   Boyd, "The Conceptual Spiral" .

22   King, *Social Science and Complexity*, p. 79.

23   "The most dangerous internal state of an OODA 'loop' occurs when the orien-
      tation process becomes so powerful that it force fits the organism's observations
      into fitting a preconceived template, even when those observations threaten the
      relevance of that template." Chuck Spinney, "Is America Inside Its Own OODA
      Loop?" (Defense and the National Interest, Jan. 26, 2005) http://www.d-n-i.
      net/fcs/comments/c536.htm.

make use of it. The world is ambiguous. [...] We never have complete and perfect information. [...] Our decisions and actions are hypotheses to be tested against this ambiguous environment. The best way to succeed in it is to revel in ambiguity.[24]

Not only are ambiguity and unpredictability the conditions of true creativity but they are also assets to be exploited against one's opponents. Indeed predictable patterns of military behaviour hand a crucial advantage to the adversary and exposes oneself to defeat. Conversely, making one's actions unpredictable unsettles the opponent's own OODA "loop" as he strives to discern a pattern amidst the "noise" created by unpredicted actions. Since war pits opposing OODA "loops", the most effective and evolutive "loop" will prevail: "you can either go through the OODA "loop" cycle faster than your opponent or you can vary your tempos and rhythms so your opponent cannot keep up with you."[25] The more overwhelmed the opponent is, the more likely he is likely to fold back on his existing schemata, desperately trying to match existing frameworks that are becoming increasingly isolated from reality until his final collapse. This is very much in accordance with a Clausewitzian understanding of war as a "clash of opposing wills" in which the ultimate target is the adversary's will and ability to resist rather than his physical capabilities.[26]

The idea that victory depends on getting inside the enemy's OODA "loop" has become commonplace in contemporary military literature, particularly in the network-centric variety, to the extent that it has

---

24   Hammond, "The Essential Boyd". For all the benefits of this condition of permanent ambiguity, there are also risks which Spinney discusses with reference to notions from chaos and complexity theory: "Boyd showed that an OODA Loop (the decision cycle of an individual or any collection of individuals) is an open, far-from-equilibrium process. This is a crucial finding: students of chaos theory, systems control theory, or the theory of evolution will immediately recognize the implications of such a construction: the OODA Loop is capable of expansion and growth, but it is also inherently unpredictable and its pathway can lead also to chaos, because it incorporates positive as well as negative feedback control loops." Spinney, "Is America Inside Its Own OODA Loop?"

25   Hammond, "The Essential Boyd".

26   While Boyd was often a fierce critic of Clausewitz and particularly of his emphasis on the destruction of the enemy's army in battle, it is this author's opinion that there are many other aspects of the Prussian's work, notably his notions of friction and the fog of war, which chime with Boyd's own conceptions.

become something of an incantation that is not always based on a consistent and faithful understanding of Boyd's ideas. This argument will be developed further below but at present one important point bears exposition. Indeed it is crucial to note that when Boyd talks about a "quicker OODA 'loop'", he does not simply mean cycling through the sequence of observation-orientation-decision-action faster but rather is referring to all the cross-referencing connections that make the OODA into a complex adaptive system. Hence, in order to confound and defeat an opponent, the OODA "loop" must be "more subtle, more indistinct, more irregular, and quicker – yet appear otherwise."[27] Initiative, surprise and deception are thus key; merely increasing the speed at which one acts by responding to stimulus from pre-establised templates (i.e. without truly orienting) is not a quickening of the OODA "loop", a point missed by many subsequent theorists.

A crucial distinction between Boyd's ideas and those governing cybernetic warfare, and one that parallels the development of chaos and complexity theories, is his focus on the conditions of emergence and transformation of systems through information rather than merely the manner in which information is processed by a fixed organisational schema. Arquilla and Ronfeldt seem to be making a similar point when they seek to distinguish the notion of information as *process* from that of *structure*. For them, the notion of information-processing, which they attribute to Shannon, Wiener and the cyberneticists, useful as it may be, tends to overemphasise the importance of technological infrastructure to the detriment of organisational arrangements.[28] They argue that:

All structures contain embedded information. Where there is structure – or pattern or organisation – there is information. Somehow the amount of structure and the amount of information go together. Embedded information is what enables a structure – be it physical, biological, or social – to hold its form, to remain coherent, even to evolve and adapt. All forms of organisation thus depend on embedded information; they do not have shape, and cannot retain their shape, without it.[29]

---

27   John R. Boyd, "Patterns of Conflict" (Presentation, Dec. 1986).

28   Arquilla and Ronfeldt, "Looking Ahead: Preparing For Information-Age Conflict" in John Arquilla and David Ronfeldt (eds), *In Athena's Camp*, pp. 442-446.

29   Ibid., pp. 444-445.

Arquilla and Ronfeldt contrast information as merely processed by a system with information as the codification of the structure of the system itself. One recognises here again the shift from the regulation of a system through information which concerned early cybernetics to the question of the self-production and self-organisation of chaoplexic systems.

Boyd's other major statement pertained to the inevitable uncertainty that permeates the activity of warfare, rejecting the drive for predictability of cybernetic warfare. This stance also echoes the discoveries of the non-linear sciences and has crucial implications for the type of control that armies should strive for. Hence we must now turn a closer eye to this new understanding of chaos and uncertainty to see how it allows for a new reading of Clausewitz and which lessons the new military theorists are drawing from it.

Embracing Uncertainty: The Chaoplexic Clausewitz

In 1992, Alan Beyerchen published an influential article that looked at Clausewitz's writings through the lens of developments in the non-linear sciences of chaos and complexity. Indeed Clausewitz's insistence on unpredictability and the imperfection of knowledge in the practice of war appears to echo similar claims made by the new sciences. Beyerchen finds in the strategist's writings three considerations of unpredictability in war: from *interaction*, from *friction*, and from *chance*.

Interaction is inherent in war as it "is not an exercise of the will directed at inanimate matter, as is the case with the mechanical arts" but rather is "directed at an animate object that reacts," effectively an opposing will (this is the crux of Clausewitz's disagreement with mechanistic theorists of war like Jomini and von Bülow).[30] This reaction locks both wills and forces into feedback loops whereby positive feedback loops can cause run-away processes – Clausewitz's tendency for war to become absolute – and make specific prediction impossible:

[Military action] must expect positive reactions, and the process of interaction that results. Here we are not concerned with the problem of calculating such

---

30   Beyerchen, "Clausewitz, Nonlinearity and the Unpredictability of War", pp. 72-73.

reactions [...] but rather with the fact that the very nature of interaction is bound to make it unpredictable.[31]

Friction is quintessentially non-linear as with it Clausewitz concerns himself with the disproportionate effect small events can have on a battle or campaign:

Success is not due simply to general causes. Particular factors can often be decisive – details only known to those who were on the spot [...] while issues can be decided by chances and incidents so minute as to figure in histories simply as anecdotes.[32]

Non-linear phenomena, characterised by positive feedback loops and sensitivity to initial conditions, are precisely those that allow for such an amplification of "minute incidents." Another way of stating this in the phraseology of complexity theory is to say that "local causes can have global effects."

As well as relating friction to the thermodynamic theories that were emerging at Clausewitz's time and notably the concept of entropy (see chapter 3), Beyerchen also connects friction to information theory:

The second meaning of "friction" is the information theory sense of what we have recently come to call "noise" in the system. Entropy and information have some interesting formal similarities, because both can be thought of as measuring the possibilities for the behaviour of systems. According to information theory, the more possibilities a system embodies, the more "information" it contains. Constraints on those possibilities are needed to extract signals from the noise. Clausewitz understands that plans and commands are signals that inevitably get garbled amid noise in the process of communicating them down and through the ranks even in peacetime, much less under the effects of physical exertion and danger in combat. His well-known discussion of the difficulty in obtaining accurate intelligence presents the problem from the inverse perspective, as noise permeates the generation and transmission of information rising upward through the ranks. From this perspective, his famous metaphor of the "fog" of war is not so much about a dearth of information as how distortion and overload of information produce uncertainty as to the actual state of affairs.[33]

---

31   Clausewitz quoted in Beyerchen, "Clausewitz, Nonlinearity and the Unpredictability of War", p. 73.

32   Clausewitz, *On War*, translated by Michael Howard and Peter Paret (Princeton University Press, 1984), p. 595.

33   Beyerchen, "Clausewitz, Nonlinearity and the Unpredictability of War", pp. 76-77.

As we saw previously with respect to the Vietnam War, misperceptions and uncertainties in military affairs are fuelled by an inability to distinguish relevant from false information (signal from noise) and excess volumes of data can hinder more than assist in this.

Chance is Clausewitz's blanket term for the uncertainty inherent to war and constitutes one part of his famous trinity, standing between the poles of irrationality (the natural force of violence, hatred and enmity among the people) and rationality (the instrumental subordination of war to government policy). The very metaphor Clausewitz employs to describe the complex interplay of the three components of the trinity – "our task therefore is to develop a theory that maintains a balance between these three tendencies, like an object suspended between three magnets" – has the potential to be read in a markedly non-linear fashion.[34] Indeed, in the popular scientific experiment the Prussian officer is referring to, a pendulum will first oscillate erratically between competing points of attraction before settling into an equidistant rest position. The pattern of oscillation taken in any given experiment is unpredictable and for all practical purpose irreproducible since a high sensitivity to initial conditions ensures that minute differences in the location of the object as it starts its motions result in wildly different patterns. This image offers a perfect illustration of Clausewitz's belief that every war is unique and will follow a singular course that cannot be predicted in detail.

In order to further unpack the notion of chance, Beyerchen calls on French nineteenth- century mathematician Henri Poincaré to distinguish between three ways in which chance manifests itself to us and which can be all found in Clausewitz:

- as a statistically random phenomenon (the traditional understanding of stochastic chaos, best analysed through the use of probabilities – Clausewitz's references to war as the play of probabilities and analogies to gambling);
- as the amplification of a micro-cause (deterministic forms of chaos in systems showing sensitivity to initial conditions, as seen in friction);
- as a function of our analytical blindness.[35]

---

34   Ibid., p. 69.

35   Beyerchen, "Clausewitz, Nonlinearity and the Unpredictability of War", p. 78.

The difference between the first two forms of chance is crucial since the former is truly random and unpredictable while the latter is actually a highly ordered form of disorder as considered by chaos theorists. If sensitivity to initial conditions and irreducible constraints on the precision of measurements impose limits on the long-term predictability of systems characterised by this form of chaos, the discovery of deterministic processes behind certain phenomena has shifted our understanding of them away from the first category of stochastic chance. This is the central paradox of chaos theory and the non-linear sciences in general: linear, Newtonian concepts and methodologies are found to be inapplicable to a vast range of phenomena which have to be tackled by approaches which cannot apprehend them in a similarly precise and predictive manner but, at the same time, the discovery has been made that phenomena which previously appeared entirely random have in fact a complex and identifiable structure. On one hand, the original promise of absolute control and omniscience of the Newtonian or cybernetic paradigms have to be abandoned. On the other, a new form of less direct and precise control and knowledge seems within reach to replace the former. In the words of Katherine Hayles, chaos has been "bound."[36] This implies new ways of directing armies on the battlefield, as will be discussed below.

The last manifestation of chance – as a function of our analytical blindness – is a result of our tendency to partition the world into discrete pieces to be analysed in isolation from one another. When two such pieces interact, we are faced with phenomena that are unexplainable to us and appear as the product of chance. What is required is a holistic approach that does not seek to isolate open systems from their environment but apprehends their profound interconnectedness, as is increasingly common in contemporary science. Clausewitz himself was clearly already aware of the limitations of traditional analysis:

It is bound to be easy if one restricts oneself to the most immediate aims and effects. This may be done quite arbitrarily if one isolates the matter from its setting and studies it only under those conditions. But in war, as in life generally, all parts of the whole are interconnected and thus the effects produced,

---

36   Hayles, *Chaos Bound.*

however small their cause, must influence all subsequent military operations and modify their final outcome to some degree, however slight.[37]

Whether mediated or not through Clausewitz, the chaoplexic lens invites an understanding of war in which uncertainty, unpredictability and change are central. This in turn implies a particular approach to the conduct of warfare and the organisation of armies, a development that is being increasingly represented in military thought. As Bar-Yam puts it:

In recent years it has become widely recognised in the military that war is a complex encounter between complex systems in complex environments. Complex systems are formed of multiple interacting elements whose collective actions are difficult to infer from those of the individual parts, predictability is severely limited, and response to external forces does not scale linearly with the applied force. It is reasonable to postulate that warfare can be better executed by those who understand complex systems than those who focus on simple linear, transparent, classically logical, Newtonian constructs.[38]

If, as the US Marine Corps's 1989 warfighting manual postulates, "the occurrences of war will not unfold like clockwork," it is futile to attempt to "impose precise, positive control over events"[39] and "it is unreasonable to expect command and control to provide precise, predictable, and mechanistic order to a complex undertaking like war."[40] As opposed to a process obeying eternal laws which can be uncovered and exploited to design infallible tactics, war is here an amorphous and constantly renewed phenomenon. Or to put it in Clausewitz's words, "war is a chameleon"; its form fluctuates and mutates, and only its basic nature is invariant. The successful army must internalise this lesson and constitute itself accordingly:

Like friction and uncertainty, fluidity is an integral attribute of the nature of war. Each episode in war is the temporary result of a unique combination of circumstances, requiring an original solution. But no episode can be viewed in

---

37   Clausewitz quoted in Beyerchen, "Clausewitz, Nonlinearity and the Unpredict-ability of War", p. 82.

38   Yaneer Bar-Yam, "Complexity of Military Conflict: Multiscale Complex Systems Analysis of Littoral Warfare", New England Complex Systems Institute, 2003, p. 1 http://necsi.org/projects/yaneer/SSG_NECSI_3_Litt.pdf.

39   *FMFM1: Warfighting*, US Marine Corps, 1989.

40   *MCDP 6: Command and Control*, US Marine Corps, pp. 46–47.

isolation. Rather, each merges with those that precede and follow it – shaped by the former and shaping the conditions of the latter – creating a continuous, fluctuating fabric of activity replete with fleeting opportunities and unforeseen events. Success depends in large part on the ability to adapt to a constantly changing situation.[41]

The ability to adapt in such fluid situations is dependent on being able to discern patterns from the seemingly random and here chaos theory provides new tools and insights. For Andrew Ilachinski, "implicit in any application of the 'new sciences' to land combat [...] is the idea that there is some latent order underlying what appears on the surface to be irregular and chaotic."[42] Ilachinski dubs "intuition" "the ability to perceive patterns in an otherwise patternless process,"[43] echoing Clause-witz's notions of "genius" and "coup d'oeil" that constitute "that superb display of divination" in the successful commander:

Circumstances vary so enormously in war, and are so indefinable, that a vast array of factors has to be appreciated – mostly in light of probabilities alone. The man responsible for evaluating the whole must bring to his task the quality of intuition that perceives the truth at every point. Otherwise a chaos of opinions and considerations would arise, and fatally entangle judgment.[44]

The recognition of truth (or pattern) is what allows for a fleeting discernment of order from the chaos of the battlefield (reflected in a conceptual chaos in the mind) and appropriate responsiveness to the ever-fluctuating conditions of war. We are reminded here of Boyd's frameworks of orientation and Gell-Mann's schemata.

Not only are closed and rigid systems unable to respond to the erup-tion of novelty and unexpected challenges but attempts to increase their performance exposes them to catastrophic breakdown. John Urry discusses this point generally in the context of complexity science but it bear clear parallels with military organisation and Boyd's own state-ments about the self-defeating nature of efforts to perfect the internal coherence of closed systems:

---

41   *Warfighting, FMFM1*, US Marine Corps.

42   Andrew Ilachinski, *Land Warfare and Complexity - Part I: Mathematical Back-ground and Technical Sourcebook* (Alexandria, VA: Center for Naval Analyses, July 1996), p. 27.

43   Ibid., p. 27.

44   Clausewitz, *On War*, p. 112.

Up to a point, tightening the connections between elements in the system will increase efficiency when everything works smoothly. But, if one small item goes wrong, then that can have a catastrophic knock-on effect throughout the system. The system literally switches over, from smooth functioning to interactively complex disaster.[45]

The implication is that the components within a system should be loosely connected together with a built-in redundancy and ability to reconfigure their positions within the network when necessary, allowing for the emergence of new behaviour and organisational arrangements. In other words, the military must be a complex adaptive system operating at the edge of chaos, a sentiment once again echoed in the Marines' doctrine:

This view sees the military organisation as an open system, interacting with its surroundings (especially the enemy), rather than as a closed system focused on internal efficiency. An effective command and control system provides the means to adapt to changing conditions. We can thus look at command and control as a process of continuous adaptation. […] Like a living organism, a military organization is never in a state of stable equilibrium but is instead in a continuous state of flux – continuously adjusting to its surroundings.[46]

In these conditions of perpetual flux, traditional conceptualisations of control have to be abandoned or redefined in favour of a more modest channelling – "the best we can hope for is to impose a general framework of order on the disorder, to prescribe the general flow of action rather than to try to control each event."[47] A new military doctrine and practice can only emerge by breaking with the command and control principles that governed cybernetic warfare during the Cold War, as suggested by Alberts and Hayes:

Control Theory requires both prediction and the existence of an adequate set of levers of control. […] [But] having effective, centrally managed levers that can control or even predictably influence a complex, adaptive system is far from guaranteed. […] In the Information Age, control needs to be thought about and approached differently. Control is not something that can be imposed on a complex adaptive system, particularly when there are many independent actors. Control, that is, ensuring that behavior stays within or moving to

---

45   Urry, *Global Complexity*, p. 35.

46   *MCDP 6: Command and Control*, United States Marine Corps, p. 46.

47   *FMFM1: Warfighting*, United States Marine Corps, 1989.

within acceptable bounds, can only be achieved indirectly. The most promising approach involves establishing, to the extent possible, a set of initial conditions that will *result* in the desired behavior. In other words, control is not achieved by imposing a parallel process, but rather emerges from influencing the behaviors of independent agents.[48]

If centralised control is no longer desirable and must give way to decentralised means for the coordination of "independent agents", a new organisational form is necessary to overcome the limitations of hierarchical structures. This form is that of the network.

The Age of the Network

The notion of the network spread rapidly throughout public and academic discourse in the last decade of the twentieth century, in no small part due to the spectacular development and diffusion of the Internet. In his seminal opus on network society, Manuel Castells argued that networks constitute no less than "the new social morphology of our societies and the diffusion of networking logic substantially modifies the operation and outcomes in the processes of production, experience, power and culture."[49] The network is now commonly argued to be the rising form of social organisation in a world perceived as increasingly globalised and interconnected through time- and space-defying technologies of transport and telecommunications.

Unsurprisingly, much of the literature on the network form therefore connects its growth with the development of information and communication technologies (ICTs), pointing to the diffusion of computers,

---

48 David S. Alberts and Richard E. Hayes, *Power to the Edge – Command ... Control... in the Information Age* (Department of Defense CCRP, 2003), pp. 206-208.

49 For Castells, the network is intimately connected to the development of capitalism and late modernity in the last decades of the twentieth century. "Networks are appropriate instruments for a capitalist economy based on innovation, globalisation, and decentralised concentration; for work, workers and firms based on flexibility; for a culture of endless deconstruction and reconstruction; for a polity geared towards the instant processing of new values and public moods; and for a social organisation aiming at the supersession of space and the annihilation of time." Manuel Castells, *The Rise of the Network Society* - second edn (Oxford: Blackwell, 2000), p. 500.

mobile telecommunications and the Internet. The Internet famously finds its roots in a military program of the 1960s and 1970s under the US Department of Defense's ARPA, an agency created in 1958 in response to the Soviet launch of Sputnik and tasked to act as a technological "engine" for the DoD by carrying out long term projects with potential military applications.[50] In 1962, ARPA created the Information Processing Technology Office (IPTO), led by J.C.R. Licklider, a veteran of the Macy Conferences on cybernetics, for the purpose of furthering research from the Semi-Automatic Ground Environment (SAGE) program, the Cold War radar and air defence system discussed previously. The resulting ARPANET became the first operational packet-switching network.[51] After the military spun off the ARPANET to the civilian sector, what was to become the Internet took on a life of its own, eventually reaching broader public awareness in the 1990s with wide-ranging effects on business practices and social interaction. Alongside the diffusion of other telecommunication systems, the Internet has become a central piece of an emerging network culture which has promoted decentralised forms of organisation and non-hierarchical channels of communication.

Castells sums up a now commonly held belief when stating that "networks are proliferating in all domains of the economy and society, outcompeting and outperforming vertically organised corporations and centralised bureaucracies."[52] While of course the network form of social organisation *per se* long predates the development and widespread diffusion of contemporary ICTs, these have certainly acted as enablers

---

50   The agency is now known as DARPA (Defense Advanced Research Project Agency) and is still an important institution within the US military.

51   An enduring myth is that the rationale behind ARPANET was to build a telecommunications network able to survive a nuclear attack. While a RAND report did consider this eventuality, the aims of the ARPANET program were more general in simply seeking to improve the resilience and cost-effectiveness of existing telecommunications based on circuit switching. Resistance to network losses was certainly part of the project but was not initially conceived for the specific context of a nuclear war. See Barry M. Leiner, Vinton G. Cerf, David D. Clark, Robert E. Kahn, Leonard Kleinrock, Daniel C. Lynch, Jon Postel, Larry G. Roberts and Stephen Wolff, "A Brief History of the Internet" (The Internet Society, 2003) http://www.isoc.org/internet/history/brief.shtml.

52   Manuel Castells, *The Internet Galaxy* (Oxford, New York: Oxford University Press, 2001), p. 1

for the formation and increased efficiency of social networks, thereby challenging the previously dominant hierarchical form.[53] For Arquilla and Ronfeldt:

The information revolution is strengthening the importance of all forms of networks – social networks, communications networks, etc. The network form is very different from the institutional form. While institutions (large ones in particular) are traditionally built around hierarchies and aim to act on their own, multi-organisational networks consist of (often small) organisations or parts of institutions that have linked together to act jointly. The information revolution favors the growth of such networks by making it possible for diverse, dispersed actors to communicate, consult, coordinate, and operate together across greater distances and on the basis of more and better information than ever before.[54]

While the technological infrastructure of the network is important, even more crucial are the actual dynamics of networks and here we find ourselves firmly within the conceptual landscape occupied by the chaoplexic sciences. Indeed the network form implies a decentralised, open, and adaptable form of organisation, naturally best suited to adjusting to a rapidly changing environment through the self-organising and emergent properties of the network. As Ian King puts it, "networking [is] a way of maintaining a low-level chaotic substrate so that – as in the brain – the chaos will from time to time give birth to an intellectual self-organising structure."[55] Similarly, for Castells, "a network-based social structure is a highly dynamic, open system, susceptible to innovating without threatening its balance."[56] In the context of military operations, the art of war becomes the harnessing of similarly fluid structures through informational exchanges between its interacting parts, a process in which information and communication technologies naturally play a vital role.

---

53   "While the networking form of social organisation has existed in other times and spaces, the new information technology paradigm provides the basis for its pervasive expansion throughout the entire social structure." Castells, *The Rise of the Network Society*, p. 500.

54   Arquilla and Ronfeldt, "Cyberwar is Coming!" in Arquilla and Ronfeldt (eds), *In Athena's Camp*, pp. 26-27.

55   King, *Social Science and Complexity*, p. 55.

56   Castells, *The Rise of the Network Society*, pp. 501-502.

Although much of this technology had been developed by the military, the latter only became aware of these social transformations belatedly, triggering animated discussion of the implications for military doctrine and practice. US practitioners looked particularly to business for inspiration, invoking Alvin and Heidi Toffler's mantra – "the way we make war reflects the way we make wealth"[57] – and emphasising the role of information superiority, adaptability, the flattening of management structures, increases in speed, and, above all, networks.

Arquilla and Ronfeldt have been among the longest-standing and most vocal proponents of networked organisation, arguing that new related types of conflict are emerging. Those actors which are most successfully adopting these new modes of conflict pose serious challenges to their more rigidly hierarchical rivals, typically established states and armies. Arquilla and Ronfeldt see these actors as particularly prominent "in the realms of low-intensity conflict – international terrorists, guerrilla insurgents, drug smuggling cartels, ethnic factions, as well as racial and tribal gangs."[58]

Since September 11, the focus has naturally been on al-Qaeda and the wider movement of radical Islamist militancy and terrorism. The nebulous and dispersed nature of these organisations has invited their analysis in terms of decentralised networks and complex adaptive systems. Thus al-Qaeda is seen as a decentralised and polymorphous network "with recursive operational and financial interrelationships dispersed geographically across numerous associated terrorist organisations that adapt, couple and aggregate in pursuit of common interests."[59] For Marion and Uhl-Bien, interactive non-linear bottom-up dynamics are behind the self-organisation of al-Qaeda in which bin Laden and the al-Qaeda leadership are an emergent phenomenon: "leaders do not create the system but rather are created by it, through a process

---

57   Alvin and Heidi Toffler, War and Anti-War: Survival at the Dawn of the 21st Century (Boston, MA and London: Little, Brown and Company, 1993).

58   Arquilla and Ronfeldt, "Cyberwar is Coming!" in Arquilla and Ronfeldt (eds), *In Athena's Camp*, p. 27.

59   Michael F. Beech, "Observing Al Qaeda Through the Lens of Complexity Theory: Recommendations for the National Strategy to Defeat Terrorism", Center for Strategic Leadership, US Army War College, July 2004 http://www.carlisle.army.mil/usacsl/Publications/S04-01.pdf.

of aggregation and emergence."[60] While a diffuse movement of Islamic radicalism coalesced to create terrorist networks from which the leadership could spring, the latter has also assisted the continued development of a decentralised movement by maintaining and fostering "a moderately coupled network, but one possessing internal structures that were loosely and tightly organised as appropriate."[61] The authors distinguish between loosely coupled networks in which the parts have functional independence, thus granting the system great resilience to large-scale perturbations, and tightly coupled networks in which the leadership imposes control mechanisms that enable it to direct activities and receive regular reports. In between these two poles, we find moderately coupled networks which allow some degree of directing by leadership but retain great resiliency. If the wider radical Islamist movement is only loosely coupled and individual terrorist cells are tightly coupled, the pre-9/11 al-Qaeda leadership network sat somewhere in between, performing the function of a galvanising interface.

Even in the case of single operation such as September 11, it has become increasingly clear that its planning and execution were far more decentralised than initially supposed. The different cells in the plot, although tightly coupled internally, functioned quasi-autonomously, and although they received some financial, logistical and training support from other parts of the organisation, were not exclusively dependent on them. Khalid Sheikh Mohammed, said to be the operational "mastermind" behind September 11 (a designation which, although commonly used in the media, is problematic as it suggests highly centralised planning and control) and now in American military custody, is alleged to have claimed that "the final decisions to hit which target with which plane was entirely in the hands of the pilots."[62] Khalid Sheikh Mohammed was only then subsequently informed of their decision in July 2001. According to this same testimony, bin Laden and the high ranks of the al-Qaeda organisation were also only very loosely informed of specific

---

60   Russ Marion and Mary Uhl-Bien, "Complexity Theory and Al-Qaeda: Examining Complex Leadership", Presentation given at Managing the Complex IV: A Conference on Complex Systems and the Management of Organizations, Fort Meyers, FL, Dec., 2002, p. 5.

61   Marion and Uhl-Bien, "Complexity Theory and Al-Qaeda", p. 27.

62   Substitution for the Testimony of Khaled Sheikh Mohammed http://news.bbc. co.uk/1/shared/bsp/hi/pdfs/06_04_06_testimony.pdf, p. 28.

details and had a very limited directing role. Many of bin Laden's close associates were never even made aware of the plot. This form of organisational and operational structure is one that is particularly alien to Western states and their hierarchical military and security apparatuses, as Mohammed himself recognises: "I know that the materialistic western mind cannot grasp the idea, and it is difficult for them to believe that the high officials in al-Qaeda do not know about operations carried out by its operatives, but this is how it works."[63]

The resilience and adaptability of the network has been further demonstrated by events following September 11 and the American response. Despite the loss of its host state of Afghanistan, a global crackdown on the organisation and its financial sources, and the military intervention of the sole superpower, it cannot be said that al-Qaeda, or at least the ideology and methods it promotes, have been defeated. If its original leadership has been mostly arrested, killed, or so severely restricted in its movements and communications as to render it operationally impotent,[64] it remains a powerful symbol for the Jihadist movement at wide. Endowed with an authority and prestige which enables it to claim responsibility for attacks in Madrid and London despite scant evidence of logistical or organisational connections to the responsible cells,[65] al-Qaeda's leadership has in a sense blended back into the loosely connected radical Islamist movement while giving a name and a face to the fluid and amorphous networks that compose it and crystallise at certain points to carry out violent actions – both for the West which tends to see al-Qaeda at every turn and for aspiring militants which see it as a model to follow.

---

63   Substitution for the Testimony of Khaled Sheikh Mohammed http://news.bbc. co.uk/1/shared/bsp/hi/pdfs/06_04_06_testimony.pdf, p. 55.

64   President Bush declared in his State of the Union address in Jan. 2004 that "We are tracking al-Qaeda around the world, and nearly two-thirds of their known leaders have now been captured or killed." George W. Bush, State of the Union Address, Jan. 20, 2004 http://www.whitehouse.gov/news/releases/2004/01/20040120-7.html.

65   "Madrid bombing probe finds no al-Qaida link", MSNBC, March 9, 2006 http://www.msnbc.msn.com/id/11753547/from/RL.1/. Mark Townsend, "Leak reveals official story of London bombings", *The Observer*, April 9, 2006 http://politics.guardian.co.uk/labour/story/0,,1750264,00.html.

A similar trend towards networked forms of organisation is presently observable across the spectrum of low-intensity conflict and criminal operations worldwide. Insurgents and guerrillas from Chechnya to Lebanon and Iraq have successfully employed small and flexible fighting units to foil the powerful state militaries of Russia, Israel and the United States.[66] In the criminal underworld, the loose confederation of organisations pursuing illicit activities which mushroomed in Russia after the collapse of the Soviet Union inaugurated a broader shift away from large centralized criminal associations. In the aftermath of the successful dismantling of the Cali and Medellín cartels in the 1990s, the Columbian drugs trade has shifted towards a network of several hundred smaller groups which spread activities more widely and is now considerably more resilient to traditional decapitation strikes aimed at taking out key leaders since operations have become far more decentralised. Likewise, the disruption of the Sicilian *Cosa Nostra* has seen ownership of the majority of the drug trade pass to the *'Ndrangheta* criminal organisation from Calabria which employs a more horizontal structure in which autonomous elements are held together by a common perspective and interests but do not form a single vertical organisation.[67]

Existing state structures remain ill-equipped to deal with these new forms of threats. For the new military theorists such as Arquilla and Ronfeldt, fire will have to be fought with fire and the changing security environment will require from states:

major innovations in organisational design, in particular a shift from hierarchies to networks. The traditional reliance on hierarchical design may have to be adapted to network-oriented models to allow greater flexibility, lateral connectivity, and teamwork across institutional boundaries. The traditional emphasis on command and control, a key strength of hierarchy, may have to give way to an emphasis on consultation and coordination, the crucial blocks of network designs.[68]

---

66   John Arquilla, *Worst Enemy: The Reluctant Transformation of the American Military* (Chicago, IL: Ivan R. Dee, 2008), pp. 158-166.

67   "Ancient Feuds and New Crimes", *GNOSIS* n. 3/2007 http://www.sisde.it/Gnosis/Rivista12.nsf/ServNavigE/13.

68   Arquilla and Ronfeldt, "Cyberwar is Coming!" in Arquilla and Ronfeldt (eds), *In Athena's Camp*, p. 45.

According to this view, the ability of the state to meet the challenges of the twenty-first century will hinge on its ability to appropriate the network form, whether in the political, administrative, policing, or military sphere. However, the authors recognise that it is not possible or even desirable for state actors to completely abandon hierarchies. The challenge facing the state is therefore to harness the flexibility and adaptability of networks while preserving some hierarchical features – hybridisation is the goal. The promise of networks in the military realm is to unlock the potential of new tactics made possible by this organisational form, chief among them that of *swarming*.

Harnessing the Swarm: Of Ants and Men

According to the new emerging military paradigm, operating as a net-worked force allows troops to act in ways which are denied to their hierarchical counterparts. Drawing further from the writings of complexity theorists and deploying biological and zoological metaphors, military theories appeal to the "swarm", the networks of distributed intelligence which enable bees, ants, and termites to evolve complex forms of collective behaviour on the basis of the simple rules of interaction of their individual members. Of particular interest is the resiliency and flexibility of these swarms as amorphous ensembles in which no single individual is critical to their continued existence and successful operation. Military swarms promise not only more adaptable and survivable forces but also new offensive and defensive tactics better suited to the contemporary battlespace.

Kevin Kelly contrasts the clock model whereby "you construct a system as a long string of sequential operations" with the swarm model, "systems ordered as a patchwork of parallel operations" where, in the absence of a chain of command "what emerges from the collective is not a series of critical individual actions but a multitude of simultaneous actions whose collective pattern is more important."[69] These two models constitute for Kelly the two theoretical poles of organisation and offer a trade-off between control and predictability on one hand and

---

69   Kevin Kelly, *Out of Control: The New Biology of Machines* (Reading: Cox and Wyman, 1994), p. 27.

adaptability and resilience on the other. Real-life systems most often lie somewhere in between these two poles and if the military is not attempting to completely dispense with hierarchy, it is now feeling the pull of the swarm pole most.

The fluidity of swarms allows these forms of social organisation to adapt more rapidly and effectively to the unforeseen. When discussing ant colonies, Nicolis and Prigogine argue that:

[a] permanent structure in an unpredictable environment may well compromise the adaptability of the colony and bring it to a suboptimal regime. A possible reaction toward such an environment is to maintain a high rate of exploration and the ability to rapidly develop temporary structures suitable for taking advantage of any favorable occasion that might arise. In other words, it would seem that randomness presents an adaptive value in the organisation of society.[70]

What enables ants to identify the optimal state of fitness in a given environment is the process of distributed computing they can be thought of as embodying. For example, despite the limited perceptive and cognitive apparatus of the single ant, a colony can identify rapidly the shortest route across a rugged landscape. This is achieved by the secretion of pheromones which serves to communicate between its members – "pheromones can be thought of as information broadcasted or communicated within the ant system."[71] In this manner, tiny pieces of local knowledge acquired by individual ants combine to constitute the emergent global knowledge that characterises the colony as a whole. The sheer number of ants allows for a process of computational trial and error which enables the colony to evolve the optimal solution to any problem. As Kelly puts it, "this calculation perfectly mirrors the evolutionary search: dumb, blind agent, simultaneous agents trying to optimise a path on a computationally rugged landscape. Ants are a parallel processing machine."[72] This distributed form of computing is what grants complex adaptive systems their ability to change and produce creative solutions to new problems.

---

70   Gregoire Nicolis and Ilya Prigogine, *Exploring Complexity* (New York: W.H Freeman, 1989), p. 233.

71   Kelly, *Out of Control*, p. 395.

72   Ibid.

For Marion and Uhl-Bien, al-Qaeda successfully constituted a distributed intelligence network which "enabled creativity and innovation on a large scale (such as that needed to pull off the 9/11 events), and helped assure the broadly based viability of the system."[73] Sageman's own account of the manner in which jihadist networks carry out operations fits this picture:

When a terrorist network embarks on a major new operation, the people involved do not know exactly how they are going to do it. No role is specified in advance. Each mujaheed starts with a general notion of what is required of him and improvises with other mujaheed as he goes along. Terrorist operations are not so frequent that they become routine, for law enforcement forces would then catch on and be able to prevent them. These operations involve much uncertainty and many unanticipated obstacles. The state of affairs requires communication among mutually dependent mujahedin, in the sense that each possesses information and resources relevant to the other and none has enough to act in isolation. At this local level, the mujahedin form a network of information processors, where the network handles large volumes of information efficiently without overloading any individual processor [...] Communications are possible horizontally among multiple nodes, allowing them to solve their problems locally without having to refer up to Central Staff and overwhelming the vertical links of communication.[74]

It is therefore through a form of parallel processing that jihadists find their way towards a solution to the organisational challenges of fulfilling a designated mission and that collective behaviour emerges without direction from a hierarchy.

Translated to the military field, swarms are the natural corollary of the constitution of networked forces, emergent phenomena produced by decentralisation and information-sharing. In the words of some of their proponents:

in the future, platforms will evolve from being networked entities to being nodes in the network, to organising efforts resembling "packs" and "swarms." This transformation will be so complete that the packs and swarms that evolve from existing platforms will bear no resemblance to their distant (in generations, not time) predecessors. Hence, in the process, the very notion of a platform will evaporate; their raison d'être will be satisfied by a new approach as a result of a

---

73 Marion and Uhl-Bien, "Complexity Theory and Al-Qaeda", p. 27.

74 Mark Sageman, *Understanding Terror Networks* (Philadelphia, PA: University of Pennsylvania Press, 2004), p. 165.

series of transformations consisting of ever-larger numbers of smaller, dumber, and cheaper components. These collections of entities will ultimately become dynamically reconfigurable packs, swarms, or other organisations of highly specialised components that work together like the cells of our bodies. As such, they will be able to be far more discriminating and precise in the effects they cause. They will become less mechanical and more organic, less engineered and more "grown."[75]

The language employed suggests that these constituent "entities" may not necessarily be human. Indeed Glenn James predicts the battlespace of the future may see what he dubs "fire ant" warfare in which swarms composed of millions of sensors, emitters, microbots, and micro-missiles and deployed via pre-positioning, burial, air drops, artillery rounds, or missiles, saturate the terrain of conflict.[76]

Beyond the flexibility and evolutionary capability that is attributed to military swarms, it is also claimed that they will also be able to bring force to bear in a new manner. Rather than throwing themselves onto the enemy in "waves", forces will be able converge on all directions for offensive bursts thereby maximising the shock effect. For Arquilla and Ronfeldt the full effects of swarming are achieved when:

the dispersed nodes of a network of small (and also perhaps some large) forces can converge on an enemy from multiple directions, through either fire or maneuver. The overall aim should be *sustainable pulsing* – swarm networks must be able to coalesce rapidly and stealthily on a target, then dissever and redisperse, immediately ready to recombine for a new pulse. A swarm network should have little to no mass as a rule (except perhaps during a pulse), but it should have a high energy potential – like a swarm of bees that can fell a mighty beast, or a network of antibodies that can attack a spreading virus.[77]

Dispersing swiftly after an attack or "pulse" also has the benefit of making troops less vulnerable to enemy attacks, particularly in the context of the high lethality and precision characteristic of contemporary and future battlefields.

Advocates of swarming do not see it merely as a military tactic of the future but as one that has been already successfully employed many times in the past, from the Mongol hordes of Genghis Khan to the

75   Alberts and Hayes, *Power to the Edge*, p. 169.

76   James, "Chaos Theory: The Essentials for Military Applications", p. 79.

77   Arquilla and Ronfeldt, "Looking Ahead", p. 465.

German U-Boat tactics in World War II. Similar tactics have also been employed in non-military contexts by diverse activists during the civil rights, anti-Vietnam war, and Seattle anti-globalisation protests.[78] While Linda Beckerman does not employ the term of swarming, the same dynamics are to be found in her description of the tactics of "mass and disperse oscillation" deployed by Somali fighters during the infamous Battle of Mogadishu in October 1993 (most commonly known as the Black Hawk Down incident).[79] This broad range of examples underlines again that such networked tactics are primarily organisationally driven rather than technologically determined, although developments in ICTs have certainly made them more widely applicable and attractive.

Arquilla and Rondfeldt have proposed a new doctrine of BattleSwarm that the US military should adopt along with a greater networking of its forces. This would entail a shift towards light networked semi-autonomous forces supported by the latest ICTs and directed by a command authority with informational topsight (a scheme that resembles very much that of network-centric warfare as discussed below). While the authors draw inspiration from complexity theory and studies of the behaviour of swarms, packs and flocks in the natural world, they recognise that the networked behaviour they are advocating is distinct in significant ways. Swarming networks in the natural world are more fluid and distributed than their military counterparts, while at the same time lacking in topsight. The swarming models created by complexity theorists and which provided the original insights into animal behaviour naturally share these features:

This theoretical and experimental work usually depicts swarming as a system in which autonomous agents interact and move around according to a set of rules and a schedule, often seeking an optimal outcome vis-à-vis another agent, set of agents, or environmental feature. The modeling allows for continual interactions among the agents, as they form and reform in fluid, shifting networks (and maybe hierarchies as well). These networks may persist for some time, or may break down and recombine into others opportunistically. Information may flow quite freely from one agent to the next about conditions near them in the model, but, in the examples we have seen, there is rarely an identifiable distribution of, or hub for distributing, topsight among all the agents. Some

---

78   Ibid.

79   Linda P. Beckerman, "The Non-Linear Dynamics of War", Science Applications International Corporation, 1999.

of the models and applications seem to be more about follow-the-leader or follow-your-neighbor "flocking" behavior than swarming conjointly to attack an adversary or other target.[80]

The behaviour these models describe does indeed seem to resemble more that of international jihadist terrorism and insurgency than the ideals of BattleSwarm in which "autonomous" agents are constrained within more formalised structures of hierarchical authority and operate on the basis of centralised information. Once again, Arquilla and Ronfeldt strive for a hybrid model in-between the poles of rigid centralisation and radical decentralisation.

The above sections have reviewed the connections between chaos theory and complexity science and new military thinking on warfare through the themes of decision cycles, uncertainty, networks, and swarming. A new set of ideas derived from the non-linear sciences are in the ascendancy and laying the ground for the emergence of a new regime of the scientific way of warfare. It remains to determine to what extent the now official Pentagon doctrine of network-centric warfare fully embraces this novel framework and breaks with cybernetic warfare, thus heralding the fully-fledged arrival of *chaoplexic warfare*. The following section argues that despite a clear move in the direction of a new non-linear way of warfare, network-centric warfare still remains critically mired in cybernetic conceptions.

Chaoplexity Goes To War? Interrogating Network-Centric Warfare

The debacle in Vietnam delivered a strong blow to cybernetic warfare and its ambitions for informational omniscience and total predictability. Uncertainty and chaos had not been banished from the battlefield after all. On the contrary, the North Vietnamese had exploited it consummately to derail the American war machine and its reliance on technology. While the defeat in Vietnam prompted some soul-searching, most of the armed forces refused to view it as a military defeat and blamed the political leadership for its inability to overcome an inferiorly equipped

---

80   John Arquilla and David Ronfeldt, *Swarming and the Future of Conflict* (RAND Corporation, 2000), pp. 48-49.

peasant guerrilla. Hence the most commonly learnt lesson was not how to effectively fight such conflicts but rather that they should be scrupulously avoided in the first place. The military could thus return to focusing on preparing for war against an opponent similar to itself, namely the Soviet Union and the Warsaw Pact, and in which it could still place hope in the principles that had been so patently ineffective in Southeast Asia.

The ideals of cybernetic warfare experienced a resurgence in the 1980s and through to the 1990s with the Strategic Defense Initiative project and debates over the forever imminent Revolution in Military Affairs (RMA). Among the key references for RMA proponents are Alvin and Heidi Toffler's *The Third Wave* (1980) and *War and Anti-War* (1995).[81] They famously argued that human civilisation was entering a third wave in its history: after the successive agrarian and industrial eras, the informational age now beckoned. Each new wave supersedes the previous one and brings with it new techniques of production and destruction since "nations make war the same way they make wealth." Although the theory has been criticised for an excessively deterministic and technocentric outlook, the Tofflers' ideas have proven to be immensely popular within the US military, to the extent that critics frequently refer to RMA advocates as Tofflerians.

In the hands of RMA evangelists, the Third Wave translated into a vision in which the future of the military was computers, information networks, and precision-guided munitions. Dreams of automated, centralised and even casualty-free wars were revived, fuelled in no small part by the spectacular success of the Gulf War. As Atkinson and Moffat put it:

[The information age] brought with it an illusion or panacea that it might be possible to exercise control from the centre after all, that new information systems, and ever greater bandwidth and computing power would enable *command* to be *controlled*, and that, somehow, technology could, in itself, create the necessary interaction across the layers to enable *automated control*: that processes could be controlled through automation and it was only a matter of devising yet more capable computers and information systems.[82]

---

81   Alvin Toffler, *The Third Wave* (London: Collins, 1980); Alvin and Heidi Toffler, *War and Anti-War*.

82   Simon Ray Atkinson and James Moffat, *The Agile Organization: From Informal Networks to Complex Effects and Agility* (Department of Defense CCRP, 2005),

Under this worldview, uncertainty and disorder are merely temporary obstacles soon to be banished, a limitation of existing technology.
Thus for Norman Davis, "what was often referred to as the "fog of war"
is in reality disorder – the inability to maintain unity of action due
to shortcomings in the C3I systems."[83] A "system of systems" which
will allow for the interoperability and synergy of Command, Control,
Computers, Communications, and Information (C4I) and Intelligence,
Surveillance and Reconnaissance (ISR) systems has been recurrently
touted as the key to "information superiority" and the eradication of
the "fog of war."[84]

The discourse of RMA supporters has followed a regular pattern over
the years: new technology is within reach that will revolutionise warfare
and will finally render it to a state of full control and predictability.
Admiral William Owens, one of its keenest advocates in recent years,
provides us here with a typical specimen:

Never in history [...] has a military commander been granted an omniscient
view of the battlefield in real time, by day and night, and in all weather conditions – as much of the battlefield and an enemy force to allow vital maneuver
and devastating firepower to deliver the coup de grace in a single blow. Today's
technology promises to make that possible."[85]

In 1997, former Air Force Chief of Staff Ronald Fogleman had already told Congress that "in the first quarter of the 21st century you will
be able to find, fix or track, and target – in near real-time – anything of
consequence that moves upon or is located on the face of the Earth."[86]
Although separated by thirty years, the rhetoric of Fogleman and Owens
has not departed in any way from the vision of Westmoreland's 1969

---

pp. 170-171.

83   Norman C. Davis, "An Information-Based Revolution in Military Affairs" in
Arquilla and Ronfeldt (eds), *In Athena's Camp*, p. 86.

84   William A. Owens with Edward Offley, *Lifting the Fog of War* (Baltimore, MD:
John Hopkins University Press, 2001).

85   Ibid., p. 14.

86   Michael O'Hanlon, *Technological Change and the Future of Warfare* (Washington, DC: Brookings Institution Press, 2000), p. 13.

speech on the automated battlefield who at the time had foreseen its arrival in "no more than ten years."[87]

In the post-Cold War environment in which military budgets were cut as part of the "peace dividend", the promises of the RMA were particularly appealing as they became a way of doing more with less and substituting technology for manpower. Owens again:

We have too much functional redundancy across our military services and agencies, particularly in support and force enhancers like intelligence, medical, logistics, and communications, and perhaps in combat areas such as air defense and long range strike. In the past, redundancy was compelling because the "fog of war" demanded it to compensate for the unexpected. Today, as a nation's information edge becomes more prominent, the extent to which we need the same level of redundancy is questionable.[88]

This view of warfare is in complete contradiction with the principles of chaos and complexity theory. Warfare cannot be completely predicted or controlled, knowledge is imperfect, and redundancy allows for great adaptability and resilience in the face of contingency. It would therefore appear that the RMA is a mere extension of the ideals of cybernetic warfare and allied with a scientific worldview that has not taken on board the most significant recent developments in the field, despite a non-negligible military literature that has attempted to draw valuable lessons from them.

However, the most recent, and now dominant, strand of the RMA literature has drawn in particular from complexity theory and sought to combine past claims from RMA prophets with an organisational doctrine inspired by the language and concepts of the non-linear sciences. According to its most vocal advocate and subsequent founding director of the Office of Force Transformation, Vice Admiral Arthur Cebrowski, "network-centric warfare looks at war as a complex, adaptive system where non-linear variables continuously interact."[89] Through the establishment of information networks, it is claimed that military organisation can be radically decentralised, allowing for processes of self-

---

87   William Westmoreland, Address to the Association of the US Army, Oct. 14, 1969.

88   Statement of Admiral William A. Owens, USN (Ret) To The US Senate, Feb. 12, 2001.

89   Gray, *Strategy for Chaos*, p. 105.

organisation and emergence. Although still in its infancy, the doctrine's ultimate ambition is nothing less than a "new theory of war."[90]

The doctrine of network-centric warfare (NCW) first appeared on the scene in the late 1990s, rapidly rising to prominence to become the new official Pentagon gospel under the agenda of "Transformation." NCW now has its counterparts in most major Western militaries with Network Enabled Capabilities (NEC) in the United Kingdom, NATO Network Enabled Capabilities (NNEC), and Network Enabled Operations (NEOps) in Canada. At first sight, network-centric warfare may appear to constitute a decisive break with established thinking, drawing explicitly from complexity theory and announcing a reversal of the dominant centralising approach. While in some respects, this is a legitimate claim, the rest of this chapter argues that although network-centric warfare has indeed appropriated the language and ideas of complexity, it has done so selectively and still rests on many of the presumptions of earlier RMA theories. Furthermore, while decentralisation – or rather self-synchronisation – appears to have become the new watchword, many of the information systems that network-centric warfare requires also allow for greater centralisation and micro-management.

Originating in the US Navy, the ideas of network-centric warfare started gaining wider attention with the proselytising of Arthur Cebrowski. In 1998, Cebrowski published with John Garstka an influential article entitled *Network-Centric Warfare: Its Origin and Future* in which he announced a decisive shift in the theory and practice of warfare. In order to bolster his claims for this RMA, Cebrowski pointed to changes in the economy and business management, a very Tofflerian move and in line with an understanding of warfare as an activity that can be reduced to production. In the midst of the Internet boom of the late nineties, the Vice Admiral waxed lyrical about a new economy that had turned the laws of supply and demand "on their heads" and was "characterised by extraordinary growth and wealth generation."[91] For

---

90   "When you rack and stack all of that what we are really talking about is a new theory of war because we are talking about new sources of power." Navy Vice Adm. Arthur Cebrowski, Speech to Network-Centric Warfare Conference, Jan. 22, 2003.

91   Arthur K. Cebrowski and John J. Garstka, "Network-Centric Warfare: Its Origin and Future", *Proceedings*, US Naval Institute, Jan. 1998.

Cebrowski, the source of this revolution was clear and available to all in the military who were willing to listen:

Central to these developments is the shift to network-centric operations, which are characterised by information-intensive interactions between computational nodes on the network. Whether these interactions are focused on commerce, education, or military operations, there is "value" that is derived from the content, quality, and timeliness of information moving between nodes on the network. *This value increases as information moves toward 100% relevant content, 100% accuracy, and zero time delay – toward information superiority.* [emphasis added][92]

Information superiority is the key concept to NCW since this is the element from which increased combat power is believed to originate.[93] Thus NCW defines itself as "an information superiority-enabled concept of operations that generates increased combat power by networking sensors, decision makers, and shooters to achieve shared awareness, increased speed of command, higher tempo of operations, greater lethality, increased survivability, and a degree of self-synchronisation."[94]

While NCW authors differ in the extent to which they believe the fog of war can be irrevocably lifted, they all share a common understanding of uncertainty as generated by a lack of information. The response is therefore consistently the same: deploy technology to acquire, process and distribute more information and ensure certain victory through information superiority. While improving the reliability of information can certainly be beneficial, the non-linear sciences point to the profound limitations of such an approach and there are three fundamental criticisms that can be levelled at the conception of information in NCW literature.

Firstly, as demonstrated within chaos theory, the sensitivity to initial conditions of non-linear systems implies that no matter how precise the information about a system's operation and its state at any given instant, long-term predictability is severely limited, if not completely

---

92   Cebrowski and Garstka, "Network-Centric Warfare".

93   Under previous incarnations of the RMA, the term 'dominant battlefield awareness' served an analogous function within the discourse.

94   David S. Alberts, John J. Garstka and Frederick P. Stein, *Network-Centric Warfare: Developing and Leveraging Information Superiority*, second edn (Department of Defense CCRP, 2000), p. 2.

inexistent. Such a conclusion applies to a perfectly transparent set of non-linear functions run through a computer, let alone to a real-world phenomenon like war in which the system's borders are uncertain, variables are undoubtedly far more numerous, and successfully identifying and measuring them is nigh impossible. However, on its own this criticism might not necessarily be fatal since short-term predictability still may be possible and an approximate long term predictability may also be achievable if the system's patterns of behaviour are identified.

Secondly, if we take Boyd's OODA "loop" seriously, we must accept that any fixed model of reality is destined to experience entropic decay – information cannot merely traverse the system, it must also be the basis on which the latter can be reshaped and reorganised. However, in appropriating the OODA "loop", NCW has merely reduced it to a greatly simplified decision cycle which acts more like a cybernetic negative feedback loop than a complex adaptive system – more shall be said on this later.

Finally, NCW proponents seem to discount completely one of Clausewitz's most famous pronouncements – "a great part of the information obtained in war is contradictory, a still greater part is false, and by far the greatest part is of doubtful character"[95] – or at least presume that it only applies to times bygone and is now rendered irrelevant by advances in ICTs. Indeed NCW puts complete faith in sensor technology and the ability of computer systems to synthesise their input into a coherent and unambiguous shared operational picture of the battlespace on the basis of which military units will be able to develop new levels of collaboration and coordination. Such a view rests on several crucial assumptions such as the infallibility of sensors and computer systems, discounting the ability of adversaries to fool sensors and create a misleading picture, and presuming that common data will necessarily be interpreted in the same manner by all units. Furthermore, NCW seems to assume that greater quantities of sensor information will result in a higher quality of information – an assumption which again rests on the belief that ambiguity and uncertainty only results from a lack of information, not from confusion produced by potentially conflicting pieces of information or failures in their interpretation. As Milan Vego points out in referring back to Clausewitz, "uncertainty is not the result of gaps

---

95   Clausewitz, *On War*

in information but largely is caused by lack of comprehension or false interpretation of the information acquired."[96] By neglecting all these insights, the US military may end up designing an organisation utterly dependent on reliable high-quality information rather than granting it the ability to adapt to uncertain conditions where information may be scarce, incomplete, or untrustworthy.

Therefore the most likely road to success lies not in attempting to attain the illusory goal of "100% relevant content, 100% accuracy, and zero time delay" which would allow the perfect operation of a friction-less cybernetic war machine, but in embracing uncertainty and design-ing a resilient and flexible military that is capable of adapting to the unforeseen and contingent. Conversely, an advantage over the adversary can be acquired not merely through targeting his information systems or accelerating the tempo of operations but by varying the tactics and offensive moves deployed against him. This would constitute a far more faithful application of chaos and complexity theory than most of the principles of NCW, despite their regular references to the aforemen-tioned sciences.

It is important to note that NCW does seem to break with previous conceptions of the RMA in its goal of self-synchronisation and draws here its inspiration and terminology directly from complexity theory. Self-synchronisation implies a radical decentralisation of the command structure by increasing the freedom of low-level forces to operate nearly autonomously and coordinate themselves on the basis of shared aware-ness, common doctrine and rules of engagement, and the commander's general intent (i.e. the overall objectives of the mission) – a set-up remi-niscent, at least on paper, of the German *Auftragstaktik*. The underlying principle is that forces will self-organise and emergent properties denied to top-down command will emerge. For Cebrowski and others, com-plexity theory is the key to unlocking increased combat power:

Military operations are enormously complex, and complexity theory tells us that such enterprises organise best from the bottom-up. Traditionally, however, military commanders work to obtain top-down command-directed synchroni-sation to achieve the required level of mass and fires at the point of contact with the enemy. Because each element of the force has a unique operating rhythm,

---

96   Milan Vego, "Net-Centric Is Not Decisive", *Proceedings*, US Naval Institute, Jan. 2003.

and because errors in force movement needlessly consume combat power, combat at the operational level is reduced to a step function, which takes time and provides opportunity to the enemy. After the initial engagement, there is an operational pause, and the cycle repeats. In contrast, bottom-up organisation yields self-synchronisation, where the step function becomes a smooth curve, and combat moves to a high-speed continuum. The "Observe-Orient-Decide-Act (OODA) Loop" appears to disappear, and the enemy is denied the operational pause.[97]

In other words, individuals units no longer need to coordinate themselves with all others, thereby slowing down the entire military machine to the "operating rhythm" of its slowest element, but can execute autonomous actions at greatest speed available to them. Self-synchronised forces can therefore "mass effects", increasing the combat tempo and raining blows on an adversary that is denied the time to respond and undergo his own decision cycle, thus leading to his collapse (the phenomenon of "shock and awe").

For its proponents, NCW marks a momentous shift from "platform-centric" organisations which privilege independent platforms (weapon systems) with their own individual sensors and weapons to "network-centric" organisations that link together sensors, decision-makers, and shooters into a single network. The network therefore constitutes the warfighting system in NCW with all nodes (platforms) on it ultimately substitutable. The principle is to create a form of distributed intelligence by sharing total information among all participants. According to the theory, this pooling of information creates a state of shared awareness among all actors which leads to self-synchronisation and emergent behaviour (Figure 14).

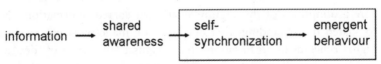

Figure 14: From information to emergence[98]

For NCW theorists, the communications network and the information superiority it provides constitute the substrate from which bottom-up

97   Cebrowski and Garstka, "Network-Centric Warfare".

98   Reproduced from Moffat, *Complexity and Network-Centric Warfare*, p. 50.

self-organisation can emerge. "NCW works because it has identified, in general terms, the initial conditions that need to exist in order to achieve effective self-synchronisation."[99]

While the notion of self-synchronisation echoes that of self-organisation and NCW advocates frequently speak of it as if it were a straightforward lesson from complexity theory, the practices it covers are in fact much more ambiguous and decentralisation does not necessarily flow from them. Self-synchronisation is presented as the coordination of units through the creation and distribution of a common operational picture by networking sensors, shooters, and decision-makers. This theoretically overcomes the limitations of platform-centric warfare in which information is "stove-piped" in each individual platform and can only be communicated in a highly inefficient manner such as voice communication. But this does not automatically mean greater autonomy and initiative for subordinate units since it also allows for a tightening of the degree of control of the command and control hierarchy over them. As Roman puts it, all too often "the seductiveness of information technology stimulates military organisational orientation towards greater centralised control and more rigid hierarchical organisations instead of the desired orientation of decentralised control and more flexible organisations."[100]

NCW talks of decoupling sensors, actors, and decision-makers for the benefit of connecting them all to a common "infostructure." However this also paves the way for an even greater differentiation between those units that command and those that merely carry out the orders. As Kolanda argues, a quite opposite argument to self-synchronisation can be made on the basis of the same technological arrangements: "the core assumptions of this argument are that shared information leads to shared understanding, that decisions are made most effectively at higher echelons of organisation, that organisations consist of "decision entities" controlling "actor entities" – and that networks permit fewer of the former to control more of the latter."[101] As some of the most prominent theorists of NCW themselves recognise, "in general, greater

---

99   Alberts and Hayes, *Power to the Edge*, pp. 208-209.

100   Gregory A. Roman, "The Command or Control Dilemma", p. 3.

101   Christopher D. Kolenda, "Transforming How We Fight - A Conceptual Approach", *Naval War College Review*, Spring 2003, Vol. LVI, No. 2.

capability to acquire, integrate, move, and process larger amounts of information rapidly makes more centralised decision-making possible."[102] Thus, when NCW advocates speak of "flattening hierarchies" in order to increase the "span of control",[103] this may entail removing layers of middle management that came with industrial age bureaucracies (the inspiration once again originating in similar changes in business organisations) but does not necessarily lead to an emancipation of lower-level forces from hierarchical control.

For one, the full operational picture constituted through the infostructure is not available to all levels of the hierarchy but only to the senior levels of command and control which can subsequently decide what picture is made available to different units. While "shared awareness" is referred to as "a type of collective consciousness",[104] in practice it implies total omniscience at the top which can then choose which parts of the picture are made available to subordinates. NCW theorists concede that "current discussion of the need for new command and control approaches in an era of Information Age Warfare explicitly considers situations where the best (most current, accurate, and complete) information may no longer be located at the subordinate command engaged in the field, but rather may be located at senior headquarters."[105] This is in marked contrast with previous cases of decentralised military organisation as employed by the German army in World War II with Blitzkrieg. The assumption then was that subordinate units possessed more accurate local knowledge than headquarters and would therefore be better able to adapt to changing circumstances and demonstrate the appropriate creativity and initiative.

Thomas Barnett expresses some serious reservations about the idea of the "common operating picture", the shared awareness which is supposed to be the catalyser for bottom-up self-synchronisation:

The common operating picture cannot really be shared in the sense that ownership will remain a top-down affair [...] NCW promises to flatten hierarchies,

---

102   David S. Alberts, John J. Garstka, Richard E. Hayes and David A. Signorip, *Understanding Information Age Warfare* (CCRP Publications, 2001), p. 177.

103   Alberts, Garstka and Stein, *Network-Centric Warfare*, p. 81.

104   Ibid., p. 135.

105   Alberts, Garstka, Hayes and Signorip, *Understanding Information Age Warfare*, p. 178.

but the grave nature of military operations may push too many commanders into becoming control freaks, fed by an almost unlimited data flow [...] The infusion of information technology into hierarchical organisations typically reduces the traditional asymmetries of information that define superior-subordinate relationships. Taken in this light, the common operating picture is an attempt by military leaders to retain the high ground of command prerogative – a sort of non-stop internal spin control by commanders on what is necessarily a constantly breaking story among all participants, given their access to information that previously remained under the near-exclusive purview of superior officers. That gets me to the question of the common operating picture's "realness", for it suggests that the picture will be less a raw representation of operational reality than a command-manipulated virtual reality.[106]

Units whose operational picture consists merely of a simplified version of that available to their superiors are effectively deprived of any ground upon which to make recommendations and exert influence on their commanding officers, particularly when local and situated knowledge not represented in the networked infosphere finds itself devalued. In other words, it negates the possibility of realising command and control as theorised by the Marine Corps:

Command and control is not so much a matter of one part of the organisation "getting control over" another as something that connects all the elements together in a cooperative effort. All parts of the organisation contribute action and feedback – "command" and "control" – in overall cooperation. Command and control is thus fundamentally an activity of *reciprocal influence*.[107]

The use of the Predator aircraft drone in Afghanistan is a case in point. Beaming images from the battlefield straight to US Central Command headquarters in Tampa and at the Pentagon, the sensor provided soldiers on the ground "little useful information and were sometimes a distraction, encouraging higher-level military staffs to try to micromanage the fighting."[108] As Vego argues, "having a common operating picture will lead operational commanders to be increasingly involved in purely tactical decisions, instead of focusing on the opera-

---

106   Thomas P. M. Barnett, "The Seven Deadly Sins of Network-Centric Warfare", *Proceedings*, US Naval Institute, Jan. 1999, pp. 36-39.

107   *MCDP 6: Command and Control*, United States Marine Corps, pp. 46-47.

108   Thomas E. Ricks, "Beaming the Battlefield Home: Live Video of Afghan Fighting Had Questionable Effect", *Washington Post*, 26 March 2002.

tional and strategic aspects of the situation within their respective areas of responsibility."[109]

This leads to the conclusion that there are in fact two fundamentally distinct approaches to networked operations, which Bar Yam sums up as follows:

The first involves networked action agents capable of individual action but coordinated for effective collective function through self-organised patterns. Analogous behaviors can be identified in swarming insects and the immune system. The second involves networked decision makers receiving information from a set of sensors and controlling coherent large scale effectors. Analogous organisational structures can be identified in the physiological neuro-muscular system. Each of these important models of networks deserves consideration for the development of networked military forces. The two paradigms are also not restrictive in the sense that there are many intermediate cases that can be considered.[110]

We see here two conceptions of warfare each with its respective scientific corpus and biological metaphors. While the former is a de-centralised, self-organised network of autonomous units, the latter is a centralised army in which the network serves only to strengthen the distinction between decision-makers and those that carry the actions out (the effectors). In the second case, there is no sense in which a true network has replaced a hierarchical structure.

Arquilla and Ronfeld also recognise that networking does not simply entail decentralisation of command and control but also greater "top-sight" for the hierarchy:

Moving to networked structures may require some decentralisation of com-mand and control, which may well be resisted in light of earlier views that the new technology would provide greater central control of military operations. But decentralisation is only part of the picture; the new technology may also provide greater "topsight" – a central understanding of the big picture that enhances the management of complexity. Many treatments of organisational redesign laud decentralisation; yet decentralisation alone is not the key issue. The pairing of decentralisation with topsight brings the real gains.[111]

---

109 Vego, "Net-Centric Is Not Decisive".

110 Bar-Yam, "Complexity of Military Conflict", pp. 23-4.

111 Arquilla and Ronfeldt, "Cyberwar is Coming!" in Arquilla and Ronfeldt (eds), *In Athena's Camp*, pp. 30-31.

Both Bar-Yam and Arquilla and Ronfeldt posit two poles to military organisation of hierarchies and networks within which the US military can fluctuate according to its needs and opportunities. Official NCW literature goes in the same direction: "NCW gives us the opportunity to explore the vast middle ground between the Industrial Age top-down hierarchical command and control approach and the highly decentralised model of small units assigned pieces of the problem with only their organic capabilities."[112]

For Bar-Yam, the merits of networks over hierarchies are to be found in the superiority of the formers' distributed information processing; while hierarchical structures can be effective at ordering large scale operations, they are far less efficient in conditions of high complexity:

Hierarchical command systems are designed for the largest scale impacts and thus *relatively* simple warfare. Indeed, traditional military forces and related command control and planning, were designed for conventional large scale conflicts. Distributed control systems, when properly designed, can enhance the ability to meet complex challenges.[113]

The real benefits of the network are to be found in its capacity for distributed computing and overcoming the limitations of hierarchical command in complex environments (Bar-Yam contrasts the simplicity of maritime combat to littoral warfare, and the simple environments of the desert and the plain to the complexity of the jungle, mountains, and urban areas):

The key to this understanding is that each individual has a limited complexity. In particular, an individual is limited in ability to process information and to communicate with others (bandwidth). In an idealised hierarchy, only the single leader of the organisation can coordinate the largest organisational units whose commanders are directly under his/her command. The coordination between these units cannot be of greater complexity than the leader. More generally, we can state that to the extent that any single human being is responsible for coordinating parts of an organisation, the coordinated behaviours of the organisation will be limited to the complexity of a single individual. Since coordinated behaviours are relatively large scale behaviours, this implies that there is a limit to the complexity of larger scale behaviours of the organisation. Thus, using a command hierarchy is effective at amplifying the scale of behaviour, but not its complexity. By contrast, a network structure (like the

---

112   Alberts, Garstka and Stein, *Network-Centric Warfare*, p. 162.

113   Bar-Yam, "Complexity of Military Conflict", p. 1.

human brain) can have a complexity greater than that of an individual element (neuron).[114]

While the logic of this argument is sound, and different organisational arrangements may indeed suit different types of war environments and situations, much will depend on the ability of the US military hierarchy to show appropriate judgement and resist the temptations of centralisation and micro-management when it is counter-productive. The historical record in this respect inspires little confidence.

On a more fundamental level, it should be underlined that to present claims that shared awareness leads to bottom-up self-organisation as a straightforward application of the principles of complexity is to profoundly misinterpret the scientific theory. As we saw in our discussion of swarming, complexity in natural or simulated systems does not emerge from a global shared situational awareness that would be available to all or any of the components of a system. This assumes a centralisation of information that precedes any decentralised action by the parts of the system. Rather, it is on the basis of localised information, calculation, and action that highly complex behaviour can emerge without any single entity possessing an overall knowledge of the system and environment. No single ant has a complete knowledge of the state of its colony or environment at any given moment – it acts on the basis of only partial knowledge of its immediate vicinity as provided by its senses and of information that has been passed to it by neighbouring ants or pheromone deposits – even if the colony as a whole appears to behave as if it did. This is how complex systems can develop emergent behaviour on the basis of localised action. Or as the Marine Corps command and control doctrine puts it with regard to military organisation, "a complex system is any system composed of multiple parts, each of which must act individually according to its own circumstances and which, by so acting, changes the circumstances affecting all the other parts."[115]

This is not to discount the potential benefits of shared informational awareness but to signal crucial divergences with the complexity sciences which NCW claims its authority from. Rather than constituting a decentralised organisation which can operate on the basis of limited and dispersed information, as in the case of al-Qaeda, the US military

---

114   Ibid., p. 8.

115   *MCDP 6 Command and Control*, United States Marine Corps, 1996, p. 41.

is developing armed forces which are dependent on large volumes of accurate information to take their decisions and act in unison. This information is to be acquired, processed and distributed through an overarching "system of systems" that has been an ambition of the military since General Westmoreland. For NCW advocates, this is the "entry fee" to the brave new military world they promise and has prompted the Pentagon to earmark $200 billion or more in expenditure for the acquisition of network hardware and software over the next decade.[116] However, reliance on this elaborate infrastructure and the skills and habits it will likely breed may in fact prevent troops from ever operating autonomously where only local or partial awareness is available. This point is all the more crucial when it becomes clear the information infrastructure will be the Achilles heel of any such army and that there exists a number of means to effectively disrupt both the hardware and software of electromagnetic equipment.[117]

Furthermore, even if we disregard its potential vulnerability to enemy targeting, the promised "system of systems" still appears dangerously captive of the illusions of the cybernetic regime embodied in Robert McNamara's failed Igloo White project, originally designed to create an impassable electronic line in Vietnam.[118] Spinney identifies four components common to all such overarching systems:

1. observation systems to identify enemy forces and targets;
2. orientation processes that filter observations through computerised target recognition templates based on the predicted "signatures" the adversary is expected to exhibit on the battlefield;
3. centralised command and control systems to orchestrate the mix of attack options on the selected set of enemy signatures (the array targets);
4. a mix of hi-tech precision-guided weapons to execute the desired attack options.[119]

---

116 Weiner, "A 'God's-Eye View' of the Battlefield".

117 Electromagnetic hardware is vulnerable to current and voltage surges through exposure to electromagnetic pulses (EMP) generated by the high-altitude detonation of nuclear weapons or other purposively designed weapons. Software can be corrupted or disabled through infection by malicious code (computer viruses, worms, or Trojan horses) or penetration by hackers.

118 See chapter 5.

119 Spinney, "Asleep at the Switch in Versailles".

Spinney points to three crucial assumptions underpinning these systems. The first is the ability to predict the signature pattern of the adversary. The second is the assumption that surveillance and reconnaissance systems will be able to distinguish enemy forces from background noise constituted by friendly forces, non-combatants, and the environment. Finally, and perhaps most importantly, the OODA "loop" which proponents of these systems refer to is:

based on a simplistic cybernetic model that assumes the conduct of war can be methodically monitored and minutely regulated by a system of sensors and negative feedback control signals, much like the temperature of a room is monitored and regulated by the predicted target temperature (or template) and negative feedback signals of a thermostat. One consequence of these assumptions is that the exclusive reliance on a negative feedback control architecture eliminates the possibility of adapting to unforeseen circumstances. This limitation can turn Boyd's conception of a dialectical non-linear OODA "loop" based on the idea of co-evolution into a one way non-adaptive road to confusion and disorder if the enemy chooses to act unpredictably.[120]

Indeed, while advocates of NCW frequently refer to Boyd and the OODA "loop", their main concern seems to be to defeat the enemy through an acceleration of the decision cycle, as opposed to the ability to act unpredictably and creatively adapt in response to contingencies. Boyd did talk of cycling through the OODA "loop" quicker but in the sense of adapting to the battle situation faster, not merely the execution of the same commands at a faster pace. By emphasising speed above everything else, NCW seeks merely to act faster by cutting down the time dedicated to all the phases in the decision cycle, including analysis and synthesis. The pronouncement of General Myers, former Chairman of the Joint Chiefs of Staff, is symptomatic: "improved joint C4ISR will allow US forces to exploit a decision cycle – to observe, decide, and act – faster than an adversary. History is pretty clear: The side that does this faster wins."[121] The omission of the orientation phase from the decision cycle in Myers's statement is revealing of the impoverished understanding of the OODA "loop" that is prevalent among NCW evangelists. RAND analyst Bruce

---

120   Ibid.
121   Richard B. Myers, "Understanding Transformation" *Proceedings*, US Naval Institute, Feb. 2003, pp. 39-40.

Berkowitz offers another example with his claims that "feedback, the basis of any guidance system, is the electromechanical equivalent of the OODA loop" and that "information warfare is whatever you need to do to get to the end of your decision cycle before your opponent gets to the end of his." [122] Rather than utilising gains in the speed of information-processing and distribution to increase the time available for orientation and thereby the ability to adapt to changing circumstances and surprise adversaries, NCW persists with a rigid cybernetic understanding of warfare that risks rendering US military operations utterly predictable to a competent opponent.

One could point to the ease with which the Serbs were able to fool NATO sensors with relatively low-tech countermeasures (decoys, camouflage, fleeting emissions) during the Kosovo War. When the smoke from the campaign had cleared, the ineffectiveness of the 78 day aerial bombardment became obvious, along with the extent to which NATO had been operating under a completely false sense of success. *Newsweek* reported in 2000 that an Air Force investigation discovered on the ground the remains of only 14 tanks (out of 120 initially "confirmed" strikes), 18 armoured personnel carriers (as opposed to 220), and 20 artillery pieces (out of the previously claimed 450).[123]

Despite such failures by electronic sensors and the systems designed to accumulate and process the information they receive, US military gluttony for ever more information has continued unabated. The new watchword is "persistent surveillance", "the ability to place intelligence assets on a target continuously or near continuously,"[124] with which a new raft of hardware and software procurement is being justified and which remains still premised on the notion that greater volumes of information will deliver greater understanding and certainty. According to network-centric warfare, these huge volumes of information and the resulting superior battlefield knowledge are supposed to be the basis on which force-multiplying decentralisation and self-syn-

---

122   Bruce Berkowitz, *The New Face of War* (New York, NY: The Free Press, 2003), p. 78.

123   John Barry and Evan Thomas, "The Kosovo Cover-Up", *Newsweek*, May 15, 2000.

124   Tamara E. McFarren, "Persistent Surveillance", *Military Geospatial Technology*, Vol. 2, Issue 3, Sept. 28, 2004.

chronisation can be achieved. However, such a scheme jars with much of the historical evidence on the successful practices pertaining to the organisation of armies.

Conclusion

In his seminal text *Command in War*, Martin van Creveld provides a masterly overview of command systems across the ages with particular attention to the manner in which they tackle the problem of uncertainty. Van Creveld concludes that when faced with a task for which insufficient information is available for its completion, a military organisation must choose from one of two approaches: "one is to increase its information-processing capacity, the other to design the organisation, and indeed the task itself, in such a way as to enable it to operate on the basis of less information."[125] The first approach results in a multiplication of communication channels (not necessarily vertically but also eventually horizontally) and results in an increase in the size and complexity of the "central directing organ." The second approach offers two further alternatives: either to simplify radically the organisation by planning everything ahead and drilling troops into a sequential number of moves to be repeated on the battlefield (such as was practised by Frederick the Great) or to establish a force composed of semi-autonomous units that can deal with parts of the task separately. Van Creveld claims that the latter approach has proven itself consistently superior to the other two throughout history. The peculiarity of network-centric warfare is that it appears to seek to chart a fourth approach by, on one hand increasing the information-processing capacity and multiplying the number of communication channels, and on the other calling for a decentralisation of military organisation.

The central purpose of decentralisation is to distribute uncertainty throughout the organisation yet NCW remains attached to the notion that a technologically-driven centralisation and fusion of information can overcome uncertainty and decisively impose order on chaos. We are far from van Creveld's exhortation to embrace the fact that "a certain amount of confusion and waste are, owing to the great uncertainty involved, in-

---

125   Van Creveld, *Command in War*, p. 269.

evitable in war; and that such confusion is not inconsistent with, and may indeed be a prerequisite for, results."[126] Nor is there any sense of a recognition of Kipp and Grau's observation that "information war has its own fog and friction that must be overcome, not assumed away."[127]

In designing a military that relies on historically unprecedented volumes of information, NCW makes the ICT infrastructure it depends on into a critical vulnerability and negates precisely the key advantage of decentralised organisations, namely their ability to operate in conditions where only limited and uncertain information is available. NCW advocates may retort that their doctrine being nothing less than a "new theory of war", we should not be surprised to see it break established moulds and that NCW will in fact achieve the synthesis of seemingly contradictory approaches. Only time will tell if this is indeed the case but for now it seems that, while appropriating some of the notions of complexity, network-centric warfare will not break decisively with the principles of cybernetic warfare. Nonetheless, the growing influence of chaos theory and complexity science on military theory and practice is clearly visible today and the current contradictions of network-centric warfare may yet come to be retrospectively viewed as merely the birth pangs of a future truly chaoplexic regime in the scientific way of warfare.

---

126   Van Creveld, *Command in War*, pp. 270-271.

127   Jacob W. Kipp and Lester W. Grau, "The Fog and Friction of Technology", *Military Review*, Sept.-Oct. 2001.

Conclusion

The scientific way of warfare is here to stay. Although it has neither consistently overshadowed all other influences on the exercise of armed force war nor been the object of a uncontested rise to prominence, one can nonetheless chart an overall ascendancy of this regime of order alongside the increasing industrial and technological dependency of war. From the early modern era onwards, scientific discourse and technological artefacts have combined to resonate with the other social and cultural developments underpinning the profound transformations of warfare in the West.

If the appeals to scientific method and prestige have endured and will continue to so, we can no longer satisfy ourselves with a monolithic treatment of the scientific way of warfare since the ideas and principles promulgated under it have fluctuated considerably as a result of both changes internal to science and war as well as to wider socio-cultural transformations. This book has proposed a rough periodisation according to the dominant scientific ideas in different eras since the onset of the Scientific Revolution and the modern age. While the distinct scientific and military regimes distinguished cannot be circumscribed by clearly delineated dates marking their beginning and end, it is nonetheless possible to point to historical intervals in which the ideas and practices characterised by a particular regime can be seen to be ascendant.

The mechanistic era can be broadly situated within the seventeenth and eighteenth centuries, present at the very foundation of modern scientific method. Organised around the clockwork metaphor, it set out a conception of the world as perfectly ordered and intricately linked together in a divine mechanism set in motion by the Creator. This worldview found its echo in the absolutist monarchical regimes which emerged in Europe at this time. Mechanistic warfare itself peaked in the second half of the eighteenth century, with Frederick the Great's army as its paradigmatic embodiment. Geometry and the newly discovered laws of motion had been already widely applied to improve fortifications and ballistics, but the Prussians did the most to turn the army itself into a giant clockwork mechanism. Via a process of intense drilling which disciplined the bodies and minds of soldiers, Frederick could not only ensure unprecedented speed and reliability in the execution of repeated firearm volleys but could also experiment with complex tactical deployments on the field. However tactics had to be almost entirely decided on before engagement as all initiative had been removed from individual soldiers and available communication technologies did not allow the commander much input once battle had begun. Only by meticulously planning ahead the course of the battle and dictating the series of manoeuvres to be carried out could the mechanistic commander chart a path to victory.

The industrialisation and motorisation of society marked the advent of the thermodynamic age, a period of great political and social upheaval. Science turned to the study of energy, articulating a new understanding of the world and of the irreversibility of certain transformational processes within it. With the formulation of entropy in particular came a probabilistic approach to scientific problems, undermining the tidy linearity and precise predictability of mechanistic models. Thermodynamic warfare saw the channelling of ever-greater flows of energy into war, whether of a ballistic, motorised, industrial or moral nature, as nation-states clashed in ever-wider conflicts which drew on all the resources at their disposal. From the onset of the French Revolutionary and Napoleonic wars to the development of nuclear weaponry, armed conflict underwent a dramatic escalation in the means of destruction deployed, almost leading to planetary annihilation. Although it was not consistently applied, a number of armies in this era experimented with tactical decentralisation to manage the uncertainty caused by the friction and fog of war theorised by Clausewitz.

If the Second World War was the apotheosis of thermodynamic warfare, it also marked the threshold of a new regime of the scientific way of warfare. Cybernetics offered a science of control and communications organised around the concept of information and embodied in advances in electromagnetic telecommunication and calculation devices made during the war, most notably the computer. Information became conceptualised as the inverse of entropy and thus the source of all order. Vast command and control architectures were established in the context of a Cold War liable to escalate into a full-blown nuclear conflict, promising centralised control and stabilising self-regulation through negative information feedback. In the elusive quest for predictability, scientific methodology was applied more systematically than ever to warfare with the comprehensive treatment by operations research and systems analysis of tactical and strategic questions.

Cybernetic warfare experienced its first serious reversal with the Vietnam War, where its analytical techniques and military systems floundered when engaged in a low-intensity conflict. Simultaneously scientists were developing their informational theories, outgrowing some of the limitations of early cybernetics. From a focus on stability and self-regulation, they turned to processes of dynamic change such as those of decentralised self-organisation. Non-linear mathematics uncovered ordered processes behind seemingly random phenomena, giving birth to chaos theory. The figure of the network allowed for the formalisation of the patterns of relations between autonomous agents which give rise to the emergence of complex adaptive entities at the edge of chaos. Contemporary to these developments are the diffusion of decentralised telecommunication networks such as the Internet and the new social assemblages which have adopted them. The emergence of a new regime of chaoplexic warfare is in evidence by the growing influence of chaos theory and complexity science on military theory and practice. On the face of it, the new doctrine of network-centric warfare would appear to mark its coming of age in the United States military with its emphasis on networked organisation, swarming and self-synchronisation. There are however serious question marks over whether network-centric warfare truly constitutes the arrival of chaoplexic warfare or whether it is little more than a repackaging of cybernetic warfare since many of the latter's centralising impulses appear alive and well in current practices. Nevertheless, the scientific discourse of chaoplexity is in the ascendancy and both Jihadist networks and the Afghan insurgency are currently demonstrating the advantages of warfare based on decentralisation and self-organisation.

It is important to note that the rise of one regime of the scientific way of warfare has not necessarily signified the disappearance of all the ideas and practices associated with the previous regimes. Some elements of past regimes remain relevant and even complementary under a new regime, albeit sometimes in a modified form. For example, the practice of intensive drilling of recruits which was so central to Frederick the Great's clockwork army has been pursued ever since to enhance discipline and reliability in the execution of orders, even if the robotic slavishness of the Prussian soldier has been generally abandoned in favour of a greater degree of autonomy and initiative of the individual in uniform. Similarly, if the drive for ever greater mobilisations and releases of energy is no longer the central focus of Western militaries, developments in the motorisation and destructive power of military force have not been cast away but rather integrated into the set of cybernetic technologies and principles which in the following era sought to bring more precise and targeted applications of this energy. And if we are to see a new era of warfare in which self-organising dynamics and decentralised tactics will be privileged, these will in all likelihood be complemented by self-regulating processes of stabilisation and a degree of top-down oversight.

One way of understanding these developments is as a process of evolution in the forms of control adopted for the purpose of handling the uncertainty inherent in the practice of warfare. While successive scientific worldviews to which specific socio-technical assemblages are associated shift the focus of scientific analysis and formulate distinct ontological claims, thereby rejecting or limiting some of the methods and assertions of previous worldviews, acquired means of control do not thereupon vanish. Instead they remain part of the ensemble of control assemblages liable to be deployed in the social field. In a sense therefore, the present work has been engaged in a genealogy of the techniques and instruments of the control and management of systems so that, as Jeremy Black puts it, "the study of Western warfare becomes an aspect of the history of systems as well as of power."[1]

Certainly developments in scientific knowledge and technological prowess have been accompanied by the constitution of new types of sociotechnical assemblages and systems. Shifts in the scientific *Weltan-*

---

1   Black, *Rethinking Military History*, p. 11

schauung have not merely transformed our perception and understanding of the processes and mechanisms of the natural world but altered our potential to act and exist within it. New forms of order and social organisation are thereupon not only made possible; their proclaimed accordance with the scientifically uncovered laws of nature acts as a potent incantation in summoning them into being. By virtue of the prestige accorded to its discourses and its close connection to technologies central to modern societies, science has through its different incarnations constituted a powerful cultural force with profound resonances beyond its original domain. Indeed Barry Barnes and Steven Shapin have observed that "any perceived pattern or organised system in nature is liable to be employed to express and comment upon social order and social experience."[2]

Through the metaphorical displacement of concepts, ideas formulated within one particular domain are transferred to another domain. Such displacements are all the more influential when they are supported by the embodied and experiential metaphors which are the technological artefacts of the clock, engine, computer, and network. As the defining machines of their time, their abstractions have taken pride of place in our conceptual frameworks. The most immediately visible impact of these technologies on the world may be their material imprint but this should not obscure their profound cultural impact, enmeshed as they are in contemporaneous discourses, whether scientific, philosophical, or other. Hence the imperative to write a history "neither of ideas alone nor of machines and their effects, but of ideas, experiences, and metaphors in their interaction with machines and material change."[3]

We have seen that underpinning each of the worldviews articulated under the scientific way of warfare is a distinct approach to control and to the problem of order and chaos. The exercise of armed force and its instrumentalisation by political entities such as the state require the establishment of an intellectual and organisational framework which provides a degree of predictability and control over its outcome.[4] In

---

2   John Rogers, *The Matter of Revolution: Science, Poetry, and Politics in the Age of Milton* (Ithaca, NY: Cornell University Press, 1996), p. 2.

3   Edwards, *The Closed World*, p. xv.

4   Black refers to the "the systematisation of knowledge, such that it is possible better to understand, and thus seek to control, the military, its activities and its

this sense warfare can be seen as part of a quest for order, the search for regularity and reliability of behaviour, common to most if not all forms of social activity. War is a particular field of human endeavour in that the nature of combat, namely the fact of two opposing wills pitted against each other and both seeking to outwit and undermine each other, entails an irreducible uncertainty and unpredictability in its pursuit and hence the permanent threat of chaos erupting among even the most ordered of arrangements. Indeed, the imposition of chaos on the adversary is generally the requisite for victory in war.

Warfare is to be distinguished here in at least one regard from both science itself and from processes of economic production which have also developed in accordance with technoscientific evolutions. One can certainly construct an account of the history of economic production according to a similar narrative of technoscientific change as has been provided for warfare. Clockwork and mechanism can be related to the principle of rationalised division of labour, the engine and thermodynamics to the motorisation and industrialisation of production, and the computer and cybernetics to automation and numerical control.

In contrast to warfare, neither science nor production finds itself pitted against a sentient foe consciously trying to disrupt its efforts to impose order. The chaos or resistance to order they seek to dispel is not the work of a trickster liable to change his ways from one moment to the next; rather it is a fixed and consistent obstacle to be overcome. Thus the scientist seeking to uncover nature's laws through the discovery of patterns of regularities takes these laws to be universal and unchanging, waiting to be discovered and not susceptible to sudden change. Likewise, production is the exertion of work on generally inanimate matter according to a general and abstract plan that divides and distributes labour. While manufacturing processes are almost always susceptible to further improvement and will incur occasional breakdowns through mechanical or operator error, the actual matter being worked upon does not wilfully vary the nature of its resistance.[5]

---

interaction with the wider world." Jeremy Black, *War: Past, Present, and Future* (Stroud: Sutton, 2000), p. 29.

5   This observation no longer holds if we shift analysis from production per se to competition between different enterprises in the marketplace. Here we see sentient opposition of a similar nature to that found in war. This may account for the widespread use of military metaphors in the language of business and

In contrast, Solly Zuckerman points out that "if ever there was a world in which situations do not repeat themselves like some mass production model, it is the military world."[6] Clausewitz echoes this notion when warning against those approaches to war that treat it as another science or art:

War is no activity of the will, which exerts itself upon inanimate matter like the mechanical arts; or upon the living but still passive and yielding subject, like the human mind and the human feelings in the ideal arts, but against a living and reacting force. How little the categories or the arts and sciences are applicable to such an activity strikes us at once; and we can understand at the same time how that constant seeking and striving after laws like those which may be developed out of the dead material world could not but lead to constant errors.[7]

Clausewitz is insisting here on precisely the distinction drawn above between science and production on one hand and warfare on the other in relation to the respective passivity and reactivity of their subject matter. This is not to say that some aspects of the requirements of modern warfare do not benefit from the application of a productivist framework, notably for the purpose of the mobilisation of a war economy or in the realm of logistics (although a higher degree of redundancy will most likely need to be built into military logistics than in regular economic activity). Attempts to bring the entire spectrum of activity of war under such a framework can only be self-defeating. James Gibson's analysis of the specific failing of "technowar" as "a production system that can be rationally managed" in Vietnam can thus be extended to a wider observation about the general unsuitability of this approach to warfare.[8]

Daniel Pick has found "two interlocking projects in the history of European culture and political thought: the one tracing the quest for a pure science of war; the other charting the dissolution of the belief

---

the current popularity of Sun Tzu in management and business strategy literature. Mark R. McNeilly, *Sun Tzu and the Art of Business: Six Strategic Principles for Managers* (Oxford University Press, 2000); Gerald A. Michaelson, *Sun Tzu: The Art of War for Managers - 50 Strategic Rules* (Adams Media Corporation, 2001).

6   Solly Zuckerman, "Judgment and Control in Modern Warfare", *OR*, Vol. 13, No. 3. (Sept. 1962), p. 266.

7   Clausewitz, *On War*, p. 103.

8   Gibson, *The Perfect War*.

that war can be reduced to laws or predictable patterns."[9] While this account of two conflicting stances in Western thought on the possibility of making warfare into a fully predictable and ordered affair is broadly correct, it is somewhat misleading to oppose scientific thought to a non-scientific outside which would be opposed to the former's totalising drive. If science has indeed most often been recruited in the attempt to bring warfare under the complete control of its practitioners, we have seen that within science itself are present currents of thought which posit intrinsic limits to predictability and ordering. In particular, we have seen how Clausewitz's ideas about friction can be related to ideas articulated in the sciences of thermodynamics, chaos theory and complexity.

The historical record certainly substantiates the idea that attempts to render war fully predictable have been largely counter-productive and that, following van Creveld, "in armed conflict no success is possible – or even conceivable – which is not grounded in an ability to tolerate uncertainty, cope with it, and make use of it."[10] The most effective forms of warfare have therefore always included recognition of the inherent unpredictability that accompanies the use of military force and built into military organisation a tolerance to uncertainty and even a capacity to profit from it.

There are great dangers in adopting a misguided faith in the efficacy and predictability of military force. Such a belief tends to make war into a more attractive option among the instruments of policy because of its presumed decisiveness and unambiguity, thereby resulting in the conceptual reduction of complex strategic problems requiring a multi-pronged approach into ones liable to be fully resolved through military intervention, and frequently leading to disastrous consequences when acted upon on this basis. It was arguably a misplaced confidence in the capabilities of the US military, buoyed by the perceived early success in Afghanistan, along with a grave underestimation of the difficulties that would arise in the phase following the toppling of the Baathist regime which led to the Iraq quagmire.[11]

---

9   Pick, *War Machine*, p. 1.

10   Van Creveld, *Technology and War*, p. 316.

11   Seemingly mindful of these lessons, Donald Rumsfeld's successor as Secretary of Defense has articulated a much more cautious view of the effects of the ap-

Related to the drive for order in military affairs is the age-old tension in the conduct of military affairs between centralisation and decentralisation of armed forces and which the scientific approaches to warfare have fully played into. This tension has always presented an acute organisational dilemma for the military with the need to conciliate the tight control of a hierarchy over its subordinates and the operational need to provide autonomy and flexibility to its constituent units. Instrumentalist military thinking is above all concerned with efficiency, namely the perceived successes and failures of respective approaches. As such, the security environment and challenges presented in any era play a crucial role in determining the direction these debates take. There is no doubt that centralised and hierarchical mechanisms were largely successful in the conduct of the large-scale conflicts that characterised the major wars of the twentieth century and in the management of the perpetual state of nuclear readiness of the Cold War. However, this approach has demonstrated severe limitations in the context of counter-insurgency operations or guerrilla warfare, the Vietnam War or second Iraq conflict potently illustrating the inadequacy of the American war machine when confronted with a decentralised and diffuse enemy operating in a complex environment. The redefinition of the security environment and the new tasks given the military following the end of the Cold War have provided a powerful impetus for new military thinking arguing for the benefits of decentralisation.

War and the threat of war have been one of the most persistent features of human societies and show little sign of setting beyond the horizon of historical experience. Notwithstanding the endurance of the general phenomenon of war, its myriad manifestations have been shaped by the diversity in the material and ideational characteristics of the societies and cultures that have waged it. Every age has grappled with the conduct of warfare in its own way, as seen through its specific historical conditions and cultural baggage, as future societies will no doubt do so in their own

---

plication of military force than his predecessor. When questioned by the Senate panel which approved his nomination about his views on possible military intervention against Iran, Robert Gates replied that "I think that we have seen in Iraq that once war is unleashed, it becomes unpredictable. And I think that the consequences of a military conflict with Iran could be quite dramatic." David S. Cloud and Mark Mazzetti, "Senate Panel Approves Defense Nominee", *New York Times*, Dec. 5, 2006.

times. With chaoplexic warfare in its infancy and military thinkers and practitioners still grappling with the full implications of the non-linear sciences, it is too early to speculate on what regime of the scientific way of warfare may follow it. The scientific discourse that took centre stage with the modern era will certainly continue exerting a powerful influence on the conduct of war as technological developments and their incorporation into military activity continue apace. As long as it endures, armed conflict will persistently invite human attempts to bring greater predictability and control to its conduct. Whatever the particulars of future sciences and technologies may be, any future regime of warfare will necessarily mark yet another chapter in the continually renewed yet never settled quest for order on the battlefield.

Bibliography

Alberts, David S. and Czerwinski, Thomas J. (eds), *Complexity, Global Politics, and National Security* (Washington, DC: National Defense University, 1997).

Alberts, David S., Garstka, John J. and Stein, Frederick P., *Network-Centric Warfare: Developing and Leveraging Information Superiority*, 2nd edn (Department of Defense CCRP, 2000).

Alberts, David S., Garstka, John J., Hayes, Richard E. and Signorip, David A., *Understanding Information Age Warfare* (CCRP Publications, 2001).

Alberts, David S. and Hayes, Richard E., *Power to the Edge – Command ... Control ... in the Information Age* (Department of Defense CCRP, 2003).

Arquilla, John, *Worst Enemy: The Reluctant Transformation of the American Military* (Chicago, IL: Ivan R. Dee, 2008).

Arquilla, John and Ronfeldt, David, "Information, Power, and Grand Strategy: In Athena's Camp" in Stuart J.D. Schwartzstein (ed.), *The Information Revolution and National Security* (Washington, DC: The Center for Strategic and International Studies, 1996).

—— (eds), *In Athena's Camp: Preparing for Conflict in the Information Age* (RAND, 1997).

—— *Swarming and the Future of Conflict* (RAND Corporation, 2000).

Ashby, W. Ross, *An Introduction to Cybernetics* (London: Chapman and Hall, 1956).

Atkinson, Simon Ray and Moffat, James, *The Agile Organization: From Informal Networks to Complex Effects and Agility* (Department of Defense CCRP, 2005).

Atlan, Henri, *L'Organisation Biologique et la Théorie de l'Information* (Paris: Editions du Seuil, 2006).

Baeyer, Hans Christian von, *Information: The New Language of Science* (London: Weidenfeld and Nicolson, 2003).

Barnett, Thomas P.M., "The Seven Deadly Sins of Network-Centric Warfare", *Proceedings*, US Naval Institute, January 1999, pp. 36-39.

Bar-Yam, Yaneer, "Complexity of Military Conflict: Multiscale Complex Systems Analysis of Littoral Warfare", New England Complex Systems Institute, 2003.

Bateson, Gregory, *Steps to an Ecology of Mind* (New York: Ballantine, 1972).

Beck, Ulrich, *Risk Society: Towards a New Modernity* (London: Sage Publications, 1992).

Beckerman, Linda P., "The Non-Linear Dynamics of War", Science Applications International Corporation, 1999. http://www.calresco.org/beckermn/nonlindy.htm (accessed January 2008).

Beech, Michael F., "Observing Al Qaeda Through the Lens of Complexity Theory: Recommendations for the National Strategy to Defeat Terrorism", Center for Strategic Leadership, US Army War College, July 2004.

Beer, Stafford, "What Has Cybernetics to Do with Operational Research?", *Operational Research Quarterly*, Vol. 10, No. 1, 1959.

―――― *Cybernetics and Management* - 2nd edn (London: English Universities Press, 1967).

Beniger, James, *The Control Revolution: Technological and Economic Origins of the Information Society* (Cambridge, MA: Harvard University Press, 1986).

Benseler, Frank, Heil, Peter and Koch, Wolfgang, *Autopoiesis, Communication, and Society: The Theory of Autopoietic Systems in the Social Sciences* (Frankfurt: Campus Verlag, 1980).

Berkowitz, Bruce. *The New Face of War: How War Will Be Fought in the 21ˢᵗ Century* (New York, NY: The Free Press, 2003).

Beyerchen, Alan D. "Clausewitz, Nonlinearity and the Unpredictability of War", *International Security*, 17:3 Winter, 1992.

―――― "Clausewitz, Nonlinearity, and the Importance of Imagery" in David S. Alberts and Thomas J. Czerwinski (eds), *Complexity, Global Politics, and National Security* (Washington, DC: National Defense University, 1997).

Bien, David D., "Military Education in 18th Century France; Technical and Non-Technical Determinants" in Monte D. Wright and Lawrence J. Paszek (eds), *Science, Technology and Warfare: The Proceedings of the Third Military History Symposium* – United States Air Force Academy, 8-9 May 1969.

Black, Jeremy, *War: Past, Present, and Future* (Stroud: Sutton, 2000).

————— *Rethinking Military History* (London: Routledge, 2004).

Black, Max, *Models and Metaphors: Studies in Language and Philosophy* (Ithaca, NY: Cornell University Press, 1962).

Blight, James G. and Lang, Janet M., *The Fog of War – Lessons from the Life of Robert S. McNamara* (Oxford: Rowman and Littlefield Publishers, 2005).

Bolter, David, *Turing's Man: Western Culture in the Computer Age* (London: Duckworth, 1984).

Boorstin, Daniel J., *The Discoverers: A History of Man's Search to Know his World and Himself* (Harmondsworth: Penguin, 1986).

Boyd, John R., "Destruction and Creation" (1976).

—————, "Patterns of Conflict" (Presentation, December 1986).

—————, "Organic Design for Command and Control" (Briefing - May 1987).

—————, "The Essence of Winning and Losing" (Briefing, January 1996).

—————, "The Conceptual Spiral" (unpublished briefing).

Brey, Philip, "Theorising Modernity and Technology" in Thomas J. Misa, Philip Brey and Andrew Feenberg (eds), *Modernity and Technology* (Cambridge, MA: MIT Press, 2003).

Bryen, Stephen David, *The Application of Cybernetic Analysis to the Study of International Politics* (The Hague: Martinus Nijhoff, 1971).

Bull, Hedley, *The Anarchical Society: A Study of Order in World Politics* (London: Macmillan, 1977).

Campbell, David, Crutchfield, Jim, Farmer, Doyne and Jen, Erica, "Experimental Mathematics: The Role of Computation in Nonlinear Studies", *Communications of ACM*, 28.4 (1985).

Campen, Alan D. and Dearth, Douglas H., *Cyberwar 3.0: Human Factors in Information Operations and Future Conflicts* (Fairfax, VA: AFCEA International Press, 2000).

Capra, Fritjof, *The Web of Life: A New Synthesis of Mind and Matter* (London: Flamingo, 1997).

Cardwell, D.S.L., *Turning Points in Western Technology: A Study of Technology, Science and History* (New York: Neale Watson Academic Publications, 1974).

Carnot, Sadi, *Reflections on the Motive Power of Fire and on Machines Fitted to Develop that Power* (1824).

Castells, Manuel, *The Internet Galaxy* (Oxford, New York: Oxford University Press, 2001).

Castells, Manuel, *The Rise of the Network Society* - 2nd edn (Cambridge, MA; Oxford, UK: Blackwell, 2000).

Cebrowski, Arthur K. and Garstka, John J., "Network-Centric Warfare: Its Origin and Future", *Proceedings*, US Naval Institute, January 1998.

Clausewitz, Carl von, *On War*, trans. Michael Howard and Peter Paret (Princeton, NJ: Princeton University Press, 1984).

———, *On War*, trans. J.J Graham (Hertfordshire: Wordsworth, 1997).

Coker, Christopher, *War and the Illiberal Conscience* (Boulder, CO: Westview Press, 1998).

———, *Waging War Without Warriors? The Changing Culture of Military Conflict* (London: Lynne Rienner, 2002).

———, *The Future of War: The Re-Enchantment of War in the Twenty-First Century* (Oxford: Blackwell Publishing, 2004).

Colburn, Timothy R., *Philosophy and Computer Science* (Armont, NY and London: M.E. Sharpe, 2000).

Constant, James. *Fundamentals of Strategic Weapons: Offense and Defense Systems* (The Hague: Martinus Nijhoff, 1981).

Craik, Kenneth J.W., "Theory of the Human Operator in Control Systems", *British Journal of Psychology*, 38 (1947).

Creveld, Martin van, *Technology and War: From 2000 B.C. to the Present* (New York: Free Press, 1989).

———, *Command in War* (Cambridge, MA and London: Harvard University Press, 2003).

Cummings, Nigel, "How the World of OR Societies Began" (The OR Society). http://www.orsoc.org.uk/orshop/(awaqdrfkrmznlwneegwigdqi)/orcontent.aspx?inc=article_news_orclub.htm (accessed Jan. 2008).

Dale, Rodney, *Timekeeping* (London: The British Library, 1992).

Davis, Norman C., "An Information-Based Revolution in Military Affairs" in John Arquilla and David Ronfeldt (eds), *In Athena's Camp: Preparing for Conflict in the Information Age* (RAND, 1997).

DeLanda, Manuel, *War in the Age of Intelligent Machines* (New York: Swerve Editions, 1991).

———, *A Thousand Years of Non-Linear History* (New York: Swerve Editions, 2003).

Dechert, Charles R., *The Social Impact of Cybernetics* (Notre Dame, IN: University of Notre Dame Press, 1966).

Deleuze, Gilles and Guattari, Felix, *A Thousand Plateaus* (London and New York: Continuum, 2003).

Deleuze, Gilles, *Foucault* (Paris: Les Editions de Minuit, 1986).

Demenÿ, Georges, *Les Bases Scientifiques de l'Education Physique* (Paris: Alcan, 1902).

Department of the Army Pamphlet 600–3–49, "Operations Research/Systems Analysis" (Washington, DC: Department of the Army, 1987).

Deutsch, Karl, *The Nerves of Government* (New York, NY: The Free Press, 1963).

Duffy, Christopher, *The Army of Frederick the Great* (Vancouver: David and Charles, 1974).

Easton, David, *A Systems Analysis of Political Life* (New York, NY: John Wiley and Sons, 1965).

———, *A Framework for Political Analysis* (Chicago, IL: University of Chicago Press, 1979).

Edwards, Paul N., "The Closed World: Systems Discourse, Military Policy and Post-World War II US Historical Consciousness" in Les Levidow and Kevin Robins (eds), *Cyborg Worlds: The Military Information Society* (London: Free Association Books, 1989).

———, "Cyberpunks in Cyberspace: The Politics of Subjectivity in the Computer Age" in Susan Leigh Star (ed.), *Cultures of Computing* (Keele, UK: Sociological Review and Monograph Series, 1995), pp. 69-84.

———, *The Closed World: Computers and the Politics of Discourse in Cold War America* (Cambridge, MA: MIT Press, 1996).

———, "Why Build Computers?" in Merritt Roe Smith and Gregory K. Clancey (eds), *Major Problems in the History of American Technology: Documents and Essays* (Boston: Houghton Mifflin, 1998).

Farrell, Theo and Terriff, Terry (eds), *The Sources of Military Change: Culture, Politics, Technology* (Boulder: Lynne Rienner, 2002).

M.D. Feld, "Military Professionalism in the Mass Army", *Armed Forces and Society*, Vol. 1, No. 2, 1975.

———, "Middle-Class Society and the Rise of Military Professionalism: The Dutch Army 1589-1609", *Armed Forces and Society* Vol. 1, No. 4, 1975.

Flesher, Maryl, "Repetitive Order and the Human Walking Apparatus: Prussian Military Science versus the Webers' Locomotion Research", *Annals of Science*, Volume 54, Number 5, 1997.

Fortun, M. and Schweber, SS., "Scientists and the Legacy of World War II: The Case of Operations Research (OR)", *Social Studies of Science*, Vol. 23, 1993.

Foucault, Michel, *Surveiller et Punir* (Paris: Editions Gallimard, 1975).

———, (ed. Donald Bouchard), *Language, Counter-memory, Practice: Selected Essays and Interviews* (Ithaca NY: Cornell University Press, 1977).

———, *Power/Knowledge* (Hemel Hampstead: Harvester Press, 1980).

———, *Discipline and Punish* (London: Penguin Books, 1991).

———, *Foucault Live – Interviews 1961-1984* (edited by Sylvère Lotringer) (New York, NY: Semiotext(e), 1996).

Franchi, Stefano, Güzeldere, Güven and Minch, Eric, "Interview with Heinz von Foerster", *Stanford Humanities Review*, Vol. 4, Issue 2, 1995.

Franklin, H. Bruce, *War Stars: The Superweapon and the American Imagination* (Oxford University Press: New York, 1988).

French, David, *The British Way in Warfare 1688-2000* (London: Unwin Hayman, 1990).

Freud, Sigmund, *Civilisation and its Discontents* (London: Penguin, 2004).

Fuller, J. F. C., *The Foundations of the Science of War* (1926).

Gaddis, John Lewis, *Strategies of Containment: A Critical Appraisal of Postwar American National Security Policy* (Oxford: Oxford University Press, 1982).

Gat, Azar. *A History of Military Thought: From the Enlightenment to the Cold War* (Oxford University Press, 2001).

Gell-Mann, Murray, *The Quark and the Jaguar: Adventures in the Simple and the Complex* (London: Little Brown and Company, 1994).

———, "Let's Call It Plectics", *Complexity Journal*, Vol. 1/ No. 5 (1995/96).

Gerovitch, Slava, *From Newspeak to Cyberspeak: A History of Soviet Cybernetics* (Cambridge, MA and London: MIT Press, 2002).

Gerth, H.H. and Wright Mills, C. (eds), *From Max Weber: Essays in Sociology* (London: Kegan Paul, Trench, Trubner and Co., 1947).

Ghamari-Tabrizi, Sharon, "US Wargaming Grows Up: A Short History of the Diffusion of Wargaming in the Armed Forces and Industry in the Postwar Period up to 1964", StrategyPage.Com. http://www.strategypage.com/articles/default.asp?target=Wgappen.htm (accessed January 2008).

———, *The Worlds of Herman Kahn: The Intuitive Science of Thermonuclear War* (Cambridge, MA: Harvard University Press, 2005).

Gibson, James, *The Perfect War: Technowar in Vietnam* (Boston, MA: Atlantic Monthly Press, 1986).

Gleick, James, *Chaos: Making a New Science* (London: Vintage, 1987).

Gleyse, Jacques and al., "Physical Education as a Subject in France (Shool Curriculum, Policies and Discourse): The Body and the Metaphors of the Engine – Elements Used in the Analysis of a Power and Control System during the Second Industrial Revolution", *Sport, Education and Society* 1, vol. 7 (2002), pp. 5-23.

Goldstein, Jeffrey, "Emergence as a Construct: History and Issues", *Emergence: Complexity and Organization*, 1:1 (1999).

Gray, Chris Hables (ed.), *The Cyborg Handbook* (New York: Routledge, 1995).

———, *Postmodern War: The New Politics of Conflict* (New York: The Guilford Press, 1997).

———, *Peace, War, and Computers* (New York: Routledge, 2005).

Gray, Colin S., *Strategy for Chaos: Revolutions in Military Affairs and the Evidence of History* (London: Frank Cass, 2002).

Griffith, Paddy, *Battle Tactics of the Western Front: The British Army's Art of Attack, 1916-1918* (London: Yale University Press, 1996).

Hacker, Barton C., "Military Institutions, Weapons, and Social Change: Toward a New History of Military Technology", *Technology and Culture*, Vol. 35, No. 4. (Oct., 1994), pp. 768-834.

Hambling, David, *Weapons Grade* (London: Constable and Robinson, 2005).

Hammond, Grant T., "The Essential Boyd" http://www.belisarius.com/modern_business_strategy/hammond/essential_boyd.htm (accessed Jan. 2008).

Harris, Carl and Gass, Saul (eds), *Encyclopaedia of Operations Research and Management Science* (Norwell, MA: Kluwer Academic Publishers, 2000).

Harris, J.P., *Men, Ideas and Tanks: British Military Thought and Armoured Forces, 1903-1939* (Manchester University Press, 1995).

Hartley, R.V.L., "Transmission of Information", *Bell System Technical Journal*, Vol.7, 1928.

Harvey, David, *The Condition of Postmodernity: An Enquiry into the Origins of Cultural Change* (Oxford: Basil Blackwell, 1990).

Hayles, N. Katherine, *Chaos Bound: Orderly Disorder in Contemporary Literature and Science* (Ithaca, NY: Cornell University Press, 1990).

———, *How We Became Posthuman: Virtual Bodies in Cybernetics, Literature, and Informatics* (Chicago, IL: University of Chicago Press, 1999).

Heidegger, Martin, *The Question Concerning Technology and Other Essays* (Harper Torchbooks, 1977).

Heim, Michael, *The Metaphysics of Virtual Reality* (New York: Oxford University Press, 1993).

Heims, Steve J., *John Von Neumann and Norbert Wiener: From Mathematics to the Technologies of Life and Death* (Cambridge, MA: MIT Press, 1980).

———, *The Cybernetics Group* (Cambridge, MA: MIT Press, 1991).

Herken, Gregg, *Counsels of War* (New York: Alfred A. Knopf, 1985).

Heuser, Beatrice, *Reading Clausewitz* (London: Pimlico, 2002).

Heylighen, Francis, "Complex Adaptive Systems" (Principia Cybernetica Web, 1996). http://pespmc1.vub.ac.be/CAS.html (accessed Jan. 2008)

Heylighen, Francis and Joslyn, Cliff, "Cybernetics and Second-Order Cybernetics" in R.A. Meyers (ed.), *Encyclopedia of Physical Science and Technology* - 3rd edn (New York: Academic Press, 2001).

Hobbes, Thomas, *Leviathan* (Oxford University Press, 1998).

Holland, John H., *Adaptation in Natural and Artificial Systems* (Cambridge, MA: MIT Press, 1995).

———, *Hidden Order – How Adaptation Builds Complexity* (Reading, MA: Addison-Wesley, 1995).

Holley Jr., I.B., "The Evolution of Operations Research and the Impact on the Military Establishment; The Air Force Experience" in Monte D. Wright and Lawrence J. Paszek (eds), *Science, Technology and Warfare: The Proceedings of the Third Military History Symposium* – United Air Force Academy 8-9 May 1969.

Horgan, John, *The End of Science: Facing the Limits of Knowledge in the Twilight of the Scientific Age* (London: Abacus, 2002).

Ilachinski, Andrew, *Land Warfare and Complexity - Part I: Mathematical Background and Technical Sourcebook* (Alexandria, VA: Center for Naval Analyses, July 1996).

James, Glenn E., "Chaos Theory: The Essentials for Military Applications" (US Naval War College, Newport, RI, Center for Naval Warfare Studies, Newport Paper No. 10, Oct. 1996).

Jenner, R A., "Dissipative Enterprises, Chaos, and the Principles of Lean Organizations", *Omega: The International Journal of Management Science*, Vol. 26, No. 4 (Dec., 1998).

Jünger, Ernst, *Der Kampf als Inneres Erlebnis* (Berlin: E. S. Mittler and Sohn, 1922)

———, *Sämtliche Werke*, vols I-IX (Stuttgart, 1980).

Kaplan, Fred, *The Wizards of Armageddon* (New York: Simon and Schuster, 1984).

Kay, Lily E., *Who Wrote the Book of Life? A History of the Genetic Code* (Stanford, CA: Stanford University Press, 2000).

Keegan, John, *The Face of Battle* (London: Cape, 1976).

———, *A History of Warfare* (London: Pimlico, 2004).

Kelly, Kevin, *Out of Control: The New Biology of Machines* (Reading: Cox and Wyman, 1994).

King, Ian T., *Social Science and Complexity: The Scientific Foundations* (Huntington, NY: Nova Science Publishers, 2000).

King, James, *Science and Rationalism in the Government of Louis XIV* (Baltimore, MD: John Hopkins Press, 1949).

Kipp, Jacob W. and Grau, Lester W., "The Fog and Friction of Technology", *Military Review*, Sept.-Oct. 2001.

Kissinger, Henry, *Agenda for a Nation* (Washington, DC: The Brookings Institution, 1968).

Klein, Gary, *Sources of Power: How People Make Decisions* (Cambridge, MA: MIT Press, 1998).

Kleinschmidt, Harald, "Using the Gun: Manual Drill and the Proliferation of Portable Firearms", *The Journal of Military History*, Vol. 63, No. 3. (July, 1999).

Koestler, Arthur, *The Sleepwalkers* (London: Arkana Books, 1989).

Kolenda, Christopher D., "Transforming How We Fight - A Conceptual Approach", *Naval War College Review*, Spring 2003, Vol. LVI, No. 2.

Kranzberg, Melvin, "Science-Technology and Warfare: Action, Reaction, and Interaction in the Post-World War II Era" in Monte D. Wright and Lawrence J. Paszek (eds), *Science, Technology and Warfare: The Proceedings of the Third Military History Symposium* - United States Air Force Academy 8-9 May 1969.

Kuhn, Thomas S., *The Structure of Scientific Revolutions* - 3rd edn (Chicago, IL: University of Chicago Press, 1996).

La Mettrie, Julien Offray de, *L'Homme Machine* (1748).

Lafontaine, Céline, *L'Empire Cybernétique – Des Machines à Penser à la Pensée Machine* (Paris: Editions du Seuil, 2004).

Lakoff, George and Johnson, Mark, *Metaphors We Live By* (Chicago, IL: University of Chicago Press, 1990).

Landes, David, *Revolution in Time: Clocks and the Making of the Modern World* (Cambridge, MA: Harvard University Press, 1983).

Laplace, Pierre Simon de, «Theorie Analytique des Probabilités», *Oeuvres Complètes de Laplace*, Vol. VII (Paris: Gauthier-Villars, 1820).

Laudan, Rachel (ed.), *The Nature of Technological Knowledge: Are Models of Scientific Change Relevant?* (Dordrecht, Holland: D. Reidiel Publishing, 1984).

Lavoisier, Antoine and Laplace, Pierre-Simon, «Mémoire sur la Chaleur» (1780).

Lawrence, Philip K., *Modernity and War: The Creed of Absolute Violence* (Houndmills, Basingstoke: Macmillan, 1997).

Lechte, John, *Key Contemporary Concepts: From Abjection to Zeno's Paradox* (London: Sage, 2003).

Leiner, Barry M., Cerf, Vinton G., Clark, David D., Kahn, Robert E., Kleinrock, Leonard, Lynch, Daniel C., Postel, Jon, Roberts, Larry G. and Wolff, Stephen, "A Brief History of the Internet" (The Internet Society, 2003). http://www.isoc.org/internet/history/brief.shtml (accessed Jan. 2008)

Levidow, Les and Robins, Kevin (eds), *Cyborg Worlds: The Military Information Society* (London: Free Association Books, 1989).

Light, Jennifer S., *From Warfare to Welfare: Defense Intellectuals and Urban Problems in Cold War America* (Baltimore, MD: John Hopkins University Press, 2003).

Luhmann, Niklas, *Social Systems* (Stanford, CA: Stanford University Press, 1995).

Lynn, John A., "The Treatment of Military Subjects in Diderot's Encyclopédie", *The Journal of Military History*, Vol. 65, No. 1. (Jan., 2001).

Lynn, John A., *Battle: A History of Combat and Culture* (Boulder, CO: Westview Press, 2003).

Macy, Samuel, *Clocks and the Cosmos: Time in Western Life and Thought* (Hamden, CT: Archon Books, 1980).

Mandelbrot, Benoit B. and Hudson, Richard L, *The (Mis)Behaviour of Markets: A Fractal View of Risk, Ruin and Reward* (London: Profile Books, 2004).

Marion, Russ and Uhl-Bien, Mary, "Complexity Theory and Al-Qaeda: Examining Complex Leadership", Presentation given at "Managing the Complex IV: A Conference on Complex Systems and the Management of Organizations", Fort Meyers, FL, Dec., 2002.

Martin, James and Norman, Adrian R.D., *The Computerised Society* (Harmondsworth: Penguin Books, 1973).

Maruyama, Magoroh. "The Second Cybernetics: Deviation-Amplifying Mutual Causal Processes", *American Scientist*, 5:2 (1963).

Maturana, Humberto and Varela, Francisco, "Autopoiesis and Cognition: the Realization of the Living" in Robert S. Cohen and Marx W. Wartofsky (eds), *Boston Studies in the Philosophy of Science*, 42 (Dordecht: D. Reidel Publishing Co, 1980).

Mayr, Otto, *Authority, Liberty and Automatic Machinery in Early Modern Europe* (Baltimore, MD: Johns Hopkins University Press, 1986).

Meyers, R.A. (ed.), *Encyclopedia of Physical Science and Technology* - 3rd edn (New York: Academic Press, 2001).

McFarren, Tamara E., "Persistent Surveillance", *Military Geospatial Technology*, Vol. 2, Issue 3, Sept. 28, 2004.

McNeill, William H., *The Pursuit of Power: Technology, Armed Force, and Society since A.D. 1000* (Chicago, IL: University of Chicago Press, 1982).

McNeilly, Mark R., *Sun Tzu and the Art of Business: Six Strategic Principles for Managers* (New York: Oxford University Press, 2000).

Michaelson, Gerald A., *Sun Tzu: The Art of War for Managers – 50 Strategic Rules* (Cincinnati, OH: Adams Media Corporation, 2001).

Misa, Thomas J., Brey, Philip and Feenberg, Andrew (eds), *Modernity and Technology* (Cambridge, MA: MIT Press, 2003).

Moffat, James, *Complexity and Network-Centric Warfare* (CCRP Publications, 2003).

Mumford, Lewis, *Technics and Civilization* (New York: Harcourt, Brace and Co., 1934).

Mustin, Jeff, "Flesh and Blood: The Call for the Pilot in the Cockpit", *Air and Space Power Journal* - Chronicles Online Journal, July 2001.

Myers, Richard B., "Understanding Transformation", *Proceedings*, US Naval Institute, Feb. 2003.

Nicholls, David and Tagarev, Todor, "What Does Chaos Theory Mean for Warfare?", *Aerospace Power Journal*, Fall 1994.

Nicolis, Gregoire and Prigogine, Ilya, *Exploring Complexity* (New York: W.H Freeman, 1989).

Nietzsche, Friedrich, *The Genealogy of Morals*, II 12 (Dover Publications, 2003). Office of Force Transformation, *The Implementation of Network-Centric Warfare* (2005). O'Hanlon, Michael, *Technological Change and the Future of Warfare* (Washington, DC: Brookings Institution Press, 2000).

Osinga Frans, *Science, Strategy and War: The Strategic Theory of John Boyd* (Abingdon, UK: Routledge, 2007).

Ott, Edward, Grebogi, Celso and Yorke, James A., "Controlling Chaos", *Physical Review Letters*, 64, 1990, pp. 1196-1199.

Owens, William A., with Offley, Edward, *Lifting the Fog of War* (Baltimore, MD: Johns Hopkins University Press, 2001).

Pacey, Arnold, *Technology in World Civilization* (Oxford: Basil Blackwell, 1990). Panel on Mathematics (Nonlinear Science and the Navy), Naval Studies Board, Commission on Physical Sciences, Mathematics, and Applications, National Research Council, "Nonlinear Science" (Washington DC: National Academy Press, 1997).

Parker, Geoffrey, *The Military Revolution – Military Innovation and the Rise of the West, 1500-1800* (Cambridge University Press, 1996).

Parsons, Talcott and Mayhew, Leon H., *Talcott Parsons on Institutions and Social Evolution: Selected Writings* (Chicago, IL: University of Chicago, 1982).

Pick, Daniel, *War Machine: The Rationalisation of Slaughter in the Modern Age* (New Haven, CT: Yale University Press, 1993).

Price, Derek J. De Solla, "Notes Towards a Philosophy of the Science/Technology Interaction" in Rachel Laudan (ed.), *The Nature of Technological Knowledge: Are Models of Scientific Change Relevant?* (Dordrecht, Holland: D. Reidiel Publishing, 1984).

Prigogine, Ilya and Stengers, Isabelle, *Order out of Chaos: Man's New Dialogue with Nature* (Fontana: London, 1985).

RAND Corporation, "A Brief History of RAND" http://www.rand.org/about/history/ (accessed Jan. 2008)

———,"Preliminary Design of an Experimental World-Circling Spaceship" (1946). http://www.rand.org/pubs/special_memoranda/2006/SM-11827part1.pdf (accessed January 2008)

Robbins, Richard H., *The Belief Machine* (1985). http://faculty.plattsburgh.edu/richard.robbins/Belief/belief-machine.htm (accessed January 2008)

Roberts, Michael, *Essays in Swedish History* (London: Camelot Press, 1967).

Rochlin, Gene I., *Trapped in the Net: The Unanticipated Consequences of Computerization* (Princeton University Press, 1997).

Rogers, John, *The Matter of Revolution: Science, Poetry, and Politics in the Age of Milton* (Ithaca, NY: Cornell University Press, 1996).

Roland, Alex, "Science, Technology, and War", *Technology and Culture*, Vol. 36, No. 2, Supplement: Snapshots of a Discipline: Selected Proceedings from the Conference on Critical Problems and Research Frontiers in the History of Technology, Madison, Wisconsin, Oct. 30-Nov. 3, 1991 (Apr. 1995).

Roman, Gregory A., "The Command or Control Dilemma: When Technology and Organizational Orientation Collide" (Maxwell AFB, AB: Air University Press, Feb. 1997).

Roszak, Theodore, *The Cult of Information* (Berkeley, CA: University of California Press, 1994)

Sageman, Mark, *Understanding Terror Networks* (Philadelphia, PA: University of Pennsylvania Press, 2004).

Schelling, Thomas C., *The Strategy of Conflict* (Cambridge, MA: Harvard University Press, 1960).

Schon, Donald A., *Displacement of Concepts* (London: Tavistock Publications, 1963).

Schrödinger, Erwin, *What is Life? And Other Scientific Essays* (Garden City, NY: Doubleday Anchor, 1956).

Schwartzstein, Stuart J.D. (ed.), *The Information Revolution and National Security* (Washington, DC: The Center for Strategic and International Studies, 1996).

Serres, Michel, *Hermes III: La Traduction* (Paris: Les Editions de Minuit, 1974).

————, *Hermes: Literature, Science, and Philosophy* (Baltimore, MD: John Hopkins University, 1983).

Shannon, Claude E., "A Mathematical Theory of Communication", *Bell System Technical Journal*, Vol. 27, 1948.

Showalter, Dennis, *The Wars of Frederick the Great* (London and New York: Addison Wesley Longman, 1997).

Shy, John, "Commentary on Western Military Education 1700-1850" in Monte D. Wright and Lawrence J. Paszek (eds), *Science, Technology and Warfare: The Proceedings of the Third Military History Symposium* – United States Air Force Academy 8-9 May 1969.

Siegfried, Tom, *The Bit and the Pendulum: From Quantum Computing to M Theory – The New Physics of Information* (New York: John Wiley and Sons).

Smith, Crosbie, *The Science of Energy: A Cultural History of Energy Physics in Victorian Britain* (London: Athlone Press, 1998).

Smith, Merritt Roe and Clancey, Gregory K. (eds), *Major Problems in the History of American Technology: Documents and Essays* (Boston, MA: Houghton Mifflin, 1998).

Speelman, Patrick J. (ed.), *War, Society and Enlightenment: The Works of General Lloyd* (Leiden, Boston: Brill, 2005)

Spinney, Chuck, "Genghis John", *Proceedings*, US Naval Institute, July 1997.

————,"Asleep at the Switch in Versailles... or ... Why Nonlinear Realities Overwhelm Linear Visions ... or ... Why did Slobo Cave?" (Defense and the National Interest, Sept. 6, 1999). http://www.d-n-i.net/fcs/comments/c317.htm (accessed Jan. 2008)

————,"Is America Inside Its Own OODA Loop?" (Defense and the National Interest, Jan. 26, 2005). http://www.d-n-i.net/fcs/comments/c536.htm (accessed January 2008)

Steele, Brett D., "Muskets and Pendulums: Benjamin Robins, Leonhard Euler, and the Ballistics Revolution", *Technology and Culture*, Vol. 35, No. 2. (Apr. 1994).

Stewart, Ian, *Does God Play Dice?: The New Mathematics of Chaos* (Malden MA: Blackwell Publishing, 2002).

Taylor, Mark C., *The Moment of Complexity – Emerging Network Culture* (Chicago, IL: University of Chicago Press, 2001).

Toffler, Alvin, *The Third Wave* (London: Collins, 1980).

Toffler, Alvin and Toffler, Heidi, *War and Anti-War: Survival at the Dawn of the 21st Century* (Boston, MA and London: Little, Brown and Company, 1993). United States Marine Corps, FMFM1: Warfighting, 1989.

————, MCDP 6: Command and Control, 1996.

Urry, John, *Global Complexity* (Cambridge: Polity, 2003).

Vego, Milan, "Net-Centric Is Not Decisive", *Proceedings*, US Naval Institute, Jan. 2003.

Virilio, Paul, *Speed and Politics: An Essay on Dromology* (New York: Semiotext(e), 1986).

————, *The Lost Dimension* (New York: Semiotext(e), 1991).

Waldrop, M. Mitchell, *Complexity: The Emerging Science at the Edge of Order and Chaos* (London: Viking, 1992).

Watts, Barry D., "Clausewitzian Friction and Future War" (McNair Paper No. 52, Oct. 1996).

Weigley, Russell F., *The American Way of War: A History of the United States Military Strategy and Policy* (Bloomington, IN: Indiana University Press, 1973).

Wertheim, Margaret, *The Pearly Gates of Cyberspace: A History of Space from Dante to the Internet* (New York: W.W. Norton, 1999).

Wiener, Norbert, *Cybernetics or Control and Communications in the Animal and the Machine* (New York: Wiley, 1949).

———, *The Human Use of Human Beings: Cybernetics and Society* (London: Eyre and Spottiswoode, 1954).

———, *God and Golem, Inc: A Comment on Certain Points Where Cybernetics Impinges on Religion* (Cambridge, MA: MIT Press, 1964).

Wiener, Norbert and Rosenbluth, Arturo, "Purposeful and Non-Purposeful Behaviour", *Philosophy of Science* 17, Oct 1950.

Winner, Langdon, *The Whale and the Reactor: A Search for Limits in an Age of High Technology* (Chicago, IL: University of Chicago Press, 1986).

Wohlstetter, Albert, "The Delicate Balance of Terror" (1958). http://www.rand.org/publications/classics/wohlstetter/P1472/P1472.html (accessed Jan. 2008)

Wright, Monte D. and Paszek, Lawrence J. (eds), *Science, Technology and Warfare: The Proceedings of the Third Military History Symposium* – United States Air Force Academy, 8-9 May 1969.

Zuckerman, Solly, "Judgment and Control in Modern Warfare", *OR*, Vol. 13, No. 3, Sept. 1962).

Index